MARGUERITE PATTEN'S
Slimming Cookbook

MARGUERITE PATTEN'S
Slimming Cookbook

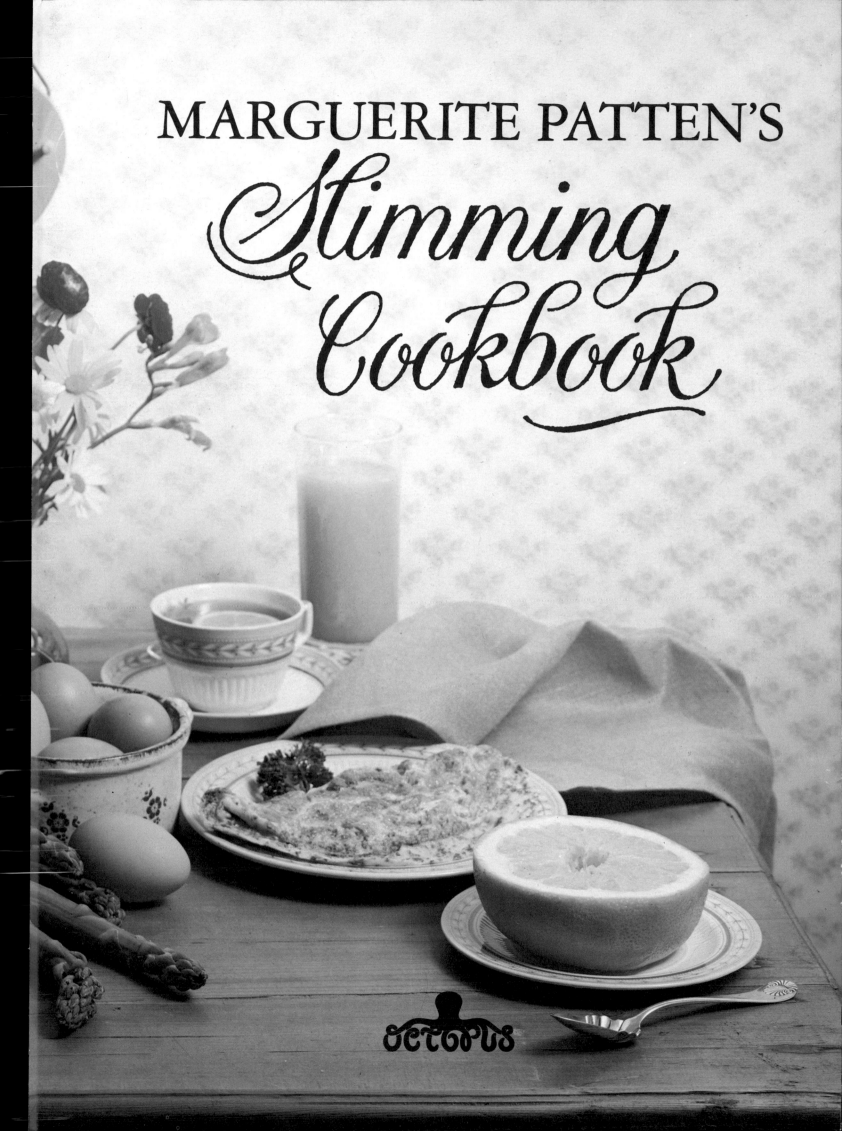

OCTOPUS

First published in 1979 by
Octopus Books Limited
59 Grosvenor Street
London W1

© 1979 Octopus Books Limited
ISBN 0 7064 0689 3

Produced by Mandarin Publishers Limited
22a Westlands Road, Quarry Bay, Hong Kong
Printed in Singapore

Contents

Introduction

The attitude towards slimming has undergone a very distinct change during the past few years. During this time a great deal of research has been carried out on the reasons for being over-weight and the ways in which a person can overcome this tendency.

Once, special slimming diets were considered a 'fad' to be followed only by those people who were very vain, or who had to keep slim for their particular job, or even were rather foolish to try and change their natural appearance.

Arguments against slimming

The arguments used against slimming were fairly strong and went something like this:

Fat people are jolly people; if you lose weight you will be thin and miserable.

You may also have come across people who believe that if you follow a slimming diet you will feel faint and lose all energy and that if you diet, you have to eat dull food and live mostly on salads – rather like a rabbit.

Let us examine some of these points and see if they are valid.

Are fat people really the happy people they appear to be? In some cases they are, but all too often over-weight men, women and children adopt a façade of jolliness to hide the fact that they hate their personal appearance and the many problems it causes them. Buying outsize or large-size clothes can be expensive, embarrassing and often difficult. Taking part in sporting activities, such as swimming, can be an unhappy experience or even a nightmare if you are at all sensitive.

Running, climbing stairs, or taking part in anything at all strenuous is often far more of an effort for the over-weight person than it is for the person with no weight problem. It is a pity that rather than admit the fact that to be fat is a liability, the over-weight often pretend to the outside world that 'everything is fine', when in fact nothing could be further from the truth.

Being jolly just because you are over-weight is not always the case. Medical opinion throughout the world now deplores the fact that one of the modern health hazards in civilized countries is that a high proportion of babies, children and adults are far too fat.

This can and does lead to emotional and physical illness. Being over-weight can be one of the reasons for diseases of the heart and it certainly does add to the fatigue of your daily routine.

Try carrying around an extra 5 or 6 pounds of food or luggage *all day long* and see how wearisome this becomes and more to the point, what a relief it is when you shed this load. Your body may be carrying not just a few surplus pounds but several extra stone (each stone being over 6 kilogrammes or 14 pounds). There is more information on being over-weight on pages 20 and 21.

Nature did not, as is often proposed by over-weight people, intend the

human body to be over-weight. It meant it to be reasonably covered with flesh and not weighed down by it. Obviously everyone's appearance will differ – some of us are short with fairly big bones; others tall with small bones, so some people will appear fatter than others, but if your doctor tells you that you are over-weight or your own *honest* appraisal of your body indicates this, then let us not deceive ourselves by blaming nature. In practically all cases it is because we are either eating *too much* food for our daily requirements and bodily functions or too much of the *wrong kind* of food.

Perhaps at the moment you *do* feel fit, in spite of being over-weight.

Why not try to lose some weight and see if your health benefits? You will feel more energetic, alert and enjoy life again. Sometimes, people assume they are too fat because of a medical disorder. In a few cases this may be correct, but in practically all instances it is *not* true. It is due to over-eating and the assumption of over-weight being due to some disorder is a very foolish and misleading one indeed.

Sensible dieting

It certainly sounds very alarming when one hears that following a slimming diet produces feelings of faintness and loss of energy. This is often the argument which persuades people *not* to follow a slimming routine. Let us think about it carefully, for it *can be true*.

If you select a badly balanced slimming diet or just decide 'not to eat' to lose weight, then undoubtedly you will feel dizzy and lethargic.

It is essential when slimming, to choose carefully the kind of dishes you eat and to watch your weight loss.

On the whole it is better to follow a plan of eating that gives a small but steady weight loss over a longer period.

This has two advantages, firstly it allows the body to become accustomed to smaller meals, so educating your system to *sensible* eating. Secondly, you are far more likely to *remain* slim if you lose weight fairly slowly. There are 'crash diets' included in this book, but, as stressed, they must only be followed for a very limited period. Pages 20 and 21 also cover this point in more detail.

Sometimes I have heard the arguments about feeling faint from over-weight people and when I have questioned them about when and how it happened, I invariably discover they

have either dieted foolishly or, in many cases, they have not dieted at all, but have just been *told* about the ill-effects of slimming and have seized upon this as a valid excuse for continuing to be over-weight and doing nothing about it.

Throughout this book it has been stressed that if you have to lose more than the odd few pounds in weight you must have medical approval and follow your doctor's advice at all times.

The idea that dieting means living on dull, uninteresting meals is of course foolishly incorrect. Today we know that slimming diets are *not* starvation diets. Obviously your intake of food must be less in calorie and/or carbohydrate content in order to lose weight. You will be adequately fed when dieting, in fact there is every chance that you will be *better* fed for you will be eating the foods that are high in nutritional value. Salads are of course useful on a weight reducing programme for generally the ingredients used are low in both calories and carbohydrates. If you dislike salads there is no need to include them in your meals.

Like many people who enjoy good food, and who spend time cooking and creating new dishes, I have always found the need to watch my weight. This means that over the years I have learned ways to lose those extra pounds and, having lost them, to choose the kind of foods that will help me to maintain a stable weight. You will notice I have said that I enjoy good food and this is one of the most important points about any successful slimming diet – the fact that you can diet and enjoy what you eat at the same time. The meals must be palatable, in fact the dishes should be as interesting and exciting as any you will find on other well planned menus.

This has been my object in writing this book, to prove to you that you *can* lose weight and indeed that you *will* lose weight if you select the right foods and the right recipes.

Let me tell you a little about the contents of this book.

I believe that in order to follow any kind of diet you must know *why* you select certain foods and *how* those foods, in the form of a diet, work to achieve their objective, in this case to make you slim and then help you *maintain* that good figure.

The first section of the book therefore deals with the theory behind slimming. You will find there are

details of the kind of foods you should choose for good health and good looks. This will enable you to learn a little about food values.

Do not be alarmed, you do not need to become a fully fledged dietician in order to appreciate the nutritional value of various foods; it is just a matter of understanding a few basic facts.

Foods to avoid

When you start your slimming routine there are certain foods it is better *NOT* to eat, or, if you find this to be a great hardship, then you may be able to eat them, but only in very small quantities. As you read about these foods you will probably recognize the fact that there are foods, such as alcohol, biscuits (cookies), cakes, bread, sweetened drinks, puddings and sweetmeats (candies), which have contributed so much to your excess weight.

The moment you decide to follow a good slimming routine you will be bombarded with suggestions, advice and various theories from friends and relatives. Listen and examine the points raised, but do not allow them to deter you from your campaign. Some of the

theories advanced by well-meaning friends will be myths and nonsense, for there are many false ideas about losing weight.

You may have read or come across the word 'Kilojoule' and wondered just what it meant. This word may well replace the better known Calorie (or Kilocalorie) and to make it more familiar you will find it is used throughout the book *with* the calorific value of recipes and foods. While on the subject of Kilojoules, calories and carbohydrates, I would like to refer you to the tables at the end of the book. These will enable you to plan your own menus and to make the wisest selection of dishes and foods when you dine out.

As you will find when you read through the book, there is a wide choice of diets to follow. You can of course, either limit your calories (Kilojoules) and base your diet on a reduced calorie count or you can follow a low-carbohydrate diet.

You are now almost ready to start on your new way of eating, but before you do so just check and see the ideal weight for your height and particular

build. Do not become too alarmed if the gap between your present weight and the one to which you aspire seems very large. You will need to follow your diet for some time to close the gap, but this is where I hope my recipes will help. By providing a variety of appealing dishes that avoid monotony, you will enjoy your cooking and eating, and lose weight.

In the second part of the book the recipes are arranged in the way in which they are found in most general cookery books, i.e. appetizers, soups, fish and meat dishes, etc. You may be a little surprised to see a section on desserts too, as these are generally assumed to be taboo for slimmers. You can eat and enjoy any of these dishes within your daily dietary needs. If however, you feel that planning your own slimming menus is difficult at this early stage then you will find a selection of balanced menus on pages 102 to 115.

As you will see each recipe has the number of calories, kilojoules and carbohydrate grammes per portion. Often these portions are generous, most recipes serve 4 people. So, if you want to make your calorie or carbohydrate intake even lower, then simply have smaller portions from the basic dish.

As I have stated previously most recipes will serve 4 people. This prevents the tiresome and time-consuming task of cooking one set of meals for slimmers and a completely different menu for non-slimmers. The meals are sufficiently interesting, nutritious and satisfying for *all* members of the family and the people who do not require to lose weight can add extra bread, potatoes or other foods as desired. Sometimes though it may benefit everyone in the family to follow the recipes in detail, for over-eating often runs in families.

Special needs

You will find a selection of short-term 'crash' diets in this book. This may help those of you who need a quick result in weight loss, for a

specific occasion, or to encourage you to *start* to lose weight.

Another section deals with the needs of children, and includes special recipes to appeal to the over-weight child or teenager. It is a sad reflection on modern eating habits that an ever-growing number of children are much too fat and parents should try and deal with this matter in a positive way. Over-weight children face health problems and could lose much of life's enjoyment.

As explained earlier, most recipes are suitable for the whole family, but in the section that begins on page 182 I have adopted a different technique. In this chapter are typical 'non slimming' family meals with extra advice on how to adapt portions for the slimmer. This means they may eat, and enjoy, everyday dishes just by making slight modifications.

Older people, who are over-weight,

may have special problems. I have tried to help senior citizens with recipes for particularly economical and easy-to-make slimming dishes. These have the added advantage of being particularly easy to digest.

Nowadays we hear a great deal about low-cholesterol foods. Often the doctor will advise both a slimming and a low-cholesterol diet. This means learning the kinds of fats and other foods to avoid or include in your daily meals. A short explanation on the meaning of low-cholesterol is found on page 130 and this is followed by a selection of suitable recipes, including some for a fat free diet.

Many of you who use this book will enjoy cooking and I hope you will find the dishes worthy of your culinary skills. Others of you may like good food but have little time, facilities or inclination for cooking. In these days when a selection of convenience foods enable one to prepare meals with a minimum of effort it is very possible to dine well, take only a little time to achieve an appetizing dish and still lose weight. If this kind of speedy meal preparation appeals to you, you will find many recipes to fulfil your requirements.

Today most homes have some labour saving appliances such as freezers, mixers, slow casseroles and pressure cookers. I have experimented and tested slimming recipes that make the best use of these modern kitchen aids.

All these sections should enable you to lose weight in a relatively pleasant way and a manner that is suitable for your particular mode of living.

Let us not pretend that slimming is really very simple. If you have to lose an appreciable amount of weight it will need will-power and perseverance to follow a fairly rigid régime for a prolonged period. The results though will give you so much pleasure that it is well worth all your efforts.

Join a slimming club

There are ways in which you can help yourself. Group therapy in the form of slimming clubs, where you meet other people with similar problems often prevents one from giving up. If you do not want to join a club then encourage other over-weight members of the family or your friends to diet too. Check regularly on your progress

towards that ideal figure; analyse any periods when you do not lose weight, discuss the reasons for this and take positive action to adapt your intake of food. All this is easier in company rather than by yourself.

On the other hand do not become a bore about slimming and talk about it all the time. If you are being entertained just eat sparingly of any fattening foods that have been provided. Probably you will have exceeded the dietary needs for that particular day, never mind you can eat less the next day and so balance the intake of food.

Keeping lost weight off

When the time arrives that you have lost the desired amount of weight, beware!!! All too often some people decide to return to their original way of eating with the result that they once more gain weight, often even more quickly than it was lost.

To maintain your weight you can obviously follow a more liberal diet than when losing those excess pounds but you must still eat wisely. On pages 194 to 211 you will find a selection of recipes that will assist you in choosing the right menus. I would like to thank the Home Economists who have produced the excellent photographs from my recipes. I am sure these will act as an incentive for most people to try out the dishes.

I have enjoyed writing this book and I would like to think it will prove a pleasure to use and be of value to a great number of people who previously have found dieting unsuccessful.

Notes

All recipes serve 4 people unless otherwise stated.

All spoon measures are level.

Ovens should be preheated to the specified temperature.

Follow only one column of measures. They are not interchangeable.

The symbols given above and below the recipes are:

■ represents calories

Kj represents kilojoules

□ represents carbohydrate grammes

Please note that the calories, kilojoules and carbohydrate grammes given are for *one* portion and not the whole dish unless otherwise stated.

Principles of Slimming

Principles of Slimming

This book contains many recipes and hints for slimmers and, as you will see from the pictures, it is full of appetizing, easy-to-make dishes that all the family will enjoy.

What are the principles of slimming? These are more fully explained in the various sections of this book. But to summarize briefly, there are a few points worth considering. The reason we are heavier, or let us use the right word, *fatter*, than we should be is a simple one, we have eaten more food than our bodies need. So, in order to lose weight we must eat less food of the right kind.

Dieting, it should be remembered, is not easy, but by following a sensible routine there is every chance of success. Keeping slim will then become a long-term process, it takes perseverance. It is a highly individual affair, no two people lose weight or maintain a good figure in the same way. It is largely governed by metabolism, explained more fully on page 21.

In following a good diet and losing excess weight you are heading towards better health, better looks, and as medical experts would agree, a longer life.

Foods for Health and Beauty

It is essential that, whilst you are dieting you eat the *right* foods so that your slimming routine makes you feel and look wonderful.

To build a healthy body as we grow or maintain this when we are adults we need *protein foods*: you will find these in: Meat and poultry of all kinds, fish of every type (ideal for slimmers), eggs, milk, milk products and cheese.

Cottage cheese is a good choice for a slimming diet.

Nuts and pulses (lentils, beans and peas) have to be eaten sparingly on some diets, so replace with other proteins, as above. Seeds, like sesame or grains, such as brown rice and wheatgerm are good, that is why bread and flour provide some of our protein; but as they are high sources of starch (a carbohydrate) so you must omit or restrict these foods. Avocados are an unusual fruit in that they are a minor source of protein.

For overall energy you need:

Protein foods as outlined above, plus foods containing the group of B vitamins. These are found in:

Wheatgerm and yeast, so when you omit bread it is a good idea to add these to soups, stews etc., they give a delicious taste (wheatgerm is available from Health Food Stores).

Meat, particularly liver, heart and brains.

To a lesser degree in the pulses, soya beans, egg yolk, nuts, yogurt, full cream milk, brown rice and seeds; there are also traces in some vegetables.

Carbohydrates and fats, like all foods, are sources of energy, but the former must be restricted on any slimming diet, and the latter on a low calorie diet.

Healthy body and mind

For a beautiful skin you should have an adequate amount of vitamin C (ascorbic acid) and foods rich in iron (which prevents anaemia). Vitamin C helps the body absorb iron so include the following foods.

Plenty of citrus fruits, blackcurrants, strawberries, green vegetables, especially parsley, spinach, watercress, tomatoes, potatoes (eat sparingly); liver, kidney, heart, turkey, egg yolks, grains.

For strong teeth you need foods rich in calcium, together with those containing vitamin D (which helps the body absorb calcium) and phosphorus. Vitamin D also is essential for good bone formation. When slimming choose from the following foods.

Cheese (cottage cheese is lowest in calories), milk, eggs, fish, poultry and meats, especially liver, fruits (cranberries very good), soya beans, olives, broccoli, sprouts.

Fluorine in water, or fish, is often recommended to prevent tooth decay.

For clear eyes you need foods that provide vitamin A as well as B, outlined on the left, so add to that list carrots, oily fish and fish liver, butter or margarine (these must be restricted on a low calorie diet).

For strong healthy hair you need a combination of all the foods outlined.

To aid mental relaxation and a good digestion, foods rich in vitamin B are important, see the list. This is aided by adding those foods that contain iodine; such as any of the following foods.

Fish, but especially cod, cod-liver, haddock, salmon, lobster and oysters, onions, bananas, strawberries and peanuts.

Foods to Restrict

If you are going to slim successfully there are certain foods you must avoid or restrict. These will depend somewhat on the *kind* of diet you have chosen, or been recommended. There are however, certain foods of which one should eat little on any form of slimming diet – these are listed first.

On any diet restrict your intake of the following foods.

Alcohol: Beer in particular, sweet wines and fortified wines, such as port. Remember if you are eating less on a slimming diet the effect of alcohol may be more marked, see also under 'Counting Calories'.

Biscuits and Cakes: As these are made basically from flour, fat and sugar they are high in both calories and carbohydrate content. Often they contain eggs, so it could be argued that they add protein, but there are many better ways of adding this to your diet.

Bread: This is both high in calories and carbohydrate content BUT does add protein plus other nutrients to the diet and therefore has important food value. This food should be restricted rather than omitted.

Cereals: Cornflakes, and rice – eat sparingly.

Cordials and sweet squashes: These often contain a high amount of sweetening so replace with unsweetened fresh fruit juices (although see comments under carbohydrates).

Dried fruits: These are high in both carbohydrate content and calories.

Flour products: In particular, puddings made with a high percentage of flour. Use as little flour or other thickening ingredients such as cornflour (cornstarch) as possible.

Jams and other preserves: These have both a high calorie and high carbohydrate content.

Lentils: Along with other pulse vegetables (beans and peas) these should be restricted, for although a valuable source of protein they are high in both calorific and carbohydrate content.

Potatoes: are one of the foods to restrict but, as shown in the table in page 218 the method of cooking is very important. If boiled they have less than half the

calories of a fried potato.

Sugar: The evil on *all* diets. Omit entirely and use sugar substitute. This applies to honey, syrups of all kinds (corn, golden, maple) and black treacle (molasses). Remember to replace sugar in all puddings, salad dressings and other forms of cookery.

COUNTING CALORIES

In addition to the above you will need to check carefully how much of the following foods you eat, all of which are high in calories.

Cheese: An important source of protein and calcium but most kinds are high in calories – choose cottage cheese.

Cream: Avoid, choose low fat yogurt instead.

Fats: All kinds, this includes oils and fatty meats and oily fish. Check the table and see the difference between fat and lean meats.

Mayonnaise: Also other oil dressings.

Nuts: These are an important source of protein and an essential food for most vegetarians but do have a high calorie value and a moderate carbohydrate content, *chestnuts* are lower in calories but higher in carbohydrate than other nuts.

Spirits: Such as whisky, brandy, gin, rum.

On a low-carbohydrate diet, in addition to the foods given for all diets – check on the content of the following.

Chestnuts: The highest carbohydrate content of any nuts.

Fruits: In particular, apples, bananas, mango, oranges, pears, raspberries.

Vegetables: Particularly those listed first, plus corn on the cob, and potatoes. Most other vegetables have some carbohydrate content, you can check on these in the tables.

Basic Principles

Your Ideal Weight

If you look at a collection of people they appear to be of entirely different shapes and sizes and yet they could be put into just three groups.

There are those who are basically long and thin, they have small frames and are described as *ectomorphic*. These people are fortunate in that, if they do put on weight, it does not show as much as in the case of their opposites.

This group are *endomorphic*, which means they have heavy bodies and may well be squat too. They are unlucky, for even a few kilogrammes or pounds of over-weight will show on their larger frames.

The third group have muscular bodies, and are known as being *mesomorphic*; they can never look as slim as the *ectomorphic* type, but on the other hand when they are at their ideal weight they look slimmer than those in the *endomorphic* group. They can consider themselves as having medium frames.

Of course you have variations on these themes, some people are half-way between a medium and a small frame or medium and large body; it is up to each individual to decide upon which set of weights to follow.

The important thing is DO NOT try and reach the ideal weight for a small frame if you know you have a large one. How can you tell? Generally by your hands and feet, or wrists and ankles. If they are slim and small in relation to your height etc., then you have a small frame.

Whether your over-weight shows to the outside world or not, YOU will know if you are carrying more weight than you should. Stand in front of a mirror, look at yourself critically, feel your flesh 'round your middle'; if you are gathering up a solid roll, then you certainly need to slim.

The word 'carrying' in the paragraph above is used advisedly, for if we are heavier than we should be, it is just as though we were carrying a heavy shopping basket or sack of coal every minute of the day.

To follow the tables, decide upon your particular frame, measure your height, *without shoes* and check upon the weight you hope to become. Remember these are only average, you could well vary by several kilogrammes or pounds.

THE TABLES

The figures are given as follows:
Metric height and weight
Height as measured in Britain and America but under this the weight is given in two ways:
UK: the British way of assessing weight, by stones (14 lb equals 1 stone) and lb.
USA: the American way of giving weight, i.e. just in pounds.

You will notice that, unlike old-fashioned weight tables, there is no column marked with your age. This is because nowadays medical opinion feels there is no reason at all why people should put on weight as they grow older, if they eat sensibly and take a reasonable amount of exercise.

Exercise has not been discussed so far in this book and it must be pointed out that ordinary walking, exercise in working, or playing a small amount of golf, or other games, will not make you lose much weight. It will however help to make you feel fit, but do not let it encourage you to eat more food than your diet states. If out in the air for any length of time one tends to feel more hungry.

Small Frame – Women

Metric		Imperial/American		
Height	Weight	Height	Weight UK st lb	USA lb
144.7 cm	43.9 kg	4 ft 9 in	6 13	97
147.3 cm	45.3 kg	4 ft 10 in	7 2	100
149.8 cm	46.7 kg	4 ft 11 in	7 5	103
152.4 cm	48.0 kg	5 ft 0 in	7 8	106
154.9 cm	49.4 kg	5 ft 1 in	7 11	109
157.4 cm	50.8 kg	5 ft 2 in	8 0	112
160.0 cm	52.1 kg	5 ft 3 in	8 3	115
162.5 cm	53.5 kg	5 ft 4 in	8 6	118
165.1 cm	54.8 kg	5 ft 5 in	8 9	121
167.6 cm	56.2 kg	5 ft 6 in	8 12	124
170.1 cm	58.0 kg	5 ft 7 in	9 2	128
172.7 cm	59.8 kg	5 ft 8 in	9 6	132
175.2 cm	61.6 kg	5 ft 9 in	9 10	136
177.8 cm	63.5 kg	5 ft 10 in	10 0	140
180.3 cm	65.7 kg	5 ft 11 in	10 5	145
182.8 cm	68.0 kg	6 ft 0 in	10 10	150

Medium Frame – Women

Metric		Imperial/American		
Height	Weight	Height	Weight UK st lb	USA lb
144.7 cm	46.2 kg	4 ft 9 in	7 4	102
147.3 cm	47.6 kg	4 ft 10 in	7 7	105
149.8 cm	48.9 kg	4 ft 11 in	7 10	108
152.4 cm	50.3 kg	5 ft 0 in	7 13	111
154.9 cm	51.7 kg	5 ft 1 in	8 2	114
157.4 cm	53.0 kg	5 ft 2 in	8 5	117
160.0 cm	54.4 kg	5 ft 3 in	8 8	120
162.5 cm	55.7 kg	5 ft 4 in	8 11	123
165.1 cm	57.1 kg	5 ft 5 in	9 0	126
167.6 cm	58.4 kg	5 ft 6 in	9 3	129
170.1 cm	60.3 kg	5 ft 7 in	9 7	133
172.7 cm	62.1 kg	5 ft 8 in	9 11	137
175.2 cm	63.9 kg	5 ft 9 in	10 1	141
177.8 cm	66.2 kg	5 ft 10 in	10 5	146
180.3 cm	68.4 kg	5 ft 11 in	10 10	151
182.8 cm	70.7 kg	6 ft 0 in	11 3	156

Large Frame – Women

Metric		Imperial/American		
Height	Weight	Height	Weight UK st lb	USA lb
144.7 cm	48.9 kg	4 ft 9 in	7 10	108
147.3 cm	50.8 kg	4 ft 10 in	8 0	112
149.8 cm	52.6 kg	4 ft 11 in	8 4	116
152.4 cm	54.4 kg	5 ft 0 in	8 8	120
154.9 cm	56.2 kg	5 ft 1 in	8 12	124
157.4 cm	58.0 kg	5 ft 2 in	9 2	128
160.0 cm	59.8 kg	5 ft 3 in	9 6	132
162.5 cm	61.6 kg	5 ft 4 in	9 10	136
165.1 cm	63.5 kg	5 ft 5 in	10 0	140
167.6 cm	65.3 kg	5 ft 6 in	10 4	144
170.1 cm	67.1 kg	5 ft 7 in	10 8	148
172.7 cm	68.9 kg	5 ft 8 in	10 12	152
175.2 cm	70.7 kg	5 ft 9 in	11 2	156
177.8 cm	72.5 kg	5 ft 10 in	11 6	160
180.3 cm	74.3 kg	5 ft 11 in	11 10	164
182.8 cm	76.2 kg	6 ft 0 in	12 0	168

Small Frame – Men

Metric		Imperial/American		
Height	Weight	Height	Weight UK st lb	USA lb
154.9 cm	52.1 kg	5 ft 1 in	8 3	115
157.4 cm	53.5 kg	5 ft 2 in	8 6	118
160.0 cm	54.8 kg	5 ft 3 in	8 9	121
162.5 cm	56.2 kg	5 ft 4 in	8 12	124
165.1 cm	58.0 kg	5 ft 5 in	9 2	128
167.6 cm	59.8 kg	5 ft 6 in	9 6	132
170.1 cm	61.6 kg	5 ft 7 in	9 10	136
172.7 cm	63.5 kg	5 ft 8 in	10 0	140
175.2 cm	65.3 kg	5 ft 9 in	10 4	144
177.8 cm	67.1 kg	5 ft 10 in	10 8	148
180.3 cm	68.9 kg	5 ft 11 in	10 12	152
182.8 cm	70.7 kg	6 ft 0 in	11 2	156
185.4 cm	72.5 kg	6 ft 1 in	11 6	160
187.9 cm	74.3 kg	6 ft 2 in	11 10	164
190.5 cm	76.2 kg	6 ft 3 in	12 0	168
193.0 cm	78.0 kg	6 ft 4 in	12 4	172

Medium Frame – Men

Metric		Imperial/American		
Height	Weight	Height	Weight UK st lb	USA lb
154.9 cm	54.4 kg	5 ft 1 in	8 8	120
157.4 cm	55.7 kg	5 ft 2 in	8 11	123
160.0 cm	57.1 kg	5 ft 3 in	9 0	126
162.5 cm	58.5 kg	5 ft 4 in	9 3	129
165.1 cm	60.3 kg	5 ft 5 in	9 7	133
167.6 cm	62.1 kg	5 ft 6 in	9 11	137
170.1 cm	63.9 kg	5 ft 7 in	10 1	141
172.7 cm	65.7 kg	5 ft 8 in	10 5	145
175.2 cm	67.5 kg	5 ft 9 in	10 9	149
177.8 cm	69.4 kg	5 ft 10 in	10 13	153
180.3 cm	71.2 kg	5 ft 11 in	11 3	157
182.8 cm	73.0 kg	6 ft 0 in	11 7	161
185.4 cm	74.8 kg	6 ft 1 in	11 11	165
187.9 cm	76.6 kg	6 ft 2 in	12 1	169
190.5 cm	78.4 kg	6 ft 3 in	12 5	173
193.0 cm	80.2 kg	6 ft 4 in	12 9	177

Large Frame – Men

Metric		Imperial/American		
Height	Weight	Height	Weight UK st lb	USA lb
154.9 cm	56.7 kg	5 ft 1 in	8 13	125
157.4 cm	58.5 kg	5 ft 2 in	9 3	129
160.0 cm	60.3 kg	5 ft 3 in	9 7	133
162.5 cm	62.1 kg	5 ft 4 in	9 11	137
165.1 cm	63.9 kg	5 ft 5 in	10 1	141
167.6 cm	65.7 kg	5 ft 6 in	10 5	145
170.1 cm	67.5 kg	5 ft 7 in	10 9	149
172.7 cm	69.4 kg	5 ft 8 in	10 13	153
175.2 cm	71.2 kg	5 ft 9 in	11 3	157
177.8 cm	73.0 kg	5 ft 10 in	11 7	161
180.3 cm	75.2 kg	5 ft 11 in	11 12	166
182.8 cm	77.0 kg	6 ft 0 in	12 2	170
185.4 cm	79.3 kg	6 ft 1 in	12 7	175
187.9 cm	81.6 kg	6 ft 2 in	12 12	180
190.5 cm	84.3 kg	6 ft 3 in	13 4	186
193.0 cm	87.0 kg	6 ft 4 in	13 10	192

Basic Principles

Myths Exploded

There are many myths and misconceptions regarding slimming and it is just as well to examine the best known before embarking on any diet, then you will know which of the many stories and theories to believe when your friends and acquaintances begin giving you good advice.

ON SLIMMING ITSELF

Theory: It does not matter if you are over-weight, as long as you feel fit. It *does* matter. There are exceptions to every rule and some very over-weight people may *appear* fit, say they *are* fit, and even *be* fit; but for the vast majority excess weight is a common factor in heart complaints and other illnesses.

Theory: Over-weight is often a family characteristic and therefore there is nothing that can be done. Over-weight in families may well be true, but the important thing is to examine the reasons for this. Generally it is because of a traditional way of eating. The parents may both have come from families who enjoyed 'good solid food' and, where there were plentiful supplies of pastry, cakes and biscuits; as everyone enjoyed this fare it was continued through the generations. It may be that the family bought a generous amount of sweetmeats to eat between meals. Also of course there may have been an inherited tendency to 'put on weight' easily. The person or people who decide to end the family tradition of being over-weight, and slim, will doubtless encounter opposition from their plump relations but they will probably find that, if they are successful, more members of the family will join them in a slimming routine.

Theory: Over-weight is because of a medical disorder and there is nothing you can do about it. There are relatively few people who *do* have a medical reason for being over-weight and your doctor will obviously have diagnosed this. In most cases we are over-weight because we eat too much food, or the wrong type of food, and if your doctor tells you that you should lose weight then follow his advice and you soon will see it was not a medical condition causing that extra fat, but just an excess of food.

Theory: If you follow a slimming diet you will feel ill and lose energy. If you are put on to a crash diet for a few days you may find you feel a little 'odd', people sometimes have a headache and feel slightly 'dizzy' but as explained on pages 118 to 126 these diets are meant for a few days only and MUST NOT BE FOLLOWED FOR LONGER.

A well balanced slimming diet will not make you feel ill or less energetic, in all honesty you may feel hungry for a while if you have been a large eater, for you are educating your body to feel satisfied with smaller quantities of food, but within a comparatively short space of time you should begin to feel very fit and very full of energy. If you do not experience a feeling of well being it is important to examine the diet and see if you are choosing the wrong kinds of foods *for you*, or, if you are following a doctor's diet sheet, it would be better to ask his advice.

Theory: A low-carbohydrate diet is more effective than a low-calorie diet.

There are three basic long-term slimming diets:

The first diet is based on *counting calories* and working out the foods that you can eat during a daily allowance. This has the disadvantage that you have to weigh or measure the food carefully (see pages 20 and 21), in order to keep a careful check on the calorific value. You also must 'add up' accurately.

The second way to diet is to check on the food with *a low* or *no carbohydrate value* and plan your diet round these. This has the disadvantage that it does mean you must limit fruits, which many people find extremely hard.

The third way is, on the whole, an expensive diet, but a very effective one. You concentrate on foods *high in protein only* (see page 12), plus a small amount of vegetables and fruit.

Each diet has, as you will see, certain advantages and disadvantages and you must weigh up just which diet will suit

you and your way of life. Some people prefer one kind of diet and find this effective; other people are more successful in adhering to one of the other kinds. The important point is to give the one recommended to you, or chosen by you, a fair trial before you decide it is not suitable for your eating habits. Do not 'chop and change' diets during a day, otherwise you have no means of checking upon the effectiveness of the particular routine.

Theory: The best way to diet is to continue eating your normal foods and just eat less of them. This could be a good way to diet, providing you have well-balanced meals originally, i.e. those high in protein and with a reasonable amount of fruit and vegetables, but if it is a badly balanced way of eating, then you are not achieving the purpose of sensible slimming, which is to establish a *permanent way of eating* so that you do not continually put on weight.

Theory: That people are over-weight because they retain fluid in the body. This may be true in some cases and your doctor will tell you to reduce the amount you drink, or whatever treatment to follow, but for most people it is quite all right to drink liquid but to check carefully on just what you are drinking. Tea

and coffee with a lot of milk and sugar is one of the most usual reasons for being over-weight. It is not the fluid content of the tea or coffee that is to blame, but the additional ingredients. Substitute skimmed milk for full-cream milk and saccharine tablets for sugar.

Check on the calorie and carbohydrate value of alcohol and fruit drinks.

Theory: It is better to eat more small meals than three larger ones. This does seem to be true in some cases, and so is ideal for the 'born nibbler'. You calculate the day's consumption of food and divide it into five or six snacks. This helps you to feel less hungry, gives you something to break the time gap between lunch and dinner and does produce a good weight loss.

ON PARTICULAR FOODS

Theory: If you rinse rice and pasta after cooking you dispose of the 'surplus starch' and the food is therefore less high in calories and carbohydrate content. Quite untrue. Tests carried out by experts dealing with both these foods have found this makes no appreciable difference to either the calorie or carbohydrate content.

Theory: If you replace sugar with honey or black treacle (molasses) you can have sweetened foods without adding weight. Quite untrue. Honey and black treacle (molasses) have *fewer* calories and a lower carbohydrate content than sugar, but still are sufficiently high to make it important to use these sparingly. Black treacle (molasses) is a valuable source of iron, but even so must be used sparingly when slimming. See the food charts, starting on page 212, for the calorific value and carbohydrate content of honey and black treacle (molasses).

Theory: If you eat grapefruit at every meal you lose weight and can eat anything else you desire. There is no food that can make you slim. Grapefruit is a good fruit to include on your diet, as it is low in calories and carbohydrate content. It has a sharp acid flavour which can assist your taste buds to shun over-sweet foods. You cannot however eat a big meal, then include a grapefruit and expect it to counteract the excess of calories and carbohydrates.

People will say 'I never eat a thing' and yet I put on weight. This is discussed more fully under the Introduction on page 6. Listen politely to all the sayings on slimming – but don't believe them all!

Basic Principles

Calories and Carbohydrates

It is important to differentiate between calories and carbohydrates and diets based upon a low intake of these.

First of all remember the common basis for both a low-calorie and a low-carbohydrate diet is to make sure that enough food of the right kind is taken to ensure good health (pages 12 and 13 deal more fully with this subject), but, at the same time, to reduce the intake of food sufficiently so you lose weight.

WHAT THEN IS A CALORIE?

A car engine needs fuel to enable it to work well. The body must have fuel, in the form of food, to provide the energy to breathe, keep the heart beating etc.

A calorie, or to give the correct title, a kilocalorie (Kcal) is a heat unit and it records the amount of energy given by food. One calorie represents the amount of heat required to raise the temperature of 1,000 g, or about 2 pints water by one degree Celcius.

Foods vary a great deal in their calorie content, some, like fat and carbohydrates, have a high value, others, such as green vegetables and most fruits, have a low one.

When you follow a slimming diet in which you count calories this is the ideal 'plan of campaign'.

Firstly, decide upon the daily number of calories you will allow yourself. A really low-calorie diet is based upon eating foods that together provide just 1,000 calories each day. This is a little on the severe side and you may well find that you can lose weight on a higher number. Most women can have between 1,000 to 1,500 calories daily while men can lose weight on 1,500 to 2,000 daily.

You must of course consult your doctor about the *ideal allowance for you.*

The reason you will lose weight on this allowance is because it has been found that most women will use 2,000 calories on an average a day in energy; most men about 3,000. This means that if you are going to *lose* weight your food needs to supply about 500 calories a day less than you need. When you have lost the weight desired then you can raise your intake of food to give just the required amount of calories to maintain your slim figure and new weight.

Secondly, while you can select any foods and count the calories, that is *bad* slimming, if you do not choose the right ones. The following is a better way:

As carbohydrate (sugar and starch) together with fat, are very high in calories avoid these as far as possible.

Instead work out your meals, based upon proteins and foods high in nutritional value (pages 12 to 15 and the various diets given on pages 102 to 115 will help you).

Count the calories of the dishes carefully, do not be tempted to cheat. Deduct the amount from your daily allowance and if you have spare calories then you can add a special 'treat'.

At first calorie counting may seem difficult, as you need to weigh or measure ingredients to have a true picture, but the recipes in this book will help as they have a clear indication of their calorific value. REMEMBER THE CALORIES ARE FOR THE BASIC DISH AND NOT THE VARIATIONS AND THEY ARE FOR A SINGLE PORTION, NOT THE COMPLETE DISH.

After a relatively short time, you will find you know exactly the weight of that slice of bread, knob or butter, or apple and it will fall into place quite easily.

You will notice there is another indication on the recipes, this is for a kilojoule. The kilojoule, or joule as it is sometimes called, has been used in nutritional data for some time, but there is every possibility that, in time, it will be the term used instead of the calorie, so it is wise to become accustomed to the name.

One kilocalorie equals 4.184 kilojoules. This makes a complicated sum when you want to work out menus for yourself, so in this book we are following the accepted practise and have based our calculations on:

One calorie equals 4.2 Kj (the abbreviation for kilojoules).

In the tables at the back of the book we have used an accurate conversion from metric to Imperial measures, i.e.

28.35 grammes equals 1 ounce

28.35 millilitres equals 1 fluid ounce. In recipes though we have returned to the method recommended in all modern recipes and given 25 g as the equivalent of 1 oz etc. The calculations on calories etc. are based on accurate conversion though.

WHAT IS CARBOHYDRATE?

Carbohydrate is taken into the body in the form of starch and sugar. These foods are then converted into simple sugars, of which glucose is the most important.

Unfortunately both starch and sugar are the foods that tend to add weight very easily and on a low-carbohydrate diet therefore these are the foods you restrict. The word 'unfortunately' has been used, since foods containing starch and sugar are very popular, but from a nutritional point of view the body will not suffer at all by the fact that the intake of these foods is drastically reduced.

The foods highest in carbohydrates are: Sweetmeats, biscuits, puddings, cakes (together with bread), anything made from flour, some fruit and vegetables and grains, such as rice.

This diet is a *low*, not 'non' carbohydrate one, you check on the carbohydrate value of foods that have this. The recipes and tables in the book will give you all the information needed.

This diet means you can have as much protein foods and fat as you wish, i.e. cheese, eggs, meat, poultry, milk etc. and butter, margarine, oil, various fats (shortenings).

It is generally recommended that the *maximum* daily allowance is 60 grammes of carbohydrate each day. It is only foods containing starch or sugar you count.

How much weight should one lose?

If you lose a kilogramme or 2 lb a week you should be satisfied. If you do not then you may have to lower either the calorie or carbohydrate content of your meals, depending upon which diet you are following. Individual weight loss depends upon the rate YOUR body uses up energy; the term used to describe this process is 'metabolism'.

One thing is certain; if you follow your selected diet sensibly you *will* slim and you *will* feel fit while doing this.

Basic Principles

Recipes for Slimming

Recipes for Slimming

The following pages give a variety of recipes for all courses of the meal and will, I hope, prove to slimmers that their food is not dull, but interesting, unusual and often a very welcome change from the more familiar fare.
The emphasis is on fresh ingredients, with the use of herbs and refreshing fruit juice, like lemon, to add flavour.
Seasoning plays an important part in recipes when you are slimming, for you need to avoid any feeling that the dish is lacking in taste. In some recipes the words 'freshly ground black pepper' are used. Do not worry unduly if you do not possess a pepper mill and peppercorns, but it is surprising just how much more taste the freshly ground peppercorns give the food. Invest in celery salt, tomato purée (paste) and a savoury Tabasco sauce, for adding a small amount often 'works wonders'.
Presentation of food is always an enjoyable part of the meal and even more so when your dishes have to be relatively simple. Use colourful salad garnishes where applicable.

APPETIZERS

The first course can add a great deal to the enjoyment of a dinner or luncheon menu and you have a surprising variety of dishes from which to choose. Try serving young vegetables separately. The most suitable are asparagus, globe artichokes, freshly cooked green beans.

ASPARAGUS POLONAISE: Top cooked hot asparagus with finely chopped hard-boiled egg and parsley; or cold asparagus with a lemon-flavoured dressing, as page 111.
GLOBE ARTICHOKES: Serve with melted butter (if you are on a low-carbohydrate diet) or well-seasoned lemon juice.
GREEN BEANS: Top hot or cold green beans with chopped parsley, chives or garlic and a little lemon juice and garnish with sliced tomatoes.
SALADS: An ideal start to the meal, especially when the ne v season's cucumber, salad greens and tomatoes arrive. Recipes for various salads are given on pages 40, 73, 147, but try simple salads, such as:
SLICED TOMATOES: Top with chopped chives, parsley and a slimmer's dressing.
CUCUMBER OR TOMATO: Slice and garnish or cut into boat shapes and fill with shrimps or cottage cheese, and top with chopped fresh herbs.
FRUIT OR FRUIT JUICES: Refreshing and relatively low in calories, but not to be taken too often if you are counting carbohydrate grammes.
FRESH GRAPEFRUIT SEGMENTS: Hot or cold. If serving hot then top the halved fruit with grated nutmeg or spice. You can add a little melted butter to encourage it to brown under the hot grill (broiler).
Mix grapefruit segments with other fresh fruits.
MELON: Scoop various types of melon into balls, flavour with orange or lemon juice and place in glasses. Top with twists of orange slices and mint leaves. A whole melon can be used as a basket and the pulp diced or scooped into balls and mixed with other fruits.

DELICIOUS PÂTÉS
A pâté can be made from a variety of ingredients: vegetables, fish and meat. These can form part of a well-balanced slimming diet if you choose suitable

Aubergine (Eggplant) Pâté; Slimmer's Liver Pâté

recipes. Those containing a high percentage of cream, brandy, etc. are not for 'calorie counters'. Remember that fish and meat are high in protein, but have no carbohydrate value.

Serve the pâté with a salad or eat with a spoon from a small dish; avoid hot toast or bread.

A few recipes are in this section, another recipe is given on page 196.

Aubergine (Eggplant) Pâté

■ 59/Kj 248 □ 10.0 g

Metric/Imperial

2 large aubergines

little olive oil

salt

pepper

2 × 15 ml spoons/2 tablespoons lemon juice

TO GARNISH:
1 lettuce heart

1 lemon, sliced

2 tomatoes, sliced

American

2 large eggplants

little olive oil

salt

pepper

2 tablespoons lemon juice

TO GARNISH:
1 lettuce heart

1 lemon, sliced

2 tomatoes, sliced

❧The best way for slimmers to cook aubergines (eggplants) in this pâté is to wrap a halved aubergine (eggplant) in lightly oiled foil. In this way you use the minimum of oil and prevent the skin from becoming hard. It then can be puréed in a blender with the soft pulp. Score the skin with a knife, sprinkle with a little salt and leave for half an hour; drain off any surplus moisture. This will make the skin lose its bitter flavour. Halve the aubergines (eggplants) lengthways. Brush with oil, sprinkle with salt and pepper and a little of the lemon juice, wrap as above. Put into an oiled dish and cover. Bake in a cool oven (140°C/275°F, Gas Mark 1) for at least an hour or until the vegetable is very soft. Then remove the soft pulp from the skin, or purée the complete vegetable in a blender or through a sieve. Mix with the remaining lemon juice and any extra seasoning required.

To serve: Either spoon into a bowl standing on a dish and arrange the lettuce leaves, lemon and tomato slices round the bowl, or place the lettuce on a flat dish and spoon the pâté over the leaves. Garnish with the lemon and tomato slices.

To freeze: The pâté freezes well. Do not freeze the salad garnish. Use within 6 months.

To thaw: Allow several hours at room temperature or longer in the refrigerator.
Variations:

1: If your diet permits using oil, blend 1–2 × 5 ml spoons/1–2 teaspoons olive or salad oil with the aubergine (eggplant) pâté.

2: Add a little curry powder and/or cayenne pepper or a few drops Tabasco sauce to the pâté.

Slimmer's Liver Pâté

■ 194/Kj 815 □ 3.6 g

Metric/Imperial

350 g/12 oz calf's or lamb's liver

1 onion, chopped

1 clove garlic, chopped

3 × 15 ml spoons/3 tablespoons beef stock

25 g/1 oz butter

salt

pepper

2 × 5 ml spoons/2 teaspoons chopped parsley

American

¾ lb calf's or lamb's liver

1 onion, chopped

1 clove garlic, chopped

3 tablespoons beef stock

2 tablespoons butter

salt

pepper

2 teaspoons chopped parsley

❧Cut the liver into thin strips, put into a saucepan with all the remaining ingredients except parsley. Simmer for 5 minutes or until the meat is just tender. Then add parsley and put everything through a mincer (meat grinder) or pound together or purée in a blender until smooth. Spoon into a dish to cool.

To serve: Spoon onto a serving plate and serve with salad or a low-calorie crispbread.

To freeze: This pâté freezes excellently for up to a month.

To thaw: Slowly in the refrigerator.

Appetizers

Fish Pâté

■ 82/Kj 344 □ 1.5 g

Metric/Imperial
few drops oil
450 g/1 lb white fish
1 lemon
3 × 5 ml spoons/3 teaspoons chopped tarragon, fennel or parsley
salt
pepper
3 × 15 ml spoons/3 tablespoons plain yogurt

American
few drops oil
1 lb lean fish
1 lemon
3 teaspoons chopped tarragon, fennel or parsley
salt
pepper
3 tablespoons plain yogurt

Brush a little oil over a plate, place the fish on this. Grate the 'zest' (yellow part of the lemon rind) and sprinkle onto the fish. Squeeze the juice and pour over fish with half the herbs, salt and pepper to taste. Cover the fish with oiled foil or a saucepan lid and place over a pan of boiling water to steam for 10 minutes or until fish is just tender. Spoon the fish, liquid and herbs into a bowl, flake, then pound until smooth, adding the yogurt.

To serve: Chill, then spoon into small dishes or onto crisp lettuce. Garnish with the rest of the herbs.

To freeze: This freezes well; use within 6 weeks.

To thaw: Slowly in the refrigerator.

Variations:

1: Add chopped chives or crushed garlic for a stronger flavour.

2: Use 25 g/1 oz to 50 g/2 oz (2 to 4 tablespoons) melted butter in place of half the yogurt.

3: Slimmer's Taramasalata: Use smoked cod's roe in place of white fish, add 1 to 2 crushed garlic cloves to the mixture.

4: Fresh Cod's Roe Pâté: Either buy ready-cooked fresh cod's roe or steam uncooked roe over boiling water for about 20 minutes until white; use as basic recipe above, but add a little tomato purée (paste).

Prawn (Shrimp) and Grapefruit Cocktail

■ 60/Kj 252 □ 6.3 g

Metric/Imperial
2 medium grapefruit
small portion of cucumber
2 small tomatoes, skinned and thinly sliced
100 g/4 oz shelled prawns
2–3 × 15 ml spoons/2–3 tablespoons lemon mayonnaise, see page 164
few lettuce leaves
TO GARNISH:
1 lemon, sliced
1 × 5 ml spoon/1 teaspoon chopped dill, fennel or parsley

American
2 medium grapefruit
small portion of cucumber
2 small tomatoes, skinned and thinly sliced
¼ lb shelled shrimp
2–3 tablespoons lemon mayonnaise, see page 164
few lettuce leaves
TO GARNISH:
1 lemon, sliced
1 teaspoon chopped dill, fennel or parsley

Cut away the skin from the grapefruit, removing the white pith at the same time, then cut out segments of the fruit, discarding any white pith and pips (pits); do this over a bowl so that no juice is wasted. Cut the cucumber into thick matchsticks, retaining the peel for colour and flavour. Mix the grapefruit segments, cucumber and tomato slices with any grapefruit juice in the bowl, most of the prawns (shrimp) – reserve 4 for the garnish, and mayonnaise. Shred the lettuce very finely, divide between four glasses, top with the grapefruit mixture and garnish with the lemon, prawns (shrimp) and herbs.

To serve: Well chilled.

To freeze: This is not a dish which will freeze.

Variations:

1: Use orange segments instead of grapefruit or a mixture of orange and grapefruit.

2: Use a peeled sliced avocado instead of the 2 tomatoes.

Prawn (Shrimp) and Grapefruit Cocktail; Les Crudités; Fish Pâté

Les Crudités

This classic French dish is an ideal appetizer. The food is interesting, varied and colourful, so full of 'eye-appeal'. As there is no cooking, the ingredients retain the maximum vitamin, mineral salt and high-fibre content. One feels well-fed and satisfied after a portion of les crudités. Fruit is not traditionally part of this dish, but some can be used if you have not enough vegetables. Do not include too much fruit if following a low-carbohydrate diet.

Buy your ingredients carefully, everything must look very fresh. Wash or peel the vegetables according to type, then cut or divide into the right shape and size to pick up with your fingers. The raw vegetables are then dipped into a dressing before being eaten; choose from the low-calorie dressing recipes on pages 80 to 81.

Arrange the food on a large dish or tray with one, or several bowls, of dressings in the centre. If you are on a strict diet, it is better to fill individual plates and bowls to give a more accurate check on the calorie and carbohydrate content. Here are some foods you might include:

Apples choose dessert varieties. Do not peel, cut into thick slices, dip into lemon juice.

Apricots halve and stone (pit).

Aubergines (**eggplants**) surprisingly good raw; slice or dice, do not peel.

Brussels sprouts choose baby sprouts.

Carrots prepare young baby carrots or cut larger ones into matchsticks.

Cauliflower divide into small florets. Dust with paprika for extra colour.

Celeriac (**celery root**) peel, cut into matchsticks. Celeriac discolours easily so *soak* in lemon juice.

Celery cut into uniform lengths or make into curls, see page 94.

Chicory (**endive**) separate the white leaves or divide the hearts into portions.

Courgettes (**zucchini**) another vegetable which can be enjoyed raw; cut into thick slices, do not peel.

Cucumber this is easier to handle if cut into thick matchsticks, rather than slices.

Leeks serve baby leeks whole or cut larger ones into thick slices.

Lettuce divide heart into portions.

Mushrooms choose firm, plump button mushrooms; wash but do not peel.

Onions choose fat spring onions [scallions], leave some of the green stalk on to make them easier to handle. The stalk can be cut to give a flower effect, see page 94.

Oranges peel and divide into segments; do not skin these, for the fruit would be too difficult to handle.

Peppers (**capsicums**) use both red and green – discard core and seeds (pits) and cut into strips.

Pineapple peel, cut into rings, then divide into portions.

Radishes leave a little stalk on these to make them easy to eat; the radishes can be cut into flower shapes as described on page 94.

Tomatoes cut into quarters, do not skin.

Turnip peel and cut into fairly thin matchsticks.

Swede (**rutabaga**) peel and cut into fairly thin matchsticks or cut fairly thick slices of the peeled vegetable, place on a chopping board then cut out fancy shapes with a small biscuit (cookie) cutter. You can prepare balls of either raw turnip or swede with a vegetable scoop.

Appetizers

SOUPS

Do not listen to people who say you cannot serve soups when slimming. It depends on the ingredients used. Hot soups can create a feeling of warmth and well-being in cold weather and may prevent you eating more fattening dishes. A cold soup is a refreshing start to any meal. Some substantial soups can form a complete meal; see pages 29 to 33.

Choose clear soups with low-calorie vegetables if counting calories, but you can add meat, fish, fat and cream if reducing the carbohydrate content of your meals. Avoid thickening soups with flour, cornflour (cornstarch) or starchy vegetables.

To Freeze Stock and Soups

Instructions on freezing soups are given in the recipes. Pack in handy-sized containers so you can defrost the mixture quickly and prepare exactly the right number of servings. As most soups contain a high percentage of liquid, allow at least 1 cm/$\frac{1}{2}$ inch to 2.5 cm/1 inch headroom in containers so the liquid can expand during freezing.

To Thaw Soups

You can often hasten the process by standing the frozen container in a bowl of cold water. Whisk or stir thawed soup briskly or purée in a blender before reheating the soup; then reheat or serve cold according to the recipe.

Consommé

■ o/Kj o □ o.o g

Consommé turns any meal into a special occasion. Full of meaty goodness, it is a soup that will satisfy the hungry slimmer.

CONSOMMÉ

This is the ideal soup for slimmers, for as you will see on this page it contains virtually no calories and has no carbohydrate content. If you add a few cooked, diced or shredded vegetables, such as carrots, onions or peppers (capsicums), to a consommé it is more interesting and you need add very few extra calories. A consommé can be served hot, cold or iced, and freezes well for 2 to 3 months.

To Make a Beef Consommé

Simmer 0.5 kg/1 lb shin, or other inexpensive stewing beef, in just enough water to cover or beef stock (made from beef bones) for several hours, or for about an hour in a pressure cooker at 15 lb/High pressure. Flavour the liquid by adding a bunch of herbs (bouquet garni), a sliced carrot and onion, or other vegetables, and salt and pepper to taste. At the end of the cooking time, strain the soup through several thicknesses of muslin or cheesecloth. For perfect clarity add the whites of 2 eggs, plus the shells, to the strained liquid, simmer for 15 to 20 minutes and strain once again. Chicken or game consommé is made in the same way as beef consommé.

Queen Soup

■ 36/Kj 151 □0.0 g

Metric/Imperial

scant 750 ml/1¼ pints beef consommé

2 egg yolks

2 × 15 ml spoons/2 tablespoons lemon juice

salt

pepper

TO GARNISH:

little chopped parsley and/or chives

twists of lemon, see page 94

American

3 cups beef consommé

2 egg yolks

2 tablespoons lemon juice

salt

pepper

TO GARNISH:

little chopped parsley and/or chives

twists of lemon, see page 94

❧Put the consommé into a saucepan. Bring almost to boiling point. Blend the egg yolks and lemon juice with a shake of salt and pepper and *whisk* into the hot, but not boiling soup. Simmer for 2 minutes only.

To serve: Pour into soup cups and top with parsley and/or chives. Arrange lemon twists on the side of the soup cups.

To freeze: This is not a soup that will freeze.

Variation:

Cold Queen Soup: Use a really good stock if possible. Chill this well then pour into a liquidizer goblet (blender jar). Add the egg yolks and lemon juice and blend for a few seconds. Serve at once topped with chopped herbs.

Consommé con Carne

■ 162/Kj 680 □5.0 g

Metric/Imperial

1 fresh or canned red pepper (capsicum)

25 g/1 oz butter or margarine

2 medium onions, chopped

100 g/4 oz minced beef, raw

3 medium tomatoes, skinned and chopped

750 ml/1¼ pints beef stock or consommé or water and 1 beef stock cube

salt

1 × 2.5 ml spoon–2 × 5 ml spoons/ ½–2 teaspoons chilli powder (see method)

150 ml/¼ pint plain yogurt

TO GARNISH:

2 × 15 ml spoons/2 tablespoons chopped parsley

From left: Queen Soup; Beef Consommé; Consommé con Carne

American

1 fresh or canned red pepper

2 tablespoons butter or margarine

2 medium onions, chopped

¼ lb raw ground beef

3 medium tomatoes, skinned and chopped

3 cups beef stock or consommé or water and 2 beef bouillon cubes

salt

½–2 teaspoons chilli powder (see method)

⅔ cup plain yogurt

TO GARNISH:

2 tablespoons chopped parsley

❧If using a fresh pepper (capsicum), discard the core and seeds and cut the pepper (capsicum) into matchstick pieces. Melt butter or margarine in a saucepan and sauté the onion for 3 to 4 minutes. Add the beef, tomatoes and pepper (capsicum), then pour in the stock, consommé or water and stock (bouillon) cube(s), add salt and chilli powder to taste. Stir once or twice. As chilli powder is *very* hot, use sparingly. Cover the pan tightly and simmer for 45 minutes.

To serve: Top with yogurt and parsley.

To freeze: Prepare then freeze. Use within 3 months. The chilli powder loses a little of its potency during freezing, so you may need to add a little extra *when* the soup has thawed.

To thaw: See comments on page 28.

Variations:

1: Omit the yogurt topping.

2: Purée the soup in a warmed blender with or without yogurt.

3: Serve the soup cold; it is then nicer if puréed in a blender, allowed to cool, then topped with yogurt and chopped chives in place of, or combined with, parsley.

Soups

Brown Fish Soup

■ 196/Kj 823 □5.0 g

Metric/Imperial

25 g/1 oz butter

1–2 rashers lean bacon, de-rinded and diced

1 medium onion, chopped

1 leek, thinly sliced

scant 1 litre/1¾ pints chicken stock or water and 1 chicken stock cube

1–2 × 15 ml spoons/1–2 tablespoons tomato purée

350 g/12 oz white fish, skinned and flaked

salt

pepper

pinch saffron powder*

2 × 15 ml spoons/2 tablespoons sherry

1–2 × 5 ml spoons/1–2 teaspoons chopped fennel

1 × 15 ml spoon/1 tablespoon chopped parsley

American

2 tablespoons butter

1–2 slices lean bacon, de-rinded and diced

1 medium onion, chopped

1 leek, thinly sliced

3¾ cups chicken stock or water and 2 chicken bouillon cubes

1–2 tablespoons tomato paste

¾ lb lean fish, skinned and flaked

salt

pepper

pinch saffron powder*

2 tablespoons sherry

1–2 teaspoons chopped fennel

1 tablespoon chopped parsley

Heat the butter over a low heat until it just turns brown, but do not allow to burn. Add the diced bacon, plus the rinds (if any), and the prepared vegetables. Cook steadily for several minutes, turning once or twice and taking care the butter does not darken any more. Remove the bacon rinds (if any). Pour in the stock, or water and stock (bouillon) cube(s). Heat for a few minutes then add the tomato purée (paste), skinned and flaked fish, salt, pepper and saffron powder. Simmer for 15 minutes, then add the sherry and the fresh herbs.

To serve: Hot with crisp toast made from starch-reduced (low-calorie) bread. This makes a light main course.

To freeze: This soup freezes well; use within 3 months. Omit sherry if possible until reheating and do not overcook the fish.

To thaw: Reheat gently from the frozen state, add the sherry to the hot soup.

Variation:

Make the soup as above up to the stage of adding the fish. Purée in a blender or through a sieve until the mixture is smooth. Return to the pan, add the flaked fish and continue as above. If preferred, the soup may be cooked completely then sieved or puréed in a blender.

* **Saffron** comes from the stamens of a crocus and is available powdered or in strands. Saffron strands could be infused with the liquid in recipes, but remove before serving if using instead of the powder.

Creamed Liver Soup

■ 198/Kj 832 □7.7 g excluding croûtons

Metric/Imperial

225 g/8 oz calf's or lamb's liver

25 g/1 oz butter or margarine

2 medium onions, finely chopped

300 ml/½ pint beef stock or water and ½ beef stock cube

450 ml/¾ pint milk

salt

pepper

TO GARNISH:

chopped chives and/or parsley

American

½ lb calf's or lamb's liver

2 tablespoons butter or margarine

2 medium onions, finely chopped

1¼ cups beef stock or water and 1 beef bouillon cube

2 cups milk

salt

pepper

TO GARNISH:
chopped chives and/or parsley

❧Cut the liver into 5 mm/¼ inch cubes or put through a coarse mincer (meat grinder). Heat the butter or margarine and cook the liver with the onions for 1 to 2 minutes only, stirring once or twice. Pour in the stock, or water with the half (whole) stock (bouillon) cube, and milk and simmer for 10 minutes or until the liver and onions are tender. Add salt and pepper to taste. Purée the soup in a warmed blender or through a sieve until smooth. Reheat and garnish with chopped chives and/or parsley.

To serve: Hot with croûtons of toasted starch-reduced crispbread or use crispbread cut into small shapes.

To freeze: This soup freezes well for 6 weeks.

To thaw: See comments on page 28.

Variations:

1: Use lamb's kidneys in place of liver in the basic recipe or variation 2.

2: Liver Soup Niçoise: Use all stock instead of stock and milk and cook 2 skinned and chopped cloves of garlic, and 2 to 3 skinned (peeled), chopped tomatoes with the liver and onion.

Lemon Avocado Soup

■ 89/Kj 374 ☐ 5.6 g

Metric/Imperial

1 large lemon

2 medium avocados

450 ml/¾ pint chicken stock

150 ml/¼ pint plain yogurt

salt

white pepper

2–3 spring onions, finely chopped

American

1 large lemon

2 medium avocados

2 cups chicken stock

⅔ cup plain yogurt

salt

white pepper

2–3 scallions, finely chopped

❧Grate enough lemon zest to give 1 × 2.5 ml spoon/½ teaspoon; be careful to use just the yellow 'zest' and none of the bitter white pith. Put into a bowl with the lemon juice. Halve the avocados, remove the stones (pits), and scoop out the pulp. Mash this with the lemon juice and grated zest. Add the cold stock and yogurt, stir or whisk until smooth. If you have a blender, put small amounts of the lemon 'zest', the lemon juice, avocado pulp, stock and yogurt into a blender goblet and purée until smooth. Add salt and pepper then the chopped spring onions (scallions). Cover and chill before serving.

To serve: As cold as possible.

To freeze: Freeze without the spring onions (scallions); add these before serving. Use within 2 months.

To thaw: For several hours in the refrigerator.

Variations:

1: Top the soup with more yogurt and paprika.

2: Curried Avocado Soup: Add 1 × 5 ml spoon/1 teaspoon curry powder to the basic ingredients.

3: Avocado Prawn (Shrimp) Soup: Make the avocado soup, use fish stock (made as page 41) rather than chicken stock if possible. Add approximately 75 g/3 oz chopped prawns (shrimp) before serving. If freezing this, use within a month.

Brown Fish Soup; Creamed Liver Soup; Lemon Avocado Soup

Soups

Tomato Soup

■ 102/Kj 428 □ 5.3 g

Metric/Imperial

25 g/1 oz butter or margarine

1 onion, chopped

1 clove garlic, chopped

450 g/1 lb tomatoes, skinned and chopped

300 ml/½ pint water or chicken or ham stock

2–3 bacon rinds

bouquet garni

salt

pepper

pinch cayenne pepper

1–2 drops liquid sugar substitute

1 × 15 ml spoon/1 tablespoon tomato purée

American

2 tablespoons butter or margarine

1 onion, chopped

1 clove garlic, chopped

1 lb tomatoes, skinned and chopped

1¼ cups water or chicken or ham stock

rind from 2–3 slices bacon

bouquet garni (bunch of herbs)

salt

pepper

pinch cayenne pepper

1–2 drops liquid sugar substitute

1 tablespoon tomato paste

❧ Melt butter or margarine in a saucepan add the onion and garlic and sauté for 3 to 4 minutes, then add the remaining ingredients. Simmer for 25 minutes. Remove the bacon rinds and *bouquet garni*. Purée the soup through a sieve or in a blender.

To serve: Although this soup is generally served hot, it is delicious chilled, but you may find you need a little extra liquid.

To freeze: This soup will freeze for up to 3 months. See also variation 3.

To thaw: See comments on page 28.

Variations:

1: Speedy Tomato Soup: Omit the tomatoes and water or stock and use 750 ml/1¼ pints/3 cups tomato juice.

2: Tomato Bouillabaisse: Prepare the basic tomato soup, cook for about 10 minutes, then add 175 g/6 oz to 225 g/8 oz skinned and diced white (lean) fish; use a mixture of fish if possible. Cook for a further 10 minutes, then add 75 g/3 oz to 100 g/4 oz prawns (shrimp) or other shellfish and heat for a few minutes.

Remove the bacon rinds and *bouquet garni*. Top with chopped parsley and/or chervil.

3: Tomato Sorbet: Prepare the basic tomato soup, freeze then fold in 2 stiffly whisked (beaten) egg whites and freeze again. Serve in glasses or chilled soup cups. Garnish with a little cottage cheese and twists of lemon.

4: Tomato Soup Hungarian Style: Add 2 × 5 ml spoons/2 teaspoons paprika and a chopped red pepper (capsicum) to the other ingredients. Top the soup with plain yogurt and paprika before serving.

5: Tomato con Carne: Omit the cayenne pepper and substitute chilli powder to taste. Just before serving add some drained, canned kidney beans and simmer gently until the kidney beans are heated through.

Spinach Soup

■ 57/Kj 239 □ 5.7 g

Metric/Imperial

2 medium onions, finely chopped

600 ml/1 pint chicken stock or water and 1 chicken stock cube

0.75 kg/1½ lb spinach, well-washed

1 bay leaf

sprig parsley

salt

pepper

pinch grated nutmeg, see method

300 ml/½ pint plain yogurt

TO GARNISH:

paprika

American

2 medium onions, finely chopped

2½ cups chicken stock or water and 2 chicken bouillon cubes

1½ lb spinach, well-washed

1 bay leaf

sprig parsley

salt

pepper

pinch grated nutmeg, see method

1¼ cups plain yogurt

TO GARNISH:

paprika

❧ Put the onion, stock, or water and stock (bouillon) cube(s), and the well-washed spinach into a pan. Add the bay leaf, parsley, salt and pepper. Cover the pan and cook steadily for 10 to 15 minutes until the spinach is tender. Remove the bay leaf and purée the soup through a sieve or in a blender.

To serve: As a hot soup: Return to the pan with the nutmeg and half the yogurt, heat without boiling. As a cold soup: Chill the purée and whisk in half the yogurt. Omit nutmeg. Spoon both soups into soup cups. Top with the remainder of the yogurt and paprika.

To freeze: Although these green vegetable soups are nicer when freshly made, they can be frozen for up to 2 months. Add the yogurt when the purée mixture has thawed.

To thaw: See the comments on page 28.

Variations:

1: Use chopped frozen spinach instead of the fresh vegetable. Finely chop or grate the onions and cook for 5 minutes in the liquid, *then* add the frozen spinach and continue as above. It is not essential to purée this soup.

2: Cabbage Soup: Substitute 350 g/12 oz to 450 g/1 lb shredded cabbage (or other green vegetable) for the spinach.

3: Cauliflower Soup: Use a medium cauliflower in place of the spinach. Chop a few of the tender cauliflower stalks and leaves and simmer in the liquid with the onions for 5 minutes to give a pronounced flavour, then divide the head of the cauliflower into small florets, add to the soup and cook until tender. Remove 4 to 6 small florets for garnishing, purée the remainder of the ingredients and proceed as spinach soup. Top with yogurt, small cauliflower florets and paprika.

4: Creamy soups: If you are on a low-carbohydrate diet, you could substitute soured (sour) or fresh cream and a little lemon juice for all, or some of the yogurt in the soup, then top with fresh cream.

Curried Cucumber Soup

■ 83/Kj 349 □ 10.49 g

Metric/Imperial
1 medium cucumber
small bunch spring onions
1–2 × 5 ml spoons/1–2 teaspoons curry powder
300 ml/½ pint plain yogurt
approximately 150 ml/¼ pint skimmed milk
salt
pepper
TO GARNISH:
1 × 15 ml spoon/1 tablespoon chopped parsley
little paprika

American
1 medium cucumber
small bunch scallions
1–2 teaspoons curry powder
1¼ cups plain yogurt
approximately ⅔ cup skimmed milk
salt
pepper
TO GARNISH:
1 tablespoon chopped parsley
little paprika

✤Peel the cucumber and grate about three-quarters; cut the remainder into matchstick-shaped pieces for garnishing. Chop the spring onions (scallions) finely, using only very little of the tender part of the green stalks; avoid the tough green portions. Mix the grated cucumber, onions, curry powder and yogurt together with enough milk to give a pouring consistency. Add salt and pepper to taste.

To serve: Chill and serve in chilled soup cups and garnish with the remaining cucumber, parsley and paprika.

To freeze: This soup does not freeze well as the raw cucumber and onions (scallions) lose their crispness.

Variations:

1: Omit the curry and flavour the soup with a little chopped mint, or other herbs.

2: Cucumber and Tomato Soup: Use tomato juice in place of the yogurt and milk.

Spinach Soup; Tomato Soup; Curried Cucumber Soup

Soups

FISH

Fish is one of the best protein foods to include in your diet. It is low in calories and has no carbohydrates. There is such a range that you can have many interesting dishes.

Many fish are lacking in natural oils, so need butter, or other fat, to give a moist texture during the cooking process. This is no problem if you are on a low-carbohydrate diet.

The hints on adapting basic cooking methods and the recipes in this chapter should solve the problems of fish cookery for slimmers.

Cooking Fish the Slimming Way

If you make certain modifications you can cook fish by most of the classic methods and still include this in a sensible slimming diet.

This method retains the good flavour of the fish, but care must be taken that it does not dry in the oven. Use a moderately hot oven (190°C/375°F, Gas Mark 5) when baking fillets or cutlets (steaks) and place just above the centre of the oven; use a slightly lower position in the oven for whole, large fish.

Allow about 15 minutes for thin fillets of fish, 20 to 25 minutes for thicker fillets or cutlets (steaks) and about 15 minutes per 0.5 kg/1 lb for whole fish. You will need to add an extra 5 to 10 minutes when baking fish wrapped in foil.

Baking can be varied in many ways. If you are on a **low-carbohydrate** diet then place the fish in a well-greased oven-proof dish; add salt, pepper, chopped herbs and/or lemon juice to flavour, then top the fish with plenty of melted butter or margarine. Do not cover the dish. Bake until tender and the fish will be golden-brown and moist.

This method is not suitable for a **low-calorie** diet, for every 25 g/1 oz/2 table-spoons butter or margarine adds 220 to 260 calories to the dish. There are, however, many ways in which baking can be used without increasing the calorie count appreciably.

Moisten the fish with skimmed milk, lemon, orange or tomato juice or a fresh purée of tomatoes, or sliced, raw tomatoes with chopped onion and garlic. Because little, if any, fat is used it is better in this instance to cover the dish; this may mean increasing the cooking time slightly.

Another excellent method of baking the fish is to first wrap it in greased foil, adding various ingredients as on page 36; these can be varied in many ways. The fish is kept moist and all the flavour is retained.

Soufflé-topped Fish

Put 4 portions of fish (e.g. flounder or sole), each weighing about 100 g/4 oz into a greased ovenproof dish. Add salt, pepper and lemon juice to flavour. Cover the dish and bake, as directed on this page, but for only 10 to 15 minutes, depending upon the thickness of the fish, until nearly tender. Separate 2 eggs; blend the yolks with 25 g/1 oz/$\frac{1}{4}$ cup grated Edam cheese, salt and pepper and 1 × 15 ml spoon/1 tablespoon chopped parsley. Fold in the stiffly whisked egg whites. Spoon on top of the fish and return to the oven, without the cover. Bake for a further 10 minutes.

To serve: At once.

■ 144/Kj605 □Trace

Stuffed Fish

Baked fish is more interesting if filled with a stuffing. There are several suitable recipes in this section. Split, bone whole fish and put in the stuffing. Spread skinned fillets with stuffing, roll or fold, or top cutlets (steaks) with stuffing. Cook as the basic directions on this page, but allow an extra 10 to 15 minutes cooking time.

Pacific Ratatouille

■ 209/Kj878 □ 9.6 g

Metric/Imperial

ingredients as for Ratatouille, see page 209.

4–6 plaice fillets (each 175 g/6 oz)

American

ingredients as for Ratatouille, see page 209.

4–6 flounder fillets (each 6 oz)

♣Prepare and cook the ratatouille, as directed on page 209. Skin the plaice (flounder) fillets and fold. Put half the ratatouille into a greased ovenproof dish, place the fish on top, then cover with the rest of the ratatouille. Cover the dish, bake for approximately 40 minutes in the centre of a moderately hot oven (190°C/375°F, Gas Mark 5).

To serve: As soon as cooked.

To freeze: The completed dish is better freshly cooked, but thawed ratatouille could be used.

POACHING

Often one hears the term 'boiling' to describe the process of cooking fish in liquid. This should never happen, for the fish is spoiled if cooked in the high temperature of a boiling liquid; the liquid should just **simmer gently**.

Slimmers can choose a variety of liquids from water, flavoured with herbs, lemon or orange juice and the 'zest' of the fruits (coloured part of the rind), to tomato juice or a mixture of wine and water. Fish can be poached in milk or milk and water.

A variety of vegetables can be cooked with the fish; if these take longer to cook then simmer in the liquid until nearly ready before adding the fish, for overcooked fish is spoiled fish.

If you place the fish in cold liquid, bring this to simmering point and allow from 3 to 5 minutes steady simmering for thin fillets; 5 to 7 minutes for thicker fillets and cutlets (steaks). Whole fish take from about 10 minutes per 0.5 kg/ 1 lb.

STEAMING

This simple way of cooking fish retains both flavour and texture, that is why it is excellent when using fish in salads or moulds. It is considered a particularly easy-to-digest method of cooking the fish, so is ideal for slimming.

Grease a plate or dish lightly and place the prepared fish on this. Add salt, pepper, a little lemon juice or milk to moisten, plus a small amount of extra butter (unless avoiding fat). Cover with another plate, foil or a saucepan lid and cook over a saucepan of boiling water until tender. Allow slightly longer than if poaching the fish.

Pacific Ratatouille; Stuffed Fish; Soufflé-topped Fish

Fish

FRYING

For 'calorie-counters', frying is definitely taboo, for the amount of fat required will add appreciably to the daily calories; although this can be minimised if you use a non-stick pan, where about half the usual amount of fat or oil will give a satisfactory result.

If you are following a low carbohydrate diet, frying fish is quite a good choice if you do not use a breadcrumb or batter coating. The classic dish on the opposite page illustrates a simple and delicious way to fry.

OVEN 'FRIED' FISH

Although the following method is not strictly frying, it is an excellent compromise, for the fish coating is crisp and it will suit the people who enjoy fish that is fried. Naturally you must consider the calorie content of the egg and crumb coating, but you reduce the total if you choose crushed low-calorie crispbread crumbs and you avoid the extra calories of oil or fat essential for true frying.

First dry the fish, then coat in beaten egg and crumbs or crushed low-calorie crispbread crumbs.

Brush a metal baking tray or sheet with a little melted fat or oil, so the tray or sheet just looks greasy, place in a hot oven (220°C/425°F, Gas Mark 7) and heat for 3 to 4 minutes. Remove from the oven and carefully place the coated fish on this.

Drizzle a little melted fat (shortening, lard or the like) or oil on top of the fish; do not brush this as it would disturb the crumbs and might cause them to come off the fish during cooking.

Return the tray or sheet to the hot oven and bake until tender.

Allow about 5 minutes cooking time for fish cakes or very thin fillets of fish; 8 to 10 minutes for thicker fillets and 15 to 20 minutes for coated cutlets (steaks). Lower the heat after 10 minutes if the coating is becoming too brown and reduce oven to moderately hot (190°C/375°F, Gas Mark 5).

There is no need to drain the crisp fish on absorbent paper.

Serve with lemon wedges and garnish with fresh sprigs of parsley.

GRILLING (BROILING)

This is another method of cooking fish for anyone who is anxious to avoid extra calories.

Grilling (broiling) uses less fat than frying, but the fish has the same firm texture and keeps most of its flavour. As well as this, grilled (broiled) fish comes to the table with a golden brown colour, which looks most appetizing.

Remember that the grill (broiler) should always be heated before cooking the fish, so it is cooked in the shortest possible time. This makes a great deal of difference to both flavour and texture.

Brush white (lean) fish with a little melted butter, margarine or oil before placing under the grill (broiler). This can be flavoured with:

1: Finely grated lemon rind (use just the 'zest' to avoid any of the bitter white pith) and lemon juice.
2: Finely grated lime rind (use just the 'zest' to avoid any of the bitter white pith) and lime juice.
3: Chopped herbs including chopped garlic.
4: A little curry powder to taste.
5: Tomato purée (paste) or anchovy essence (paste).
6: Worcestershire, Soy or Tabasco sauce; use these sparingly, so they do not override the taste of the fish.

Another way to keep fish moist when grilling (broiling) with little if any fat, is to marinate it in a little wine, lemon juice or milk, to which you add a generous shake of salt and pepper. Leave the fish in the liquid for an hour, remove, then drain and cook under the grill (broiler).

When grilling (broiling) fish allow about 3 minutes cooking time for very thin fillets, do not turn; about 5 to 6 minutes for thicker fillets (give 3 minutes on a very high heat, then lower the heat for 2 to 3 minutes). Allow thick cutlets (steaks) about 10 minutes cooking time and turn halfway through this period to brown both sides of the fish.

The scallop kebabs show another way of presenting grilled (broiled) fish, i.e. on skewers. Never eat the fish from the skewers, for this could burn your mouth badly.

Scallop Kebabs

■ 358/Kj 1504 □ 0.25 g

Metric/Imperial
8 de-rinded rashers bacon, halved
8 medium scallops, sliced
8–12 button mushrooms
25 g/1 oz butter, melted (optional)
1 × 15 ml spoon/1 tablespoon lemon juice
salt
pepper

American
8 slices bacon, halved
8 medium scallops, sliced
8–12 mushrooms
2 tablespoons butter, melted (optional)
1 tablespoon lemon juice
salt
pepper

Form bacon into rolls, thread scallop slices, bacon rolls and mushrooms on to skewers alternately. Brush with butter if desired, sprinkle with lemon juice, salt and pepper. Cook under the hot grill (broiler) for about 5 minutes, turning several times.

To serve: Hot with a very small amount of cooked rice. Ideal for a barbecue.

To freeze: Should be freshly cooked, although thawed scallops could be used.

Variation:

Use pieces of skinned, boneless white (lean) fish instead of the scallops.

Below: Scallop Kebabs
Right: Sole Meunière

Sole Meunière

■ 398/Kj 1671 □ 0.5 g

Metric/Imperial

8 fillets sole (about 75 g/3 oz each)

salt

pepper

100 g/4 oz butter

2 × 15 ml spoons/2 tablespoons lemon juice

1 × 15 ml spoon/1 tablespoon chopped parsley

1 × 5 ml spoon/1 teaspoon capers

American

8 sole fillets (about 3 oz each)

salt

pepper

8 tablespoons butter

2 tablespoons lemon juice

1 tablespoon chopped parsley

1 teaspoon capers

Skin the fillets, sprinkle the fish with a little salt and pepper. Heat the butter in a large frying pan, fry the fish until just tender. Lift on to a hot dish and keep warm. Add the rest of the ingredients to the butter left in the pan. Heat until the butter turns a dark golden brown in colour.

To serve: Spoon the butter sauce over the fish. Garnish with a lemon twist and a few fresh parsley sprigs, if liked. Serve with a green vegetable such as broccoli, spinach or cabbage.

To freeze: This dish is not suitable for freezing.

Fish

FISH VARIETY

Fish lends itself to being used in a great variety of ways, as the recipes on this and the following pages indicate.

Seafood and Cheese Soufflé

■ 293/Kj 1231 □ Trace

Metric/Imperial

15 g/½ oz butter

100 g/4 oz fresh or canned crabmeat

25 g/1 oz–50 g/2 oz shelled prawns, shrimps or other shellfish

0.5 × 15 ml spoon/½ tablespoon lemon juice

1 × 5 ml spoon/1 teaspoon chopped fennel or dill

4 eggs

50 g/2 oz Parmesan cheese, grated

salt

pepper

American

1 tablespoon butter

¼ lb fresh, canned or frozen crabmeat

1–2 oz shelled shrimp or other shellfish

½ tablespoon lemon juice

1 teaspoon chopped fennel or dill, fresh or dried

4 eggs

½ cup Parmesan cheese, grated

salt

pepper

Spread the butter over the bottom of an 18 cm/7 inch soufflé dish. Add the flaked crabmeat, whole prawns (shrimp) or shrimps and sprinkle with the lemon juice and the chopped fennel or dill. Put a piece of foil over the fish and heat in a moderately hot oven (190°C/375°F, Gas Mark 5) for 5 to 6 minutes.

Meanwhile separate the eggs; mix the yolks, cheese, salt and pepper together. Whisk the egg whites until very stiff, then fold into the egg yolk mixture. Spoon over the hot fish, return to the centre of the oven and bake for 20 minutes until well risen and golden brown.

To serve: As soon as cooked.

To freeze: This dish cannot be frozen.

Variation:

Use diced lightly cooked white (lean) fish or flaked cooked or canned salmon or other shellfish in place of crab.

Seafood Mould; Seafood and Cheese Soufflé; Stuffed Tomatoes

Stuffed Tomatoes

■ 45/Kj 189 □ 4.7 g

Metric/Imperial

4 large tomatoes

salt

pepper

4 medium plaice fillets

1 small onion, grated

1 × 15 ml spoon/1 tablespoon chopped parsley

American

4 large tomatoes

salt

pepper

4 medium flounder fillets

1 small onion, grated

1 tablespoon chopped parsley

Halve the tomatoes, scoop out the pulp and sprinkle the halved cases with a little salt and pepper. Skin and halve the plaice (flounder) fillets; put into the halved tomatoes. Chop the tomato pulp, mix with the onion and parsley, add salt and pepper to taste and spoon over the fish in the halved tomatoes. Lift the tomatoes into a greased casserole, cover with a lid and bake for 20 minutes in the centre of a moderately hot oven (200°C/400°F, Gas Mark 6).

To serve: Hot with a green salad or vegetable.

To freeze: Not suitable for freezing.

Variations:

1: Plaice (Flounder) Parcels: Slice the whole tomatoes. Use 4 large squares of foil and brush lightly with oil. Put half the sliced tomatoes in the centre of each piece of foil. Put the fish on top of the tomatoes, season well and top with the grated onion and parsley, then the remaining sliced tomatoes and season again. Fold the foil to encase the fish and seal the ends of the foil. Put on to a baking sheet and bake for approximately 25 minutes at the temperature above. There is no need to halve the fish fillets in this variation.

2: Stuffed cucumbers: Trim a cucumber and cut in half lengthways. Carefully scoop out the seeds and a little of the flesh and discard. Prepare the filling as above, but combine the flaked fish with the onion, parsley and seasoning. Cut the cucumber into boat-shaped pieces then fill and bake as the recipe above.

Courgettes (zucchini) are a good alternative to cucumber.

Seafood Mould

■ 138/Kj 580 □ 11.9 g

Metric/Imperial

350 g/12 oz uncooked white fish (weight without skin and bone)

4 large tomatoes, skinned and chopped

4 × 15 ml spoons/4 tablespoons fresh breadcrumbs

salt

pepper

2 × 5 ml spoons/2 teaspoons chopped parsley

little lemon juice

FOR THE TOPPING:

50 g/2 oz shelled prawns

4 × 15 ml spoons/4 tablespoons plain yogurt

American

¾ lb uncooked lean (flounder or sole) fish (weight without skin and bone)

4 large tomatoes, skinned and chopped

⅓ cup fresh breadcrumbs

salt

pepper

2 teaspoons chopped parsley

little lemon juice

FOR THE TOPPING:

2 oz cooked, shelled shrimp (¼ lb raw in the shell)

¼ cup plain yogurt

Mince (grind) or chop then pound the uncooked fish in a bowl until smooth. Mix the fish and tomatoes with all the other ingredients, then put into a bowl, cover with greased foil. Steam over a saucepan of boiling water for 40 minutes. Turn out; this may be a little difficult, since the bowl is not greased, but let the mould wait a few minutes, then it should come out of the container without much difficulty. Garnish with the prawns (shrimp) and yogurt.

To serve: Hot or cold.

To freeze: Freeze the cooked mould in the bowl, turn out and wrap. Use within 2 months.

To thaw: If serving hot, steam for 10 to 15 minutes.

Variation:

If you are on a low-carbohydrate diet, substitute soured (sour) cream for the yogurt and sprinkle with a little paprika pepper.

Fish

39

COLD DISHES WITH FISH

Most fish can be served cold as a main dish and the ways of preparing these are very varied.

Never overcook fish when you want it cold, for the fish continues to soften as it cools, and overcooked fish loses both its flavour and shape.

Piquant Seafood Salad

■ 158/Kj 664 □ 8.5 g

Metric/Imperial

300 ml/½ pint plain yogurt

1 × 2.5 ml spoon/½ teaspoon Soy sauce

1 × 2.5 ml spoon/½ teaspoon curry powder

1 × 15 ml spoon/1 tablespoon chopped spring onions

1 green pepper (capsicum), de-seeded and chopped

2 medium tomatoes, skinned and chopped

0.5 kg/1 lb cooked white fish, diced

2 × 15 ml spoons/2 tablespoons chopped celery

50 g/2 oz peeled prawns

TO GARNISH:

lettuce

1 lemon, sliced

American

1¼ cups plain yogurt

½ teaspoon Soy sauce

½ teaspoon curry powder

1 tablespoon chopped scallions

1 green pepper, de-seeded and chopped

2 medium tomatoes, skinned and chopped

1 lb cooked lean (flounder or sole) fish, diced

2 tablespoons chopped celery

2 oz shelled shrimp (¼ lb raw in the shell)

TO GARNISH:

lettuce

1 lemon, sliced

☙ Mix the yogurt with all the other ingredients except garnish.

To serve: Spoon onto a bed of lettuce and garnish with the lemon slices.

To freeze: An excellent way to serve thawed fish.

Variation:

Salad Parmesan: Omit the curry powder and Soy sauce and add 50 g/2 oz/½ cup grated Parmesan cheese to the plain yogurt.

Herb and Fish Mousse

■ 159/Kj 668 □ 2.9 g

Metric/Imperial

450 g/1 lb white fish

150 ml/¼ pint water

150 ml/¼ pint skimmed milk

salt

freshly ground pepper

1 packet aspic jelly (to set 600 ml/1 pint)

2 × 15 ml spoons/2 tablespoons dry sherry

1 × 5 ml spoon/1 teaspoon chopped dill

1 × 5 ml spoon/1 teaspoon chopped parsley

2 eggs

TO GARNISH:

lettuce, shredded

1 lemon, sliced

few cucumber slices

American

1 lb lean (flounder or sole) fish

⅔ cup water

⅔ cup skimmed milk

salt

freshly ground pepper

lemon rind, grated (optional)

bouquet garni (bunch of herbs) (optional)

4 teaspoons unflavored gelatin

2 tablespoons dry sherry

1 teaspoon chopped dill

1 teaspoon chopped parsley

2 eggs

TO GARNISH:

lettuce, shredded

1 lemon, sliced

few cucumber slices

☙ Poach the fish very gently in the water and milk. Add only a very little salt and pepper as the aspic is highly flavoured. (Add lemon rind and bouquet garni to the fish if gelatin is used.) Lift the fish from the liquid. (Remove lemon rind and bouquet garni if used.) Soften the aspic jelly (gelatin) in the sherry, then stir into the hot liquid in the saucepan; stirring continuously until the aspic jelly (gelatin) is thoroughly dissolved. Add the herbs. Separate the egg yolks from the whites. Whisk the yolks in a basin (bowl), then whisk in the warm aspic (gelatin) mixture. Chill until just setting. Whisk the egg whites stiffly and fold in with the flaked fish to the aspic (gelatin) mixture. Spoon into one 1.25 litre/2 pint/5 cup mould or six individual moulds and leave to set. Turn out and garnish with the lettuce and twists of lemon and cucumber.

Summer Chaudfroid; Herb and Fish Mousse; Piquant Seafood Salad

To serve: Either as an appetizer or a light main dish.

To freeze: If using aspic, open-freeze, then wrap or freeze in mould(s), turn out and wrap. Use within 2 months. Do not freeze if using unflavored gelatin.

To thaw: Allow to thaw in the refrigerator.

Variation:
Use shellfish in place of fish. Simmer the shells in water to give just under 300 ml/½ pint/1¼ cups of liquid, strain and use in place of the water and milk, or make only 150 ml/¼ pint/⅔ cup stock and add nearly 150 ml/¼ pint/⅔ cup milk. Dissolve the aspic or ordinary gelatine (gelatin) in this.

Summer Chaudfroid

■ 192/Kj 806 □ 3.7 g

Metric/Imperial

4 portions white fish (each 175 g/6 oz)
generous 300 ml/½ pint water
salt
pepper
fish stock (see method)
aspic jelly to set 300 ml/½ pint
150 ml/¼ pint plain yogurt
3 × 15 ml spoons/3 tablespoons low-calorie mayonnaise

TO GARNISH:
1 lettuce
¼ cucumber, thinly sliced
1 lemon, thinly sliced

American

4 portions lean (flounder or sole) fish fillets or steaks (each 6 oz)
generous 1¼ cups water
salt
pepper
fish stock (see method)
2 teaspoons unflavored gelatin
⅔ cup plain yogurt
3 tablespoons mayonnaise

TO GARNISH:
1 head lettuce
¼ cucumber, thinly sliced
1 lemon, thinly sliced

Remove any skin and bones from the fish, but keep the fillets or cutlets (steaks) a good shape. Poach the fish in the water or water and wine, as page 35, adding only a very little salt and pepper. Do not over-cook the fish, for it is important that it keeps a firm texture. Lift the fish from the liquid and cool on a plate. Put the bones and skin of the fish into the liquid in the pan, cover the pan and simmer for 15 minutes until reduced to approximately 12 × 15 ml spoons/12 tablespoons/¾ cup of good fish stock. Strain carefully. Soften, then dissolve, the aspic jelly (gelatin) in this liquid, allow to cool; blend with the plain yogurt and mayonnaise, whisking or mixing until very smooth. Allow the sauce to become quite cold until it stiffens slightly, then spread over the fish.

To serve: When quite set, lift onto a bed of lettuce and garnish with the slices of cucumber and lemon.

To freeze: Do not freeze.

Variation:
Chaudfroid Mould: Cook and flake the fish. Make the aspic mixture as above, add the fish, 2–3 × 15 ml spoons/2–3 tablespoons diced cucumber and 2 chopped hard-boiled eggs. Spoon into an oiled mould and leave to set. Turn out onto a bed of green salad.

Fish

FISH WITH A BITE

Some people complain that fish is lacking in a strong taste, but they forget it can combine with many other more piquant flavours. You can add onion, garlic, curry powder, a variety of herbs (dill, fennel and parsley are particularly good flavourings for fish) without appreciably increasing the calories. The recipes on these pages give some suggestions which can be adapted for most fish.

Curried Trout

■ 233/Kj 979 □ 8.1 g including sultanas

Metric/Imperial

4 smoked trout (about 175 g/6 oz each)

4 × 15 ml spoons/4 tablespoons low-calorie mayonnaise, see page 164

3 medium spring onions, finely chopped

1 × 5 ml spoon/1 teaspoon curry powder

pinch of dry mustard

¼ medium cucumber, peeled and finely chopped

pinch of ground ginger

1 × 5 ml spoon/1 teaspoon capers

2 × 5 ml spoons/2 teaspoons chopped parsley

1 × 15 ml spoon/1 tablespoon sultanas (optional)

TO GARNISH:
1 lemon, sliced

¼ medium cucumber, thinly sliced

1 lettuce heart

American

4 smoked trout (about 6 oz each)

¼ cup low-calorie mayonnaise, see page 164

3 medium scallions, finely chopped

1 teaspoon curry powder

pinch of dry mustard

¼ medium cucumber, peeled and finely chopped

pinch of ground ginger

1 teaspoon capers

2 teaspoons chopped parsley

1 tablespoon seedless white raisins (optional)

TO GARNISH:
1 lemon, sliced

¼ medium cucumber, thinly sliced

1 lettuce heart

❧Cut off the heads and split the trout. Remove the back bones. Mix the mayonnaise with the rest of the ingredients except garnish. Spread half of the mixture onto the split fish, then fold over to form the original shape. Lift onto the

serving dish and top with the remaining mixture.

To serve: Cold, garnished with twists of lemon, sliced cucumber and lettuce.

To freeze: Do not freeze the prepared dish, but this is an excellent way to serve thawed smoked trout.

Variation:

Using fresh trout or herrings: Clean the fish, remove the heads, then split and take out the intestines, including the roes. Remove the back bones. Chop the roes, mix with the curried mixture. Put all the mixture over the split fish, fold over and put into a greased ovenproof dish. Cover with greased foil and bake for 25 to 30 minutes in the centre of a moderately hot oven (190°C/375°F, Gas Mark 5). Serve hot or cold.

Devilled Fish; Curried Trout. Far right: Savoury Roes

Devilled Fish

■ 267/Kj 1121 □ 16.3 g

Metric/Imperial

450 g/1 lb–1.5 kg/1¼ lb white fish (weight without skin and bone)

40 g/1½ oz butter or margarine

2 medium onions, finely chopped

1–2 cloves garlic, crushed

1 × 5 ml spoon/1 teaspoon curry powder

few drops Tabasco sauce

150 ml/¼ pint plain yogurt

3 × 15 ml spoons/3 tablespoons finely chopped celery

1 × 15 ml spoon/1 tablespoon finely chopped canned red pepper (capsicum)

salt

pepper

shake cayenne pepper

FOR THE TOPPING:
2–3 × 15 ml spoons/2–3 tablespoons crisp breadcrumbs

American

1–1¼ lb lean (flounder or sole) fish (weight without skin and bone)

3 tablespoons butter or margarine

2 medium onions, finely chopped

1–2 cloves garlic, crushed

1 teaspoon curry powder

few drops Tabasco sauce

⅔ cup plain yogurt

3 tablespoons finely chopped celery

1 tablespoon finely chopped canned red pepper

salt

pepper

shake cayenne pepper

FOR THE TOPPING:
2–3 tablespoons crisp breadcrumbs

❧Cut the fish into neat pieces and steam as on page 35 until just soft. Do not over-cook. Melt the butter or margarine in a saucepan. Toss the onion and garlic in this until soft, then lower the heat and mix in the curry powder, Tabasco sauce, plain yogurt, celery and red pepper (capsicum). Add salt, pepper and the cayenne pepper, then the cooked fish.

Heat gently, taste and add more curry powder or other seasoning, if required. Spoon into a flameproof dish, sprinkle top with the breadcrumbs and place under a hot grill (broiler) for a few minutes.

To serve: Hot or cold with a green salad.

To freeze: Not suitable for freezing.

Savoury Roes

■ 327/Kj 1374 ☐ 7.6 g

Metric/Imperial
450 g/1 lb soft herring roes
50 g/2 oz butter or margarine
2 onions, finely chopped
4 tomatoes, thickly sliced
salt
pepper
25 g/1 oz breadcrumbs

American
1 lb soft herring roes or fish sticks
4 tablespoons butter or margarine
2 onions, finely chopped
4 tomatoes, thickly sliced
salt
pepper
½ cup breadcrumbs

❧If the roes are frozen allow to thaw and strain off the surplus liquid. Heat the butter or margarine in a saucepan and toss the onions in this for 2 to 3 minutes. Put half the tomatoes and half the onions into a shallow ovenproof dish, top with the roes, sprinkle with salt and pepper to taste; add the rest of the onions, the tomatoes and finally the breadcrumbs. Bake in the centre of a moderately hot oven (190°C/375°F, Gas Mark 5) for about 30 minutes.

To serve: Hot, with a green vegetable such as broccoli or spinach.

To freeze: This dish freezes well for up to 2 months.

To thaw: Reheat gently.

Variations:

1: Use fingers of skinned white fish (fish sticks) in place of the roes.

2: Flavour the dish with fresh herbs of your choice (parsley, sage, lemon thyme). Add with the roes and finish as above.

Fish

MEAT AND POULTRY

Unless you are a vegetarian you will be able to enjoy a variety of dishes based on meat, poultry and game in your slimming diet. All forms of meat are of high protein value and meat, especially liver, heart and kidneys, are valuable sources of iron.

The method by which you cook meat, poultry or game will determine the suitability of the dish for a low-calorie or low-carbohydrate diet.

Often it will be necessary to change the familiar accompaniments to meat and poultry to the special slimming stuffings and sauces. However, these will make a pleasant change for all the family.

Cooking Meat the Slimming Way

There is a belief that the only way to present meat for slimmers is to grill (broil) expensive steak and cutlets (chops) of lamb. These meats *are* a good choice, for their high quality makes them suitable for this simple, appetizing mode of cooking. They are costly, though, and in this book there are many recipes based upon cheaper meat and poultry. The recipe that follows *is* a luxury one, but the second can be made with inexpensive minced (ground) beef.

Steak Tartare

■ 282/Kj 1185 □ 1.3 g

Metric/Imperial

450 g/1 lb raw minced fillet steak

4 egg yolks plus two egg shells, halved

4 gherkins, diced

1 onion, finely diced

capers

salt

pepper

American

1 lb ground raw filet of beef

4 egg yolks plus two egg shells, halved

4 small sweet dill pickles, cubed

1 onion, finely chopped

capers

salt

pepper

❧ Arrange 4 rounds of raw steak on individual dishes topped with an egg yolk in half the shell. Garnish each dish with the diced gherkins (cubed sweet dill pickles), onions and capers, adding salt and pepper to taste.

To serve: As soon as prepared.

To freeze: Do not freeze.

Meat Loaf; Steak Tartare; Hamburgers; Golden-topped Shepherd's Pie

Hamburgers

■ 238/Kj 998 □ 0.0 g

Metric/Imperial

450 g/1 lb minced beef

salt

pepper

American

1 lb ground beef

salt

pepper

❧ Mix all the ingredients together and form into 4 flat cakes. Grease a frying pan, heat, then fry the hamburgers.

To serve: With vegetables, or on toast or in hot split hamburger rolls.

To freeze: Freeze on flat trays, lift off, separate by squares of waxed paper, then wrap. Use within 3 months. Cook from the frozen state.

Variations:

1: Add herbs and an onion chopped.

2: Add an egg for a softer mixture.

BAKING

In this method of cooking the meat can be combined with other ingredients, as in the Meat Loaf recipe below.

Meat Loaf

■ 456/Kj 1916 □ 10.5 g

Metric/Imperial

1 × 15 ml spoon/1 tablespoon oil

2 large tomatoes, skinned and chopped

1 medium onion, chopped

0.75 kg/1½ lb raw minced beef

1 × 2.5 ml spoon/½ teaspoon chopped fresh sage or pinch of dried sage

salt

pepper

150 ml/¼ pint beef stock or water and ½ beef stock cube

50 g/2 oz fresh breadcrumbs

2 eggs

American

1 tablespoon oil

2 large tomatoes, skinned and chopped

1 medium onion, chopped

1½ lb raw ground beef

½ teaspoon chopped fresh sage or pinch of dried sage

salt

pepper

⅔ cup beef stock or water and 1 beef bouillon cube

1 cup fresh breadcrumbs

2 eggs

❧ Heat the oil in a frying pan and toss the tomatoes and onion in this for 2 to 3 minutes. Mix with the rest of the ingredients. Brush a 1 kg/2 lb loaf tin with oil, put in the mixture, smooth flat on top and cover with oiled foil. Stand the tin in a dish of cold water (this keeps the loaf moist during cooking). Bake in the centre of a moderate oven (160°C/325°F, Gas Mark 3) for 1½ hours. Lift the tin from the water and place a weight on top. Allow to become quite cold before turning out of the tin.

To serve: Reheat to serve hot with tomato or brown sauce, see page 79.

To freeze: This meat loaf freezes well for up to 3 months.

To thaw: Reheat very slowly to serve hot, or allow to thaw in the refrigerator.

Variations:

1: Other meats may be used in place of beef; for example, try a mixture of lean ham and chicken or ham and veal.

2: Make a more piquant loaf by adding 2–3 × 15 ml spoons/2–3 tablespoons finely chopped pickled onions, gherkins (sweet dill pickles), etc.

3: Coat the loaf with half-set aspic jelly (gelatin), or a jelly made from meat stock, then allow this to set firmly. Attractive garnishes can be dipped in liquid aspic jelly (gelatin) and placed on top or round the sides of the loaf.

USING COOKED MEAT

There are many ways to use cooked meat, one of the easiest being to make a good salad, see page 146.

Slimmers' Rissoles

Blend cooked minced (ground) meat with salt, pepper, chopped herbs, an egg yolk or a little yogurt to bind. Form into flat cakes, put on a greased and heated baking tray. Bake in a moderate oven (180°C/350°F, Gas Mark 4) until hot and browned.

Golden-topped Shepherd's Pie

Simmer skinned chopped onions and tomatoes in a little stock, add minced (ground) or chopped cooked meat, salt and pepper. Heat well, put into an oven-proof dish and top with 2 beaten eggs and bake in a moderate oven (160°C/325°F, Gas Mark 3) for about 15 minutes.

Meat

From left: Glazed Beef Roll; Boiling Meat; Savoury Beef

COOKING MINCED (GROUND) BEEF

Minced (ground) beef is a general favourite with adults and children and is a versatile meat. The recipe on page 47 is similar to the famous Bolognese sauce. The meat mixture can be served on toast, as a topping on spaghetti, a filling in pancakes (crêpes) or omelettes; or served with vegetables. Meat loaves, as the recipes on page 45 or below, can be served as a hot or cold dish.

Glazed Beef Roll

■ 456/Kj 1915 □ 26.3 g

Metric/Imperial

450 g/1 lb carrots, chopped

salt

pepper

40 g/1½ oz butter or margarine

2 medium onions, finely chopped

50 g/2 oz fresh breadcrumbs

3 × 15 ml spoons/3 tablespoons milk

pinch of dried thyme

350 g/12 oz raw minced beef

100 g/4 oz raw minced pork

1 egg

1 × 15 ml spoon/1 tablespoon chopped parsley

TO GLAZE:

3–4 × 15 ml spoons/3–4 tablespoons tomato ketchup

1 × 5 ml spoon/1 teaspoon brown sugar

generous pinch of dry mustard powder

TO GARNISH:

8–10 small onions or shallots

350 g/12 oz fresh or frozen green beans

American

1 lb carrots, chopped

salt

pepper

3 tablespoons butter or margarine

2 medium onions, finely chopped

1 cup fresh breadcrumbs

3 tablespoons milk

pinch of dried thyme

¾ lb raw ground beef

¼ lb raw ground pork

1 egg

1 tablespoon chopped parsley

TO GLAZE:

3–4 tablespoons tomato ketchup

1 teaspoon brown sugar

generous pinch of dry mustard powder

TO GARNISH:

8–10 small onions or shallots

¾ lb fresh or frozen green beans

❧ Cook the carrots in a little water, with salt and pepper to taste, until just tender. Drain and mash to a smooth purée. Heat the butter or margarine in a frying pan, fry the onions until soft, add half to the carrot purée.

Put the breadcrumbs into a bowl, add the milk, thyme, the meats, egg, parsley and the remaining chopped fried onion and salt and pepper and mix together. Place the mixture on a sheet of grease-proof or waxed paper over a *damp* working surface; cover with a second sheet of paper. Roll out to an oblong shape about 23 cm/9 inches × 15 cm/6 inches. Re-

move the top sheet of paper. Spread the remaining carrot mixture evenly over the meat. Roll up like a Swiss (jelly) roll. Line a roasting tin with foil, lightly grease the foil then lift the roll onto this.

Mix the ketchup, brown sugar and mustard together. Brush over the meat roll, do not cover this. Bake in the centre of a moderately hot oven (180°C/350°F, Gas Mark 4) for 45 to 50 minutes. Meanwhile peel the onions or shallots and prepare the beans. Cook each vegetable separately in boiling salted water until tender.

To serve: Arrange the roll on a dish surrounded by the onions and beans.

To freeze: The roll can be prepared (but not cooked) and frozen for 6 weeks. It is better to add the glaze when ready to cook the meat roll.

To thaw: There is no need to thaw this roll; add the glaze and cook as above.

Savoury Beef

Put 2 onions, peeled and chopped, 2 tomatoes, skinned and sliced, 300 ml/ ½ pint (1¼ cups) beef stock, or water and a beef stock cube (2 bouillon cubes), into a pan. Add 450 g/1 lb minced (ground)

beef, stir briskly to mix the meat with the liquid. Add salt and pepper to taste, 1 × 15 ml spoon/1 tablespoon chopped parsley, 1 × 15 ml spoon/1 tablespoon tomato purée (paste). Simmer steadily in a covered pan stirring from time to time, for 45 minutes to 1 hour. Remove the lid towards the end of the cooking period to allow any excess liquid to evaporate, so that the meat mixture becomes the consistency of a thick sauce.

To freeze: This dish freezes well for up to 3 months.

Variations:

1: Add cubed green or red pepper (capsicum) and/or a peeled and crushed clove of garlic to the mixture.

2: If you are on a low-carbohydrate diet the vegetables and meat can be fried in 25 g/1 oz to 50 g/2 oz fat (1–2 tablespoons butter before adding the liquid and other ingredients.

3: Add finely sliced or chopped mushrooms and flavour the mixture with Soy sauce to taste. Season lightly with salt.

■ 227/Kj953 □ 4.0 g

BOILING MEAT

This name indicates that meat and poultry are cooked in boiling liquid, this is incorrect; the liquid must be kept at simmering point only, to ensure the meat is evenly tenderized.

Many meats can be cooked by this method, the most suitable being brisket or silverside (corned beef), tongue, bacon joints or neck of lamb.

If the meat is salted, soak in cold water to cover for 12 hours. Discard the water, put the meat into a pan with fresh water, herbs, vegetables and pepper to taste. When cooking fresh meat add both salt and pepper.

Allow per 450 g/1 lb: brisket, silverside, and tongue, 40 minutes; bacon 20 to 30 minutes (depending upon cut) and neck of lamb a total of about 1½ hours. See pressure cooker section, pages 166 and 169.

To serve: With the vegetables and the unthickened liquid as a sauce if it is not too salty; otherwise gravy.

Meat

FRYING MEAT

This method of cooking is really only worth considering if you are following a low-carbohydrate rather than a low-calorie diet, every 25 g/1 oz fat (2 tablespoons butter) adds 240 calories, but no carbohydrates. Do not coat meat in breadcrumbs though.

Fry steak in butter or fat until cooked to your personal taste. You can then add a little made mustard (Dijon mustard) and plain yogurt to any fat remaining, heat, and spoon over the steak.

When frying lamb or veal you could use the same flavourings as for steak.

Steak au Poivre

Press crushed peppercorns or shake black pepper onto both sides of pieces of fillet or rump steak (shell, hip or shoulder blade steak). Fry the steaks until tender, remove from the pan, and serve or add a little soured cream (sour cream) plus a *small* quantity of brandy to any butter remaining in the pan, heat and spoon over the steaks.

Steak Diane

Fry finely chopped onions in the butter before frying thin pieces of steak. Add a little Worcestershire sauce, salt and pepper, heat and serve.

Paprika Veal

Sprinkle salt and pepper over thin fillets of veal. Fry in butter until tender, add plain yogurt, tomato purée (paste) and a little paprika to the pan and heat.

Lamb Cutlets in Herb Sauce

■ 351/Kj 1476 □ 5.4 g

Metric/Imperial

8 lamb cutlets (each about 100 g/4 oz)

2 onions, thinly sliced

1–2 cloves garlic, chopped

3 large tomatoes, skinned and sliced

1 × 15 ml spoon/1 tablespoon chopped parsley

1 × 2.5 ml spoon/½ teaspoon chopped mint

1 × 2.5 ml spoon/½ teaspoon chopped rosemary or tarragon

150 ml/¼ pint white stock or use water and ½ chicken stock cube

salt

pepper

TO GARNISH:
12 black or green olives

American

8 lamb cutlets (each about ¼ lb)

2 onions, thinly sliced

1–2 cloves garlic, chopped

3 large tomatoes, skinned and sliced

1 tablespoon chopped parsley

½ teaspoon chopped mint

½ teaspoon chopped rosemary or tarragon

⅔ cup white stock or use water and 1 chicken bouillon cube

salt

pepper

TO GARNISH:
12 black or green olives

❧ Fry the cutlets steadily for 3 minutes on either side in a large pan; do this slowly for the first 2 to 3 minutes, so the natural fat will flow to stop the meat sticking to the pan. Lift out of the pan onto a plate. Put the vegetables, herbs (fresh if possible), stock or water and stock cube into the frying pan and heat for a few minutes. Return the cutlets to the pan, add a little salt and pepper. Simmer for 10 minutes or until the meat is tender and the vegetable mixture reduced to a rather thin purée.

To serve: Place the cutlets on the vegetable base and garnish with olives.

To freeze: This dish can be frozen for 2 to 3 months.

To thaw: Heat gently from frozen.

Steak au Poivre. Above right: Paupiettes of Veal; Lamb Cutlets in Herb Sauce

Paupiettes of Veal

■ 309/Kj 1298 □ 8.4 g

Metric/Imperial

4 thin slices fillet of veal (each about 100 g/4 oz)

100 g/4 oz mushrooms, chopped

2 medium tomatoes, skinned and chopped

1 × 15 ml spoon/1 tablespoon chopped parsley

salt

pepper

1 × 15 ml spoon/1 tablespoon flour

1 × 2.5 ml spoon/½ teaspoon finely grated lemon rind

50 g/2 oz butter or margarine

150 ml/¼ pint stock

1 × 15 ml spoon/1 tablespoon tomato purée

2 × 15 ml spoons/2 tablespoons white wine

150 ml/¼ pint plain yogurt

TO GARNISH:
chopped parsley

paprika

American

4 thin slices veal scallops (each about ¼ lb)

¼ lb mushrooms, chopped

2 medium tomatoes, skinned and chopped

1 tablespoon chopped parsley

salt

pepper

1 tablespoon flour

½ teaspoon finely grated lemon rind

4 tablespoons butter or margarine

$\frac{2}{3}$ cup stock

1 tablespoon tomato paste

2 tablespoons white wine

$\frac{2}{3}$ cup plain yogurt

TO GARNISH:

chopped parsley

paprika

❧Flatten the veal with a rolling pin. Mix the mushrooms, tomatoes and chopped parsley, add salt and pepper to taste. Spread over the veal and roll each piece firmly. Secure with wooden cocktail sticks or fine string. Blend the flour, salt and pepper and lemon rind. Roll the veal in this. Heat the butter or margarine in a pan and brown the meat rolls gently and slowly. Add the stock, tomato purée (paste) and wine. Cover the pan and simmer gently for 20 minutes. Lift out of the pan onto a hot dish. Stir the yogurt into the stock and heat gently without boiling.

To serve: Spoon the sauce over the meat and sprinkle with parsley and paprika.

To freeze: This dish does not freeze well as it is better when freshly cooked.

Variation:

Paupiettes of Beef: Use thin slices of topside (top round) of beef instead of veal.

GRILLING (BROILING) MEAT

The grill (broiler) is the ideal place in which to cook tender pieces of meat for slimmers. If you compare the calorie content of fat and lean meat you can save calories by avoiding excess fat. On the other hand you need some fat to keep the meat pleasantly moist. Grill (broil) chops and cutlets with the natural fat on the meat and discard this when you eat the meal.

To grill (broil) food correctly place on a preheated grill (broiler) except for slices of bacon and gammon (ham), for if the grill (broiler) is very hot the fat has a tendency to curl and burn. (Snip the rind to prevent curling.)

If the meat is lean, brush with the minimum quantity of melted butter or fat (oil or shortening). Cook quickly on either side until browned, then lower the heat and continue cooking to personal taste. You will have a more moist piece of meat if it is not overcooked.

To add flavour to meat before it is grilled (broiled) soak it in a marinade.

Low-calorie marinade: Sieve or purée 4 large tomatoes, add a little salt, pepper, a crushed clove of garlic, 1 × 15 ml spoon/ 1 tablespoon of lemon juice or white wine vinegar and a little made mustard (Dijon mustard). If you are on a low-carbohydrate diet you could add 1 × 15 ml spoon/1 tablespoon of oil. Leave 4 portions of meat in this for an hour, turn once or twice, remove and grill (broil). If any marinade is left spoon onto the cooked meat.

ROASTING MEAT

A roast joint is appreciated by all the family and can be quite suitable for most slimming diets. Those of you who are counting calories should cut away excess fat from the meat; but this does not make any difference on a low-carbohydrate diet.

Wrap the meat in lightly greased foil, or place in a greased roaster bag or use a covered roasting tin. Both the foil and the covered tin mean you need to add about 15 minutes to the cooking time.

Meat

USING STUFFINGS

An interesting stuffing gives added fla-vour, a more moist texture and a more satisfying dish when used with meats, fish and poultry.

The three stuffings on this page are excellent 'mixers'.

The mixture of Celery and Pepper (capsicum) is excellent with chicken, turkey, lamb or white (lean) fish; while the Apple and Onion Stuffing is a perfect partner to pork, beef, duck or goose and the richer oily fish, such as herrings.

Choose the Mushroom and Tomato stuffing for lamb or veal, it is also excel-lent with game and chicken, or with most white (lean) fish.

Celery and Pepper (Capsicum) Stuffing

■ 66/Kj 277 □ 2.4 g with butter

Metric/Imperial
2 onions, chopped

150 ml/¼ pint water

salt

pepper

small celery heart, chopped

2–3 celery leaves, chopped

1 green pepper (capsicum), de-seeded and diced

1 × 15 ml spoon/1 tablespoon chopped parsley

25 g/1 oz butter or margarine (optional)

American
2 onions, chopped

⅔ cup water

salt

pepper

small celery heart, chopped

2–3 celery leaves, chopped

1 green pepper, de-seeded and cubed

1 tablespoon chopped parsley

2 tablespoons butter or margarine (optional)

From left: Apple and Onion Stuffing; Celery and Pepper (Capsicum) Stuffing; Fruity Lamb; Mushroom and Tomato Stuffing

❧ Simmer the onions in the water, adding salt and pepper to taste, until the onions are half-cooked and the liquid absorbed. Mix with the celery, cubed pepper (capsicum), parsley and butter or mar-garine if wished. Use this as a stuffing for poultry or bake as the apple stuffing.

Fruity Lamb

■ 616/Kj 2586 □ 27.7 g

Metric/Imperial
1 large breast of lamb, boned

FOR THE STUFFING:
225 g/8 oz prunes, soaked overnight in cold water

2 medium onions, chopped

1 large cooking apple, peeled, cored and diced

1 × 15 ml spoon/1 tablespoon chopped parsley

1 × 2.5 ml spoon/½ teaspoon chopped sage or pinch of dried sage

salt

pepper

TO GARNISH:
watercress

American
1 large breast of lamb, boned

FOR THE STUFFING:
½ lb prunes, soaked overnight in cold water

2 medium onions, chopped

1 large baking apple, peeled, cored and cubed

1 tablespoon chopped parsley

½ teaspoon chopped sage or pinch of dried sage

salt

pepper

TO GARNISH:
watercress

❧ Drain the prunes reserving a little juice for gravy. Stone (pit) and chop half of these, leave the remainder whole. Blend the chopped prunes, onion and apple with the parsley, sage, salt and pepper. Spread over the lamb, roll firmly and tie. Weigh the stuffed joint (roast) and roast in the centre of a moderately hot oven (180°C/350°F, Gas Mark 4), allowing 35 minutes per 450 g/1 lb and 35 minutes over. Add the whole prunes to the roast-ing tin about 25 minutes before the end of the calculated cooking time.

To serve: Carve the lamb into thin slices and garnish with the whole prunes and watercress. If making a gravy to serve with this add a little prune juice to the stock.

To freeze: This dish is better if prepared then frozen rather than freezing the cooked joint.

To thaw: Leave uncovered, overnight, in the refrigerator.

Variation:
This stuffing can also be used for boned leg or shoulder of lamb.

The calorie and carbohydrate count is based on 0.5 kg/1¼ lb fairly fat meat.

Apple and Onion Stuffing

■ 45/Kj 189 □ 10.6 g

Metric/Imperial

2 large onions, chopped

150 ml/¼ pint water

salt

pepper

2 large cooking apples, peeled, cored and diced

1 × 2.5 ml–1 × 5 ml spoon/½–1 teaspoon chopped sage or pinch of dried sage

American

2 large onions, chopped

⅔ cup water

salt

pepper

2 large baking apples, peeled, cored and cubed

½–1 teaspoon chopped sage or pinch of dried sage

🍃 Simmer the onions in the water with salt and pepper to taste until half-cooked and the liquid absorbed. Mix with the apples and sage. Use this as a stuffing for pheasant or pork or put into a shallow ovenproof dish, cover and bake for 1 hour in a moderate oven (180°C/350°F, Gas Mark 4).

Mushroom and Tomato Stuffing

■ 11/Kj 46 □ 1.1 g

Metric/Imperial

175 g/6 oz mushrooms, chopped

225 g/8 oz tomatoes, skinned and chopped

salt

pepper

1 × 15 ml spoon/1 tablespoon chopped chives

1 × 15 ml spoon/1 tablespoon chopped parsley

American

6 oz mushrooms, chopped

½ lb tomatoes, skinned and chopped

salt

pepper

1 tablespoon chopped chives

1 tablespoon chopped parsley

🍃 Mix all the ingredients together. Use this as a stuffing for white (lean) fish, meat or poultry or put into a shallow ovenproof dish, cover and bake in a moderately hot oven (180°C/350°F, Gas Mark 4) for 40 minutes.

Meat

Beef with Sour Cream Sauce

■ 410/Kj 1722 □ 4.6 g

Metric/Imperial

1 kg/2 lb topside beef

2 medium onions, sliced

2–3 sticks celery, chopped

6–8 small carrots, cut in strips

300 ml/½ pint beef stock or water and 1 beef stock cube

1 bay leaf

salt

pepper

1 × 15 ml spoon/1 tablespoon·lemon juice or white wine vinegar

50 g/2 oz mushrooms

150 ml/¼ pint soured cream

American

2 lb top round of beef

2 medium onions, sliced

2–3 stalks celery, chopped ·

6–8 small carrots, cut in strips

1¼ cups beef stock or water and 2 beef bouillon cubes

1 bay leaf

salt

pepper

1 tablespoon lemon juice or white wine vinegar

½ cup mushrooms

⅔ cup sour cream

❧Put the beef with the onions, celery, carrots, stock, or water and stock cube(s), into a casserole. Add the bay leaf, salt and pepper and lemon juice or vinegar. Cover the casserole and cook for 1½ to 1¾ hours in the centre of a moderate oven (160°C/325°F, Gas Mark 3).

To serve: Lift the meat from the casserole, slice neatly and arrange on a warmed serving dish with the well-drained onions, celery and carrots. Put 150 ml/¼ pint/ ⅔ cup of the stock with the mushrooms into a pan, simmer for 5 minutes. Add the soured (sour) cream and heat gently for 2 to 3 minutes without boiling. Spoon over the meat.

To freeze: This dish is better eaten when freshly cooked.

OFFAL (VARIETY MEATS)

Variety meats can make all diets more interesting and more satisfying nutritionally. See also pages 186 and 187.

From rear: Beef with Sour Cream Sauce; Curried Kidneys; Liver Quenelles

Curried Kidneys

■ 210/Kj882 □ 13.0 g

Metric/Imperial

8 lamb's kidneys (about 50 g/2 oz each)

1 medium onion, chopped

50 g/2 oz butter or margarine

½–1 × 15 ml spoon/½–1 tablespoon curry powder

1 × 15 ml spoon/1 tablespoon flour

300 ml/½ pint brown stock or water and ½ beef stock cube

1 × 15 ml spoon/1 tablespoon sultanas

1 × 15 ml spoon/1 tablespoon desiccated coconut

1 × 15 ml spoon/1 tablespoon sweet chutney

salt

pepper

American

8 lamb's kidneys (about 2 oz each)

1 medium onion, chopped

4 tablespoons butter or margarine

½–1 tablespoon curry powder

1 tablespoon flour

1¼ cups brown stock or water and 1 beef bouillon cube

1 tablespoon seedless white raisins

1 tablespoon shredded coconut

1 tablespoon sweet chutney

salt

pepper

❧ Skin and halve the kidneys. Fry the kidneys and onion in the butter or margarine. Stir in the curry powder and flour, cook gently for 1 to 2 minutes. Gradually blend in the stock or water and ½ stock (1 bouillon) cube. Bring to the boil, stir until thickened. Add the sultanas (raisins), coconut, chutney, salt and pepper, cover the pan, simmer for 25 minutes.

To serve: With cooked rice.

To freeze: This dish does not freeze well and is better served freshly made.

Liver Quenelles

■ 211/Kj886 □ 14.2 g

Metric/Imperial

350 g/12 oz calf's or lamb's liver

100 g/4 oz fresh breadcrumbs

1–2 × 5 ml spoons/1–2 teaspoons chopped fresh herbs or pinch mixed dried herbs

1 egg

TO POACH:

450 ml/¾ pint beef stock or water and 1 beef stock cube

American

¾ lb calf's or lamb's liver

2 cups fresh breadcrumbs

1–2 teaspoons chopped fresh herbs (parsley, thyme, bay leaf, etc.) or pinch dried herbs

1 egg

TO POACH:

2 cups beef stock or water and 2 beef bouillon cubes

❧ Put the liver through the mincer (grinder or food processor) twice so it is very fine in texture. Mix the liver with the rest of the ingredients. Form into eight sausage shapes. If the mixture is slightly sticky, you will find it helpful to dampen your fingers before handling the mixture. Pour the stock, or water and stock cube(s), into a frying pan and bring to boiling point. Put in the quenelles then lower the heat, so that the stock simmers gently, and poach the sausage shapes for 8 minutes, turning once or twice.

To serve: Hot with mixed vegetables.

To freeze: Either prepare and open-freeze then wrap, or cook and freeze in the stock. Use within 6 weeks.

To thaw: Cook or heat from the frozen state.

Variations:

1: Omit breadcrumbs and use 225 g/8 oz/1 cup minced (ground) liver and 225 g/8 oz/1 cup sausage meat.

2: Liver and Bacon Rolls: Use the basic recipe above or half liver and half sausage meat. Form into sausage shapes. Roll thin rashers (slices) of bacon round each quenelle, secure with cocktail sticks (wooden toothpicks) and bake for approximately 20 minutes in the centre of a moderately hot oven (200°C/400°F, Gas Mark 6).

Meat

Ways to Cook Poultry

The recipes on this page use young chicken joints for frying or grilling (broiling). These chicken joints cook quickly and can be served in many ways.

The calories etc. above each recipe assume portions of 100 g/4 oz (¼ lb) of edible chicken flesh.

Chicken, turkey and game can be roasted without adding too many extra calories; especially if you choose the low-calorie stuffings on the previous pages. As these are lean meats cook in a greased roaster bag, or greased foil or a covered roasting tin.

Duck and goose are high in calories, but have no carbohydrate content.

Chicken is delicious cooked by simmering in liquid with vegetables and herbs to flavour. Allow 15 to 20 minutes per 450 g/1 lb for a young bird, but up to 40 minutes per 450 g/1 lb for an older fowl; or until the bird is quite tender.

Citrus Chicken Espagnole

Citrus Chicken Espagnole

■ 153/Kj645 □2.2 g

Metric/Imperial

1 garlic clove, crushed

3 × 15 ml spoons/3 tablespoons lemon juice

4 × 15 ml spoons/4 tablespoons orange juice

salt

pepper

pinch of ground cinnamon

4 joints frying chicken, skinned

very little oil

American

1 garlic clove, crushed

3 tablespoons lemon juice

¼ cup orange juice

salt

pepper

pinch of ground cinnamon

1 broiling chicken, skinned and quartered or 4 pieces of chicken

very little oil

Mix the garlic with the lemon and orange juice, add salt, pepper and the cinnamon. Pour this mixture into a shallow dish and put the joints of chicken (chicken pieces) in this. Leave for several hours, turning several times. Lift the chicken out of the marinade, drain well and brush with the minimum of oil. Grill (broil) quickly on either side then lower the heat and cook slowly for 10 minutes.

To serve: With a salad or green vegetable. If any marinade is left, it can be poured over the chicken before serving.

To freeze: The completed dish will not freeze well.

West Indian Chicken

■ 278/Kj 1169 □11.6 g

Metric/Imperial

4 joints frying chicken

salt

pepper

25 g/1 oz butter

1 large onion, thinly sliced

150 ml/¼ pint chicken stock or water and ½ chicken stock cube

1 × 5 ml spoon/1 teaspoon Soy sauce

3 × 15 ml spoons/3 tablespoons dry white wine or dry cider

2 thin slices fresh pineapple, diced

1 medium avocado, skinned and sliced

about 18 grapes, de-seeded

American

1 broiling chicken, quartered, or 4 pieces of chicken

salt

pepper

2 tablespoons butter

1 large onion, thinly sliced

⅔ cup chicken stock or water and 1 chicken bouillon cube

1 teaspoon Soy sauce

3 tablespoons dry white wine or dry cider

2 thin slices fresh pineapple, cubed

1 medium avocado, skinned and sliced

about 18 grapes, de-seeded

Above: West Indian Chicken
Right: Curried Chicken Kebabs

🍂Sprinkle the chicken joints (pieces) with salt and pepper; there is no need to skin them. Heat the butter in a frying pan, cook the chicken joints (pieces) in this for a few minutes until golden on all sides, turn once or twice. Add the onion slices to the frying pan, together with the stock, or water and stock cube, Soy sauce and wine. Simmer gently, turn the chicken once or twice. When the chicken is tender, add the pineapple, avocado and grapes. Heat through for 2 to 3 minutes only.

To serve: With a green salad or cooked cauliflower.

Note: The amount of stock is relatively small and by the time the chicken is tender almost all the liquid will have been absorbed. If you like a more moist dish, use double the amount of liquid.

To freeze: Do not freeze this dish, it is better eaten freshly cooked.

Variation:
Slices of veal or lean lamb could be used instead of chicken.

Curried Chicken Kebabs

■ 322/Kj 1352 □2.9 g

Metric/Imperial
12 tiny onions or shallots
salt
pepper
4 small joints chicken breast
4 chicken livers
50 g/2 oz butter or margarine
2 × 5 ml spoons/2 teaspoons curry powder
squeeze of lemon juice
8 button mushrooms
1 green pepper (capsicum), de-seeded and diced

American
12 tiny onions or shallots
salt
pepper
breasts from 2 chickens
4 chicken livers
4 tablespoons butter or margarine
2 teaspoons curry powder
squeeze of lemon juice
8 mushrooms
1 green pepper, de-seeded and cubed

🍂Peel the onions or shallots and simmer in a very little water with salt and pepper to taste for 3 to 4 minutes only. Drain well. Cut the chicken breasts into 2.5 cm/1 inch pieces, skin and halve the chicken livers. Melt the butter or margarine and blend with the curry powder, lemon juice, salt and pepper. Place the cubed chicken in this for 5 to 10 minutes.

Meanwhile wash and dry, but do not skin, the mushrooms; the stalks should be removed, but mushrooms have much more flavour if the skins are left on. Lift the chicken pieces from the curry mixture. Thread all the ingredients alternately, including the green peppers (capsicums), onto 4 metal skewers. Brush the liver and vegetables with any curried butter left. Cook for 8 to 10 minutes under a hot grill (broiler) or over a barbecue fire, turning several times.

To serve: With a mixed salad.

To freeze: Kebabs must be eaten when freshly cooked and not frozen.

Variation:
Use cubed calf's or lamb's liver instead of chicken livers. Substitute garam masala (mixed spices) for the curry powder, this gives an authentic 'curry' flavour.

Meat

COOKING TURKEY

Turkey is low in calories and has no carbohydrate content, so it is a wise choice for most diets. See points on cooking chicken.

Using Cooked Turkey Choose methods of heating cooked turkey that do not dry the meat.

Buying Turkey Joints It is now possible to purchase portions of fresh or frozen turkey, which must be completely thawed in the refrigerator before cooking. These are very useful for smaller families.

The portions can be roasted, or diced and cooked as the recipes on this page.

Turkey Milanaise

■ 170/Kj714 □5.2 g

Metric/Imperial

1–2 onions, peeled and thinly sliced

450 g/1 lb tomatoes, skinned and sliced

300 ml/½ pint chicken stock or water and ½ chicken stock cube

1 green pepper, de-seeded and diced

salt

pepper

1 × 1.25 ml spoon/¼ teaspoon chopped fresh rosemary or pinch of dried rosemary

450 g/1 lb raw turkey meat, diced

American

1–2 onions, peeled and thinly sliced

1 lb tomatoes, skinned and sliced

1¼ cups chicken stock or water and 1 chicken bouillon cube

1 green pepper, de-seeded and cubed

salt

pepper

¼ teaspoon chopped fresh rosemary or pinch of dried rosemary

1 lb turkey meat, cubed

❧Separate the sliced onion into rings. Put the onion rings and tomatoes into a deep frying pan with the stock, or water and stock cube, green pepper (capsicum), salt, pepper and rosemary. Simmer for 10 minutes, stirring frequently, then put in the turkey. Cook the diced turkey in the sauce, turning once or twice, for 15 minutes until it is tender and the sauce has thickened.

To serve: With a green vegetable and a very little cooked rice.

To freeze: This dish freezes well for 2 to 3 months.

To thaw: Reheat gently.

Variations:

1: Add 1 to 2 cloves crushed garlic plus a good pinch chilli powder.

2: Lamb Milanaise: Cook 8 lamb cutlets in a similar sauce.

Turkey Kebabs

■ 360/Kj1512 □4.7 g

Metric/Imperial

450 g/1 lb cooked turkey

50 g/2 oz small button mushrooms

1 green pepper (capsicum), de-seeded and diced

4 medium tomatoes, quartered

salt

pepper

1 × 15 ml spoon/1 tablespoon oil

FOR THE DRESSING:

100 g/4 oz cottage cheese

4 × 15 ml spoons/4 tablespoons plain yogurt

1–2 × 5 ml spoons/1–2 teaspoons made mustard

American

1 lb cooked turkey

½ cup small mushrooms

1 green pepper, de-seeded and cubed

4 medium tomatoes, quartered

salt

pepper

1 tablespoon oil

FOR THE DRESSING:

¼ lb cottage cheese

¼ cup plain yogurt

1–2 teaspoons Dijon mustard

❧Cut the turkey into fairly thick strips or squares. Wipe, but do not skin the mushrooms. Put the turkey and all the vegetables onto 4 to 6 metal skewers. Add a little salt and pepper to the oil and brush the ingredients with this. Cook under a hot grill (broiler) for about 5 minutes, turning once. Blend the ingredients for the dressing together.

To serve: Spoon the dressing into a small bowl and arrange on a dish with the kebabs.

To freeze: This dish is not suitable for freezing as previously cooked turkey is used.

Variation:

Use pieces of fruit, e.g. cubed pineapple, cooked and well-drained prunes, sliced bananas (dipped in lemon juice) with, or instead of, the vegetables.

From rear: Turkey Milanaise; Gingered Turkey; Turkey Kebabs

Gingered Turkey

■ 306/Kj1285 □17.0 g

Metric/Imperial

2 × 15 ml spoons/2 tablespoons oil

2 medium onions, thinly sliced

100 g/4 oz button mushrooms

1 × 15 ml spoon/1 tablespoon cornflour

1–2 × 5 ml spoons/1–2 teaspoons ground ginger

300 ml/½ pint turkey or chicken stock

350 g/12 oz cooked turkey

300 ml/½ pint plain yogurt

salt

pepper

cayenne pepper

TO GARNISH:

25 g/1 oz stem ginger, thinly sliced

25 g/1 oz blanched almonds, flaked and browned

American

2 tablespoons oil

2 medium onions, thinly sliced

¼ lb mushrooms

1 tablespoon cornstarch

1–2 teaspoons ground ginger

1¼ cups turkey or chicken stock

¾ lb cooked turkey

1¼ cups plain yogurt

salt

pepper

cayenne pepper

TO GARNISH:

⅛ cup stem ginger, thinly sliced

¼ cup blanched, flaked almonds, browned

❧Heat the oil in a pan, fry the onions and mushrooms for 5 minutes, stirring well, so they do not discolour. Lift into a heated serving dish and keep hot. Blend the cornflour (cornstarch) and ginger with the turkey stock. Pour into the pan and cook until thickened. Cut the turkey into long strips, or neat uniform-sized cubes. Add the turkey and yogurt to the sauce, with salt, pepper and cayenne pepper to taste. Heat gently for 10 minutes. Spoon the turkey and sauce into the serving dish; top with the sliced ginger and almonds.

To serve: With a green vegetable.

To freeze: This dish is better eaten freshly cooked.

Meat

VEGETABLE DISHES

Vegetables must play an important part in any slimming diet, for they add interest to meals and give one a feeling of being satisfactorily fed. Most vegetables also provide essential vitamins and minerals.

It is *always* important to cook vegetables correctly, but even more essential if you are omitting the usual gravies and sauces. An overcooked vegetable loses much of its pleasant taste, texture and nutritional value.

This chapter, plus the one that follows, includes salads with raw vegetables, as well as cooked dishes.

Cooking Vegetables

There are many interesting ways of cooking vegetables; and you will find some suggestions in these pages. The basic method though is to cook in boiling salted water.

Use the minimum quantity of water, this means being sparing with salt. Make sure the water is boiling *before* you add the vegetables. If you are cooking a 'family-sized' quantity of a vegetable add it *steadily*, rather than all at once, to the boiling water; this will make sure that the water continues to boil. Cover the pan; cook green vegetables as quickly as possible. Some other vegetables, particularly potatoes, should then be cooked steadily to prevent the outside breaking before the inside is tender.

The old-fashioned adage was 'to put everything that grew above the ground into boiling water; everything that came from below the ground into cold water and bring it to the boil'. We now realise that by plunging the vegetable into boiling water we retain the vitamin C content.

Other points that are important when preparing vegetables are:

1: Shop critically for really fresh food.

2: Cook as soon as you can after purchase.

3: Never leave shredded green vegetables standing or soaking in water before cooking. Shred, wash, then cook as soon as possible after preparation.

Frozen vegetables retain much of their original vitamins, for they are frozen when freshly picked. If you freeze your own vegetables follow this advice. As the vegetables are 'blanched' (i.e. partially cooked in boiling water before being frozen) the cooking time when they are prepared for serving is appreciably shorter than for a fresh vegetable.

Canned vegetables have been subjected to heat for some period and therefore need heating only. They then have about the same amount of vitamin C as cooked vegetables.

WEIGHT OF VEGETABLES

It is not easy to buy exactly the right sized onion or tomato, as specified in a recipe and sometimes you may find you have to use a slightly smaller or larger vegetable. This should not spoil the recipe, but remember it will affect the calorie and carbohydrate content.

In some recipes in this book there is no mention of the size of onion or tomato, etc. used; this indicates that varying quantities of that vegetable will not spoil the taste of the dish; but in order to calculate the approximate calories and carbohydrates as accurately as possible I have assumed a 'medium onion' weighs about 100 g/4 oz/¼ lb and a tomato just under this weight. In other recipes I state specifically 'medium', 'large' or 'small'; this means that particular dish is more successful if you try and use this size.

Globe Artichokes with butter

Globe Artichokes

These are ideal for slimmers as they take a long time to eat (a more important point than one sometimes imagines, for often slimming dishes seem eaten all too quickly); they are relatively low in both calories and carbohydrate content too. They can be served hot or cold.

When one buys artichokes they look large, but there is a great deal of waste, so that a vegetable that weighs about 225 g/8 oz/½ lb before cooking will probably only produce half this amount i.e. edible flesh. The calories, etc. of the cooked artichoke given are based on 4 medium artichokes plus 75 g/3 oz/4 tablespoons melted butter for 4 portions.

To Cook Globe Artichokes

The simplest way to cook and serve globe artichokes is to trim away the bottom of the stalk and any rather tough outer leaves, the tips of the leaves may be cut level by cutting with a pair of kitchen scissors too, but this is not essential. Put the artichokes into boiling salted water and boil until tender. This varies, a small young artichoke takes about 25 minutes, but large ones need 35 to 40 minutes. If you use an enamel saucepan the vegetable keeps its colour better than when cooked in an aluminium (aluminum) saucepan. Globe artichokes may also be cooked in a pressure cooker.

Lift the artichokes out of the water and drain.

To serve: If serving hot heat a little butter and add salt and pepper to taste. Spoon the hot butter on the side of the plate, pull away the outer leaves and dip these into the butter. Eat the base of the artichoke.

To freeze: Always freeze before cooking, as whole artichokes freeze well for 6 months; 'blanch', then pack.

■ 206/Kj 865 □ 3.2 g

Variations:

1: Serve cold with a little oil and vinegar dressing as page 81. If serving cold pull out the centre of the artichoke while the vegetable is warm, then pour the dressing in the centre.

2: Stuffed artichokes: Cool the artichokes, pull out the centre. Make one of the savoury stuffings on pages 50 and 51, cook in a covered dish until soft, fill the centres of the artichokes with the hot stuffing and serve.

3: To reduce calories serve the hot or cold artichoke with lemon juice, flavoured with salt, cayenne pepper or paprika and chopped fresh herbs.

4: Artichokes au gratin: Cook the artichokes, pull out the centres and fill with the slimmer's cheese sauce, given on page 78. Top with a little grated cheese and heat for a few minutes under the grill (broiler).

5: Cook the artichokes and cut away the leaves leaving just the tender base (called the heart or bottom). Use these as a filling in omelettes; cool and add to salads; top with cheese and brown under the grill (broiler).

Vegetables

Jerusalem Artichokes

This vegetable is low in both calories and carbohydrate content so it makes a wise alternative to potatoes. Scrape the vegetables, put immediately into water with a little lemon juice or white vinegar, to retain the white colour. Drain and place in boiling salted water to cover to which should be added 1 × 5 ml spoon/1 teaspoon of lemon juice or white vinegar. Cook steadily for about 20 minutes, until tender.

To serve: Strain and top with chopped parsley or chives. Non-slimmers can add plenty of melted butter and so can those of you who are on a low-carbohydrate diet. The calories and carbohydrate figures *are based on* 100 g/4 oz/¼ lb *cooked vegetable plus the herbs.*

To freeze: Jerusalem artichokes freeze well. Prepare as above, 'blanch' as usual. They are best if used within 3 to 4 months.

Variations:

1: Baked artichokes: Par-boil for 5 minutes, drain then roast in a little hot fat.

2: Cheese purée: Boil and mash the artichokes with grated cheese, then put into a dish, top with more grated cheese and sliced tomatoes and brown under the grill (broiler).

3: Top the artichokes with plain yogurt, blended with a little fresh tomato purée (paste) and chopped parsley and/or basil.
■ 22/Kj92 □ 3.6 g

Asparagus with Butter

This luxury vegetable is ideal on a diet, for as you will see from the figures even 100 g/4 oz/¼ lb when cooked is low in both calories and carbohydrate content. The figures also allow 75 g/3 oz/6 tablespoons melted butter for 4 portions.

The secret of cooking asparagus is to stand it upright, so the tender tips are not spoiled. Use an asparagus boiler or the basket in which you blanch vegetables for freezing makes a splendid alternative. Scrape the outside of the white part of the stalks and trim the bottom ends so the stems are of equal length. Put into the basket or tie in bundles, to keep the stems upright and cook in boiling salted water. You should cover the pan, but if the saucepan is not sufficiently deep and the lid would break the tips arrange foil

loosely over the top or invert a light saucepan over the cooking pan. The purpose is to keep in all the steam. Allow 20 to 30 minutes cooking, depending upon the thickness of the stems.

To serve: Drain and serve hot or cold with melted butter or the special Hollandaise sauce on page 80.

To freeze: Asparagus freezes well, use within a year.

Variations:

1: Asparagus Polonaise: Top hot or cold asparagus with chopped hard-boiled eggs and parsley. Non-slimmers could add fried breadcrumbs too.

Asparagus with Butter; Aubergine (Eggplant) and Tomato Bake; Cheese Medley

2: Hungarian Asparagus: Top hot asparagus with soured (sour) cream, blended with paprika. Plain yogurt could be used instead of the sour cream.

3: Parmesan Asparagus: Top cooked asparagus with a sprinkling of grated Parmesan cheese and a little melted butter or margarine and heat under the grill (broiler). This could be served with poached eggs.

4: Asparagus and Egg salad: Scramble eggs lightly, adding chopped parsley and a little chopped red pepper (capsicum). As the egg mixture cools, blend in enough yogurt to give a creamy texture. Spoon onto a bed of lettuce, garnish with cooked asparagus and sliced tomatoes.
■ 215/Kj903 □ 1.2 g

Aubergine (Eggplant)

Originally from India, aubergine (eggplant) with its distinct purple coloured skin, is a popular vegetable with many people. It is one of the important ingredients in Ratatouille, page 209 and the Moussaka on page 152, and is a very versatile vegetable. Aubergine (eggplant) makes a delicious pâté too, see page 25.

One of the favourite ways of serving

this is to cut the aubergine (eggplant) into unpeeled slices, toss in seasoned flour and fry, but if you are trying to avoid extra calories this is not for you. Those of you on a low-carbohydrate diet can fry the slices, but toss the sliced unpeeled aubergine (eggplant) in a little salt and pepper instead of flour, then fry in hot oil or fat until tender. Drain on absorbent paper and serve. The calories, etc. for this method of cooking are on page 212.

Aubergine (Eggplant) and Tomato Bake

Wipe 2 medium aubergines (eggplants) and cut into thin slices. Skin and slice 450 g/1 lb tomatoes. Arrange the aubergine (eggplant) and tomato slices in layers in an ovenproof dish beginning and ending with tomatoes and adding a little salt and pepper to each layer. Cover the dish and bake for $1\frac{1}{4}$ hours in the centre of a moderate oven (160°C/325°F, Gas Mark 3).

To serve: Top with chopped basil or parsley and serve hot or cold as an accompaniment to most main dishes.

To freeze: This dish freezes well for 12 months.

■ 40/Kj 168 □ 7.2 g

Bamboo Shoots

This vegetable is an essential ingredient in Chinese cooking, and also good as an accompaniment in main meals. As it is generally obtained in canned form, heat until as tender as desired, and top with chopped herbs. The figures given *assume* 100 g/4 oz/$\frac{1}{4}$ *lb* per portion plus the herbs.

To freeze: Bamboo shoots are better not frozen.

Variations:

1: Cheese Medley: Heat the Bamboo shoots until as tender as desired, cool, mix with cubed Cheddar and Danish Blue Cheese, skinned tomatoes and canned red pepper (capsicum). Serve on a bed of mixed salad.

2: Bamboo shoots with mushrooms: Cut the Bamboo shoots across into slices. Fry in a little oil with sliced mushrooms until tender. Add a little chicken stock flavoured with Soy sauce and Oyster sauce and simmer until heated through.

■ 36/Kj 151 □ 9.0 g

Green Beans

The green type of bean is extremely versatile and should be included in slimmer's meals, for it is a good source of protein. Prepare the beans, cut away the 'stringy' ends and sides, and slice runner beans (Italian beans) but leave the French type and haricots verts (ordinary stringbeans) whole. Cook in boiling salted water and drain when tender. The figures given *assume* 100 g/4 oz/$\frac{1}{4}$ *lb* per portion when cooked.

To serve: Hot or cold, flavoured with chopped chives and parsley.

To freeze: Blanch, pack and use within a year.

Variations:

1: Tuscany Beans: Skin and chop several tomatoes, add a little chopped basil and parsley, simmer to a purée, mix with the cooked beans.

2: Beans with Onion sauce: Add several peeled and sliced onions and 1 to 2 crushed cloves garlic to the water in which you are cooking the beans. Let this evaporate towards the end of the cooking period; but drain away any surplus. Combine the bean mixture with plain yogurt and chopped chives and serve hot or cold.

3: Bean Salad: Green beans are a good salad accompaniment to hot or cold dishes. Cook the beans, toss in chopped parsley and savory when hot, plus a little oil and lemon juice. Allow to cool and serve on a bed of lettuce heart, garnished with sliced tomatoes.

4: Beans with Almonds: This is a good accompaniment to the Christmas turkey or any other poultry. Cook the beans and drain well, keep hot. Peel and finely slice a medium onion and crush a clove of garlic. Heat 1×15 ml spoon/1 tablespoon oil and fry the onion and garlic until soft. Add the beans and toss to coat well in the flavoured oil. Place on a serving dish and sprinkle with a small amount of almonds (toasted under the grill/broiler) and grated Parmesan cheese. For those members of the family not slimming, add some breadcrumbs which have been fried in butter.

■ 16/Kj 67 □ 3.2 g

Vegetables

Other Beans

There are many popular types of bean, including lima, haricot (navy), butter beans, etc. As these are high in both calories and carbohydrate content they must be eaten sparingly, whilst trying to reduce weight.

Haricot (Navy) Beans

These are an excellent source of protein and popular with children; recipes using them as a main ingredient of the meal rather than an accompaniment are on page 151.

Soya Beans

These are used for T.V.P. (Textured Vegetable Protein) a food that is being used today to replace, or extend, the meat content of some dishes. See the recipe on page 152.

Broad Beans

These are delicious when young, and you can cook both the pods as well as the bean. Boil in salted water, drain, top with a little plain yogurt and paprika or just with chopped parsley.

Broad beans make an excellent meal topped with cheese sauce or poached eggs.

One of the most interesting ways to cook broad beans is as follows:

Beans Americano

De-rind and chop 25 g/1 oz (chunk) bacon, peel and chop an onion, 2 stalks of celery and 4 large tomatoes. Put the bacon into a saucepan and cook for 2 to 3 minutes, add the vegetables and simmer until a thick pulp. Mix with 1 × 15 ml spoon/1 tablespoon chopped parsley and 450 g/1 lb cooked broad beans.

To serve: With meat or fish or as a separate course.

To freeze: This dish can be frozen. Use within 3 months.

Variations:

1: Serve the dish cold, garnished with watercress and chopped hard-boiled eggs.

2: Add a chopped canned or fresh red pepper (capsicum), discard the core and seeds if a fresh pepper (capsicum), and chop 2 garlic cloves; add to the tomato mixture.

■ 108/Kj 455 □ 11.7 g

Carrots

Never overcook carrots, for they are much nicer when slightly firm in texture.

Try cooking the carrots in a little chicken or other stock instead of salted water; lift the lid off the pan towards the end of the cooking time, so the liquid evaporates.

Mash carrots with a small amount of butter, chopped parsley, a very little chopped tarragon and grated nutmeg.

Cook 1 or 2 chopped onions with the carrots and mash together when tender.

Carrot and Yogurt Bake

Cook 450 g/1 lb peeled, sliced carrots until tender. Drain, put into an oven-proof dish, top with plain yogurt and grated cheese. Heat for 10 minutes in a hot oven (220°C/425°F, Gas Mark 7), or try the Egg and Carrot Bake, page 64. Calorie and carbohydrate figures given assume 150 ml/¼ pint/⅔ cup plain yogurt and 50 g/2 oz/½ cup grated cheese to serve 4 people.

■ 98/Kj 411 □ 7.7 g

Carrot Ring

Cook 450 g/1 lb peeled carrots in the minimum quantity of water with salt and pepper to taste, strain and save the liquid. Sieve or purée the carrots in a blender then add enough of the carrot stock to give just under 600 ml/1 pint/2½ cups of purée. Soften 15 g/½ oz/2 envelopes of gelatine (gelatin) in 2 × 15 ml spoons/2 tablespoons water, add to the reheated carrot purée and stir until dissolved, then blend in 150 ml/¼ pint/⅔ cup milk. Spoon into a lightly oiled ring mould. Leave to set in a cool place.

To serve: Turn out and fill the centre with 3 halved or quartered hard-boiled eggs and a chopped head of chicory (endive).

■ 108/Kj 452 ☐ 8.5 g

Celeriac

This rather ugly looking root (it is like a large badly shaped turnip) has the good flavour of celery, but the texture of a turnip when cooked. It is delicious raw but equally good when it is cooked. It does discolour badly, so have the boiling salted water, plus 1×5 ml spoon/1 teaspoon lemon juice, all ready and drop the peeled and cubed, or sliced, celeriac into this at once. When cooked, toss in butter and chopped parsley or other herbs. Celeriac can be mashed with a little chopped mint, or parsley or chives, and a generous amount of butter or margarine.

Scalloped Celeriac

Arrange 450 g/1 lb peeled and thinly sliced celeriac in an ovenproof dish, cover with 150 ml/¼ pint/⅔ cup milk heated with a little salt and pepper, then top with 15 g/½ oz/1 tablespoon butter or margarine. Bake for 1¼ to 1½ hours in the centre of a very moderate oven (160°C/325°F, Gas Mark 3) by which time the milk will have been absorbed and the top layer of celeriac will be golden in colour.

To serve: With cold meats, salads or fish.

To freeze: Celeriac is always better freshly cooked.

■ 61/Kj 256 ☐ 4.2 g

Cucumber

Cucumber is generally considered a salad vegetable, but it is excellent if cooked.

You can use cucumber instead of courgettes (zucchini) in the Ratatouille recipe on page 209, an advantage if you grow cucumbers and have a good crop. Cucumbers can be skinned, sliced and boiled in salted water until softened or, as they contain so much water, they can be steamed over a pan of boiling water. Top with chopped fennel and dill if serving with fish.

For those of you who are not counting calories, but carbohydrate content, you can slice the peeled cucumber and fry in a little butter or margarine or oil.

Cucumber Salad

Shell 3 hard-boiled eggs. Chop the whites and sieve the yolks into a bowl. Blend 300 ml/½ pint/1¼ cups plain yogurt with the egg yolks, add 2×5 ml spoons/2 teaspoons white wine vinegar, salt and pepper to taste. Cut a medium cucumber into thick slices, then into matchstick shapes. Pile onto a dish, top with the dressing and garnish with 50 g/2 oz of watercress sprigs and the egg whites.

To serve: With other salads or curries or as an appetizer.

To freeze: Salad is not suitable for freezing.

■ 114/Kj 481 ☐ 6.1 g

Beans Americano; Carrot Ring; Scalloped Celeriac

Vegetables

Courgettes (Zucchini)

These are cooked as marrow (squash), but since you do not remove the peel you retain rather more flavour. Courgettes (zucchini) are in Ratatouille and in Courgettes (Zucchini) à la Grècque on page 179.

TAKE A NEW LOOK AT VEGETABLES

Since vegetables are so important when slimming try new ways of serving them. The Cucumber Cream Ice on this page is a good example of an unexpected way to eat this familiar vegetable, and so is the Egg and Carrot Bake, also on this page.

Cucumber Cream Ice

■ 84/Kj 354 □ 4.0 g

Metric/Imperial

1 medium cucumber

juice of 1 lemon

150 ml/¼ pint soured cream

ice-cold water

salt

pepper

TO GARNISH:
1 lemon, sliced

American

1 medium cucumber

juice of 1 lemon

⅔ cup sour cream

ice-cold water

salt

pepper

TO GARNISH:
1 lemon, sliced

Peel most of the cucumber, save just a little with the peel on, as this gives a better colour to the ice. Chop the cucumber into pieces and blend with the lemon juice, soured (sour) cream and enough water to give a fairly thick purée. Season well with salt and pepper. Freeze until the consistency of a sorbet, then spoon into glasses.

To serve: Top with twists of lemon.

To freeze: This ice can be frozen in a refrigerator or freezer. Serve when lightly frosted.

Variations:

1: Flavour the ice with a pinch of curry powder.

2: Flavour with a little chopped mint.

3: To make the ice more creamy, use 300 ml/½ pint/1¼ cups soured (sour) cream.

Egg and Carrot Bake

■ 222/Kj 933 □ 6.0 g

Metric/Imperial

350 g/12 oz carrots, diced

225 g/8 oz sweeds, diced

salt

2 × 15 ml spoons/2 tablespoons single cream

1 × 15 ml spoon/1 tablespoon chopped mixed herbs

pepper

6 hard-boiled eggs, halved

100 g/4 oz Cheddar cheese, grated

50 g/2 oz cream cheese

150 ml/¼ pint plain yogurt

American

¾ lb carrots, cubed

½ lb swedes (rutabagas), cubed

salt

2 tablespoons light cream

1 tablespoon chopped mixed herbs

pepper

6 hard-boiled eggs, halved

1 cup grated Cheddar cheese

¼ cup cream cheese

⅔ cup plain yogurt

Cook the diced (cubed) carrots and swedes (rutabagas) in boiling salted water until just tender. Strain and mash; add the cream, herbs and pepper to taste and reheat. Spoon the hot mixture into a greased ovenproof dish; press the eggs into the mixture with the cut sides downwards. Mix the cheeses together, blend with the yogurt. Cover the top of the pie with this mixture. Bake in the centre of a moderately hot oven (200°C/400°F, Gas Mark 6) for about 15 minutes; lower the heat after 10 minutes if the topping is becoming too brown.

To serve: With baked or grilled (broiled) tomatoes.

To freeze: Do not freeze.

Variations:

1: If the vegetables and eggs are both very hot, they could be put into a flame-proof dish and placed under the grill (broiler) for a few minutes, instead of baking in the oven.

2: Egg and pumpkin bake: Pumpkin is a good alternative to carrot. Peel and remove the seeds to make 350 g/12 oz finished pumpkin. Cook and mash as above, then finish with the cheese topping. Bake as above.

Note: This is a dish that may encourage children to eat and enjoy carrots.

Fennel

This is one of the most interesting of all root vegetables. The white root has a very pronounced aniseed taste, and the delicate 'feathery' leaves, a less strong, but similar taste.

The leaves are chopped and put into sauces and mayonnaise to serve with fish, but they are also excellent in a dressing for egg and cheese salads.

The root can be chopped and used raw in salads; you can use just a very little to add interest to a rice salad or a Russian salad.

The root can be cut into slices and simmered in well-seasoned water and strained, then tossed in melted butter or margarine. It is the ideal root vegetable to serve with fish.

Fennel and Cauliflower Salad

Cook the florets of a 450 g/1 lb cauliflower. Blend with about 100 g/4 oz of the sliced root of fennel. Add 4 × 15 ml spoons/4 tablespoons chopped spring onions (scallions) and carrot matchsticks. Pile onto a dish and top with the Hollandaise sauce on page 80. This gives 4 portions.

To freeze: Do not freeze as it is better served when freshly made.

Variation:

Fennel blends well with cooked turnip or kohlrabi. Cook and dice (cube) either of these vegetables and use instead of the cauliflower. Substitute mayonnaise for Hollandaise sauce.

■ 134/Kj 563 □ 5.3 g

From rear: Fennel and Cauliflower Salad; Egg and Carrot Bake; Cucumber Cream Ice

Vegetables

Endive and Chicory

Often there is confusion between these two vegetables, for in Britain endive is the name given to the vegetable that looks like a curly lettuce, while chicory is the name given to the white vegetable. In France and America the two names are reversed. Both vegetables are relatively low in calories and carbohydrate and excellent in salads; but you can cook a green endive (chicory) for a short time and serve it instead of cabbage, although this is an acquired taste.

Chicory (endive) can be cooked in a little lemon flavoured water, to which is added salt and pepper to taste. Do not overcook for if you do the vegetable becomes bitter in taste. It can be topped with butter or cheese or Hollandaise sauce, see pages 78 and 80.

Chicory (endive) is an excellent ingredient in a salad with sliced fresh oranges and green endive (chicory), lettuce or watercress.

Green Vegetables

All green vegetables are low in calories, but are higher than many people realize in carbohydrates, even so they add important vitamins and fibre to any diet, or mode of catering, and so are an important ingredient to include in your meals.

You can vary the dishes by the way in which they are served; cabbage or any cabbage greens taste interesting if mixed with chopped spring onions (scallions) and diced dessert apple; or you can fry the onion and apple if you are able to include some butter or margarine in your diet.

There is a recipe on page 175 for Stuffed Cabbage and a number of ideas using green vegetables are included throughout this book.

Children often prefer green vegetables raw and this is a splendid way of serving them in salads instead of using lettuce.

You will find that watercress, lettuce and parsley have been used generously in recipes. This is because they add flavour and also are low in both calorie and carbohydrate content.

Leeks and Onions

Both these vegetables add flavour to so many dishes and both are excellent as a separate vegetable.

If you boil the vegetables be careful not to overcook them or use too much water, for both contain a high percentage of water and you can so easily spoil them if they are 'swimming' in liquid.

Young leeks are delicious in a salad, they can be topped with yogurt and paprika or a little grated cheese for a light dish or turned into a supper dish (see recipe on this page).

Leek and Bacon Savoury

Prepare 8 leeks so each weighs about 100 g/4 oz/¼ lb and cook in boiling salted water until just tender, drain well. Remove the rinds from 8 thin rashers (slices) of streaky bacon weighing about 225 g/8 oz/½ lb. Stretch the bacon by stroking firmly with a knife in one direction, this makes it even thinner. Wrap the bacon rashers (slices) round the leeks. Put into a flameproof dish and cook under a hot grill (broiler) for several minutes, then turn and cook on the other side.
To serve: As soon as cooked.
To freeze: This dish does not freeze well.
■ 346/Kj 1453 □ 13.6 g

Leek and Orange Salad

Blend 1 × 15 ml spoon/1 tablespoon oil with 2 × 15 ml spoons/2 tablespoons lemon juice, salt, pepper and a little made (Dijon) mustard. Prepare and slice 4 raw young leeks, each weighing about 75 g/3 oz and the pulp from 4 medium oranges. Mix with the dressing and garnish with watercress.
To serve: With cheese or meat dishes.
■ 91/Kj 382 □ 15.1 g

Leek and Mushroom Salad

Wash, but do not peel, 100–175 g/4–6 oz/1–1½ cups small mushrooms and use raw in the salad above, with, or instead of, the oranges. Raw mushrooms are delicious, but they *must* be very fresh.

Leek and Pepper (Capsicum) Salad

Cube a red, green and yellow pepper (capsicum), discard the core and seeds and use in the salad above, with, or instead of, the oranges.

Mushrooms

This vegetable gives flavour to many dishes and fortunately adds few calories and has no carbohydrate content. The method in which they are cooked, i.e. frying, for example, will add calories, but the fat does not change the carbohydrate content.

Raw mushrooms are delicious in salads; wash, dry, trim the ends of the stalks, but do not peel; for this contains a lot of the flavour.

If you simmer mushrooms in a little stock, strain, then toss in plain yogurt, blended with paprika, you have a very pleasant hot or cold dish. This is based upon a traditional Hungarian way of serving mushrooms.

Stuffed Peppers (Capsicums)

Leek and Orange Salad; Leek and Bacon Savoury; Hungarian Mushrooms

Peppers (Capsicums)

These sweet peppers (capsicums) have become a very interesting ingredient in cooking in most countries. They add colour, as well as flavour and a crisp texture. Fortunately they are one of the fairly few vegetables that have no carbohydrate content, although they provide a medium number of calories.

Peppers (capsicums), green, yellow or red are excellent in salads, stews, etc. If you like the crisp texture of the pepper (capsicum) then you will only need to dice (cube) or chop the pulp and discard the core and seeds. If, however, you find this pulp a little too crisp then 'blanch' the vegetables for 2 to 3 minutes in boil-ing salted water, then strain, cool and chop. If you want to discard the very thin outer skin then heat for a few minutes in the oven and slip off.

Stuffed Peppers (Capsicums)

Cut the tops from 4 fairly large green peppers (capsicums); scoop out the seeds and cores; discard these. Cook the peppers (capsicums), plus the tops, in a pan of boiling salted water for 3 to 5 minutes, then strain. Prepare the selected filling; this could be one of the stuffings on pages 50 or 51 or a small amount of cooked rice and chopped grilled (broiled) bacon, diced cooked meat, flaked cooked fish or grated cheese. Chop the tops and add to the filling. Put the mixture into the pepper (capsicum) cases and stand in a lightly greased ovenproof dish. Top with a lid or greased foil and bake for approximately 30 to 35 minutes in the centre of a moderate oven (180°C/350°F, Gas Mark 4). The calorie and carbohydrate content will depend upon the filling used.

Vegetables

Parsnips

The sweet flavour of parsnips lend themselves to roasting and serving with the roast joint; they are particularly good with beef. Par-boil the vegetable first until half cooked, then strain, dry on absorbent paper and put into the hot fat; this gives a much more tender texture. Their sweetness may suggest that parsnips are higher in calories than potatoes but they are considerably lower, so make a good alternative.

Parsnips are excellent boiled and mashed with chopped chives and a very little mint.

Parsnip Loaf

Cook and mash 450 g/1 lb parsnips (weight when peeled). Mix with 2 × 15 ml spoons/2 tablespoons chopped parsley and 2 eggs. Put into a well greased 0.75 kg/1½ lb to 1 kg/2 lb loaf tin, covered with greased foil and bake for an hour in the centre of a very moderate oven (160°C/325°F, Gas Mark 3).

To serve: Turn out onto a bed of shredded lettuce and garnish with chopped parsley. Serve hot or cold.

To freeze: Use within 3 months.

■ 102/Kj428 □ 13.1 g

Parsnip Loaf

Potatoes

Often people say that one must not touch a potato when slimming. It may be necessary if your diet is to be very restricted, but on the other hand if you are used to having potatoes every day you may find it better to allow yourself just one small potato, weighing about 50 g/2 oz, rather than omitting them altogether.

This is particularly important when dealing with children, and you will find a recipe for a potato dish, using jacket potatoes on page 151.

If you cook the potatoes in their skins, either by boiling, steaming or baking you have a more satisfying dish.

Peas

As peas are one of the most popular of cooked vegetables it may be very hard to omit these from your meals. Remember too that peas, like beans and lentils, are an excellent source of protein, so they are important from this point of view. Peas, however, are a 'starchy' vegetable and, as such, high in carbohydrate content, also in calories too, so serve them sparingly and on occasions when you want to increase the total protein content of the dish, or meal.

Salsify

This unusual root vegetable can be cooked as celery or celeriac, and is excellent in the following way.

Salsify Vinaigrette

Peel the vegetable, cook until just soft in well seasoned water. Strain, halve, then toss in an oil and vinegar dressing as page 81. Either serve at once with crisp

fried bacon or allow to cool. The vegetable can be topped with mayonnaise or Hollandaise sauce, see page 80. Garnish with lemon and watercress.

Swedes (Rutabagas) and Turnips

Both these vegetables are lower in both calorie and carbohydrate content than potatoes, so could be served as an alternative to those of you wanting to lose weight gradually.

Tomatoes

There is no need to stress the versatility of tomatoes, they are invaluable for adding flavour and colour to hot and cold dishes. The Tomato Ice on this page is a new, and very suitable way, to use tomatoes for slimmers, and the mould makes a satisfying main dish.

Tomato Ice

■ 127/Kj535 □8.8 g

Metric/Imperial
0.75 kg/1½ lb ripe tomatoes
bunch spring onions, finely chopped
1 clove garlic, crushed (optional)
2 × 15 ml spoons/2 tablespoons salad or olive oil
salt
pepper
iced water
TO GARNISH:
little parsley
2 green peppers, de-seeded and chopped

Tomato Ice; Cheese and Tomato Moulds

¼ medium cucumber, diced

4 × 15 ml spoons/4 tablespoons plain yogurt

American

1½ lb ripe tomatoes

bunch scallions, finely chopped

1 clove garlic, crushed (optional)

2 tablespoons salad or olive oil

salt

pepper

iced water

TO GARNISH:

little parsley

2 green capsicums, de-seeded and chopped

¼ medium cucumber, cubed

¼ cup plain yogurt

♣ Skin the tomatoes and purée or sieve in a blender, add some of the chopped onions (scallions) and crushed garlic, then add the oil, season well with salt and pepper and stir in enough iced water to make a pouring consistency. Spoon into freezing trays and freeze until just lightly frosted. Meanwhile, dip the rims of soup cups or glasses into water or egg white and then into chopped parsley.

To serve: Spoon the ice into the dishes and garnish with the chopped spring onions (scallions) and peppers (capsicums), cubed cucumber and plain yogurt.

To freeze: Use within 3 months. Add garnish when serving.

To thaw: Slightly to be a soft ice.

Variations:

1: If using gelatine (gelatin), allow 1 × 5 ml spoon/1 teaspoon to each 600 ml/1 pint/2½ cups tomato mixture. Soften the gelatine (gelatin) in 2 × 15 ml spoons/2 tablespoons cold water, stand over a bowl of boiling water and leave until dissolved.

2: Tomato and Orange Ice: Omit the vegetables and mix the very finely grated 'zest' of an orange with the tomato purée and orange juice to give the desired blending of flavours and consistency. Freeze and garnish with orange twists.

Cheese and Tomato Moulds

■ 190/Kj 797 ☐ 11.2 g

Metric/Imperial

3 tomatoes, skinned and chopped

little water if necessary

25 g/1 oz margarine

25 g/1 oz flour

salt

pepper

25 g/1 oz fresh breadcrumbs

75 g/3 oz Cheddar cheese, grated

American

3 tomatoes, skinned and chopped

little water if necessary

2 tablespoons margarine

¼ cup flour

salt

pepper

½ cup fresh breadcrumbs

¾ cup grated Cheddar cheese

♣ Sieve or liquidize the tomatoes to give a smooth purée, add water, if necessary, to give 200 ml/⅓ pint/⅞ cup. Heat the margarine in a saucepan, stir in the flour and cook for several minutes. Remove the saucepan from the heat and gradually add the tomato purée. Bring the sauce to the boil, stirring all the time, and continue cooking until it thickens. Add salt and pepper to taste then the breadcrumbs, while the sauce is still hot. Cool slightly then add the cheese. Pour into a 600 ml/1 pint/2½ cup mould or 4 individual moulds and allow to set.

To serve: Turn out and garnish with tomato slices, lemon wedges and watercress sprigs. Serve with salad or with cold meat.

To freeze: Do not freeze for longer than one month.

Vegetables

VEGETARIAN DISHES

It is possible to follow a vegetarian diet and still lose an appreciable amount of weight. It is essential though to check you are having enough of the important nutrients.

The protein foods, such as cheese, eggs, milk and fish (if you are not a strict vegetarian) are perfect foods on a low-carbohydrate diet as they are a good source of nutrients and filling.

Unfortunately nuts and the protein vegetables (beans, lentils, peas, soya beans) are fairly high in calories and a moderate source of carbohydrate, except chestnuts, which are high in carbohydrates as well, so use these sparingly.

STARTERS FOR VEGETARIANS

Many dishes in this book are suitable as appetizers for vegetarians, but those on these pages are particularly suitable; they are unusual and add relatively few calories.

Avocado Cream

■ 233/Kj 980 □ 3.4 g

Metric/Imperial

juice of 1 lemon

2 ripe avocados

150 ml/¼ pint single cream

4 × 15 ml spoons/4 tablespoons mayonnaise

50 g/2 oz Cheddar cheese, finely grated

salt

pepper

2–3 drops Tabasco sauce

1 × 2.5 ml spoon/½ teaspoon Worcestershire sauce

American

juice of 1 lemon

2 ripe avocados

⅔ cup light cream

¼ cup mayonnaise

½ cup finely grated Cheddar cheese

salt

pepper

2–3 drops Tabasco sauce

½ teaspoon Worcestershire sauce

❧ Put the lemon juice into the bowl (this stops the avocados discolouring). Halve the avocados, remove the stones (pits) and skin, then mash into the lemon juice and add the rest of the ingredients.

To serve: Freeze lightly, spoon into glasses. Serve with a teaspoon.

To freeze: Do not freeze for any period, but only just before serving.

Variations:

1: Spoon into grapefruit skins and top with the grapefruit segments.

2: Do not freeze, but spoon into one bowl, stand on a large tray and arrange florets of raw cauliflower, cubes of baby carrots, pieces of celery and spring onions (scallions) around. Serve as a dip.

Spinach Pâté

■ 83/Kj 349 □ 4.0 g

Metric/Imperial

450 g/1 lb young spinach

1–2 cloves garlic, chopped

1 medium onion, chopped

salt

pepper

2 × 15 ml spoons/2 tablespoons chopped parsley

3 × 15 ml spoons/3 tablespoons plain yogurt

1 × 15 ml spoon/1 tablespoon lemon juice

2 hard-boiled eggs

TO GARNISH:

1 small carrot, grated

American

1 lb young spinach

1–2 cloves garlic, chopped

1 medium onion, chopped

salt

pepper

2 tablespoons chopped parsley

3 tablespoons plain yogurt

1 tablespoon lemon juice

2 hard-boiled eggs

TO GARNISH:

1 small carrot, grated

❧ Wash the spinach, drain but do not dry. Put into a saucepan with the water adhering to the leaves but no extra liquid. Add the garlic, onion, salt and pepper. Cover the pan, cook over a moderate heat for about 10 minutes until just tender. Add the parsley towards the end of the cooking time. Strain thoroughly, sieve or purée and blend with the yogurt and lemon juice. Allow to cool. Shell and chop one egg and mix with the spinach purée. Put into individual dishes. Separate the white from the yolk of the remaining egg and chop each finely. Spoon the egg yolk, egg white and grated carrot over the top of the pâté.

To serve: Chill well and serve with a teaspoon.

To freeze: This dish will not freeze, but frozen spinach could be used.

Variation:

Add finely chopped anchovy fillets, smoked or cooked fish or cottage cheese to the spinach mixture. Add a little grated nutmeg before sieving or puréeing. Other herbs, such as thyme or sage, may be used in place of the parsley.

Peanut Soup

■ 299/Kj 1256 □ 9.4 g

Metric/Imperial

25 g/1 oz margarine

2 medium onions, chopped

750 ml/1¼ pints water

little yeast extract

225 g/8 oz peanuts

2 medium carrots, grated

salt

pepper

TO GARNISH:

150 ml/¼ pint plain yogurt

2 tomatoes, skinned and chopped

American

2 tablespoons margarine

2 medium onions, chopped

3 cups water

little yeast extract

1⅛ cups peanuts

2 medium carrots, grated

salt

pepper

TO GARNISH:

⅔ cup plain yogurt

2 tomatoes, skinned and chopped

♣ Heat the margarine, fry the onions for several minutes, taking care they do not brown. Add nearly all the water and simmer for 10 minutes. Stir in a small amount of yeast extract, to give more flavour, and the peanuts. Simmer for only 2 to 3 minutes then rub through a sieve or put into a warmed blender goblet and blend to make a smooth purée. Return to the saucepan. Add the grated carrots and heat, but do not cook as these provide a contrast in texture. Taste and add any salt and pepper desired.

To serve: Top each portion with the yogurt and chopped tomato.

To freeze: This soup can be frozen for 4 to 6 weeks.

Variations:

1: Omit the margarine to reduce the calories and just simmer the onions in the liquid.

2: Omit the margarine, simmer the onions in the liquid, then add 25 g/1 oz/ 2 tablespoons peanut butter (this adds protein, but is not suitable for frying).

Spinach Pâté;
Avocado Cream

Vegetarian Dishes

Aubergine (Eggplant) Pâté

Halve aubergines (eggplants) lengthways. Sprinkle the cut surfaces with a little oil, lemon juice, salt and pepper. Put in foil, wrap and bake for 1 to 1½ hours in a cool oven (150°C/300°F, Gas Mark 2). By wrapping in this way the skins as well as the pulp soften. Unwrap, cool and serve as other pâtés.

Tomato Mousse

■ 76/Kj 320 □ 4.1 g

Metric/Imperial

3 medium tomatoes

water

pinch celery salt

shake cayenne pepper

pinch dry mustard

few drops Worcestershire sauce

2 × 5 ml spoons/2 teaspoons lemon juice

2 eggs

1 × 5 ml spoon/1 teaspoon gelatine

150 ml/¼ pint plain yogurt

few lettuce leaves

American

3 medium tomatoes

water

pinch celery salt

shake cayenne pepper

pinch dry mustard

few drops Worcestershire sauce

2 teaspoons lemon juice

2 eggs

1 teaspoon gelatin

$\frac{2}{3}$ cup plain yogurt

few lettuce leaves

❧Chop, then sieve the tomatoes to make a smooth purée. Sieving is easier if you first purée the tomatoes in a blender, but you need to sieve afterwards to remove all the seeds and tiny particles of skin. Add water if necessary to the purée to make up to 300 ml/$\frac{1}{2}$ pint/$1\frac{1}{4}$ cups; pour into a bowl, add the salt, pepper, mustard, Worcestershire sauce and lemon juice. Separate the eggs and whisk the yolks into the tomato purée. Stand the bowl over a saucepan of hot but NOT boiling water, whisk briskly until the mixture is sufficiently thick to coat the back of a wooden spoon.

Meanwhile soften the gelatine (gelatin) in 2 × 15 ml spoons/2 tablespoons water, add to the warm egg and tomato mixture and stir over the hot water until dissolved. Remove the bowl from the pan, continue whisking until the mixture is cold; stir in the yogurt. Whisk the egg whites, fold into the tomato mixture, leave in the refrigerator until beginning to set.

To serve: Chill the mixture. Shred the lettuce leaves finely and put into shallow glasses. Spoon the mixture on top.

To freeze: Do not freeze.

Variation:

Use 300 ml/$\frac{1}{2}$ pint/$1\frac{1}{4}$ cups tomato juice in place of the tomato purée and additional water.

From rear: Tomato Mousse; Nut Coleslaw; Potted Cheese

Potted Cheese

■ 137/Kj 573 □ 2.9 g

Metric/Imperial

25 g/1 oz butter or margarine

225 g/8 oz cottage cheese

1 × 15 ml spoon/1 tablespoon lemon juice

salt

pepper

pinch grated nutmeg.

2–3 spring onions, chopped

2 × 5 ml spoons/2 teaspoons chopped parsley

1 small green pepper (capsicum), de-seeded and chopped

1 lettuce

TO GARNISH:
1 lemon, cut in wedges

American

2 tablespoons butter or margarine

$\frac{1}{2}$ lb cottage cheese

1 tablespoon lemon juice

salt

pepper

pinch grated nutmeg

2–3 scallions, chopped

2 teaspoons chopped parsley

1 small green pepper, de-seeded and chopped

1 head lettuce

TO GARNISH:
1 lemon, cut in wedges

❧Melt the butter or margarine until just softened; do not overheat. Sieve the cottage cheese, or put into a blender until smooth. Mix with the lemon juice, salt, pepper and nutmeg, then add the spring onions (scallions), parsley and chopped pepper (capsicum). Spoon into 4 to 6 individual dishes and top with the melted butter or margarine.

To serve: Turn out onto a bed of lettuce and garnish with the lemon.

To freeze: Do not freeze.

Variations:

1: Omit the lemon juice and use 2 × 15 ml spoons/2 tablespoons sieved tomato purée instead.

2: Add finely chopped gherkin (sweet dill pickle) or cucumber instead of the green pepper (capsicum).

3: Use cream or grated hard cheese instead of cottage cheese.

Nut Coleslaw

■ 150/Kj 631 □ 20.9 g

Metric/Imperial

350 g/12 oz white cabbage

1 large dessert apple, peeled, cored and diced

25 g/1 oz seedless raisins

100 g/4 oz cashew nuts, chopped

FOR THE DRESSING:
5 × 15 ml spoons/5 tablespoons plain yogurt

1 × 15 ml spoon/1 tablespoon olive oil

2 × 5 ml spoons/2 teaspoons chopped parsley

salt

pepper

1 × 5 ml spoon/1 teaspoon made mustard

American

$\frac{3}{4}$ lb white cabbage

1 large apple, peeled, cored and cubed

3 tablespoons seedless white raisins

1 cup chopped cashew nuts

FOR THE DRESSING:
$\frac{1}{3}$ cup plain yogurt

1 tablespoon olive oil

2 teaspoons chopped parsley

salt

pepper

1 teaspoon Dijon mustard

❧Wash and dry the cabbage, shred very finely. Mix the cabbage, apple, raisins and chopped nuts. Mix the yogurt, oil, parsley, salt, pepper and mustard together. Add the dressing to the coleslaw as soon as it is made, allow to stand for about 30 minutes before serving. The apple does not discolour once it is put in the dressing, but will go brown otherwise.

To serve: On individual plates.

To freeze: Not suitable for freezing.

Variations:

1: Add segments of orange to the coleslaw.

2: Mix grated raw carrot into the coleslaw.

3: Add a little curry powder to the dressing.

4: Use raw spinach instead of cabbage.

5: It makes an interesting dressing if a little black treacle (molasses) is added to the yogurt, etc.

Vegetarian Dishes

EGGS AND CHEESE

These two important protein foods can combine to give interesting and nutritious dishes. Fortunately eggs are low in calories.

From left: Swiss Omelette; Cauliflower and Eggs au Gratin; Cauliflower Cheese; Tomato Cheese Pudding

Tomato Cheese Pudding

■ 238/Kj999 □ 14.1 g

Metric/Imperial

300 ml/½ pint milk

2 eggs, beaten

50 g/2 oz fresh breadcrumbs

100 g/4 oz cheese, grated

salt

pepper

pinch dry mustard

3 large tomatoes, thinly sliced

American

1¼ cups milk

2 eggs, beaten

1 cup fresh breadcrumbs

1 cup grated cheese

salt

pepper

pinch dry mustard

3 large tomatoes, thinly sliced

Warm the milk, whisk onto the beaten eggs. Add the breadcrumbs, allow to stand for 30 minutes. Stir in the cheese, salt, pepper and mustard. Line a greased dish with the sliced tomatoes and pour in the cheese mixture. Bake in the centre of a moderately hot oven (190°C/375°F, Gas Mark 5) for 30 minutes until well risen and golden brown.

To serve: As soon as the dish is cooked, with a green salad or creamed spinach.

To freeze: This dish cannot be frozen.

Variations:

1: Omit the sliced tomatoes.

2: Ham and Cheese Pudding: Add 50 g/ 2 oz/¼ cup diced cooked ham.

3: Increase the amount of breadcrumbs to 100 g/4 oz/2 cups.

Cauliflower Cheese

A familiar dish is a cauliflower topped with cheese sauce, but a more unusual version is to scoop out the centre from a whole cooked cauliflower, chop this, blend with the cheese sauce (recipe page 78), chopped hard-boiled eggs, nuts or prawns (shrimp), (if you eat fish) and chopped herbs, then spoon back into the centre of the cauliflower.

Cauliflower and Eggs au Gratin

■ 335/Kj 1409 □ 13.7 g

Metric/Imperial

1 cauliflower, about 450 g/1 lb

salt

2 hard-boiled eggs

50 g/2 oz margarine

15 g/½ oz cornflour

150 ml/¼ pint milk

pepper

100 g/4 oz cheese, grated

2 × 15 ml spoons/2 tablespoons dried breadcrumbs (raspings)

American

1 cauliflower, about 1 lb

salt

2 hard-boiled eggs

4 tablespoons margarine

2 tablespoons cornstarch

⅔ cup milk

pepper

1 cup grated cheese

2 tablespoons dry breadcrumbs

❧ Divide the cauliflower into florets and cook quickly in boiling salted water to retain the maximum vitamins. Keep 150 ml/¼ pint/⅔ cup of the water, put the drained vegetable into a hot flame-proof dish, cover with the sliced hard-boiled eggs. Heat 25 g/1 oz/2 tablespoons margarine in a saucepan, stir in the cornflour (cornstarch), and cook gently for a few minutes. Remove the pan from the heat and gradually stir in the milk and vegetable stock. Return to the heat and bring to the boil, stirring all the time. Cook until thickened then add salt and pepper and half the cheese. Pour over the cauliflower, sprinkle the top with breadcrumbs, the rest of the cheese and remaining margarine. Brown under a hot grill (broiler).

To serve: As soon as cooked.

To freeze: This dish cannot be frozen.

Swiss Omelette

□ 175/Kj 735 □ Trace

Metric/Imperial

4 eggs

50 g/2 oz Gruyère cheese, grated

salt

pepper

15 g/½ oz butter

American

4 eggs

½ cup grated Gruyère cheese

salt

pepper

1 tablespoon butter

❧ Beat the eggs, add the cheese, salt and pepper. Grease 4 scallop shells (or individual ovenproof dishes) with the butter. Spoon in the egg and cheese mixture. Bake towards the top of a moderately hot oven (190°C/375°F, Gas Mark 5) for 10 to 15 minutes until as firm as desired.

To serve: With a teaspoon. The dish can be garnished with tomatoes or asparagus tips.

Variations:

1: Add 1 × 15 ml spoon/1 tablespoon single (light) cream to each egg.

2: Add a finely chopped canned red pepper (capsicum) to the eggs and cheese.

Vegetarian Dishes

Page 12 gives details of the various foods and the job they have to do in maintaining good health as you slim, but vegetarians need to check carefully on these facts to ensure a well-balanced diet while slimming.

Most vegetarian diets include an excellent amount of fresh fruits and green vegetables, so there is a more than adequate amount of Vitamin C (ascorbic acid).

As you will probably be cutting down on bread, pasta and flour products this means you are losing some of the B vitamins, so purchase wheat germ and brewer's yeast from a Health Food store, or use a good amount of yeast extract in cooking. You can add the wheat germ and yeast to soups; they both give a very pleasant taste. You can also obtain this important group of vitamins from brown rice, egg yolk, milk, plain yogurt, nuts, soya, the pulses (dried beans) and there are traces in some vegetables such as cabbage, carrots, spinach, cauliflower, onion and beetroot.

Cheese, eggs and margarine (or butter) contain vitamin A. Carrots, leafy vegetables and some fruits, such as lemons and oranges, contain carotene, which is a precurser of vitamin A. The carotene is converted into vitamin A in the body.

If you eat fish in your diet then the oily variety provide vitamin D, and so does margarine (or butter), milk, egg yolk and flower seeds. Sunlight is also an essential source of this vitamin.

Vegetarians will be able to obtain the other vitamins, described on page 13, in their normal diet, together with most of the essential minerals.

One point upon which vegetarians, whether slimming or not, should check is that they are having adequate amounts of iron. This is provided very largely by meats, so you must ensure that your diet includes this mineral by eating generous amounts of spinach, watercress, and including such foods as dried apricots, dried prunes, black treacle (molasses), egg yolk, the various grains, honey and peanuts in your vegetarian meals.

Recipes using these foods will be found throughout this book, see pages 32, 82, 183 and 211, but you will need to 'cut down' on high-calorie or high-carbohydrate foods until you have lost the required weight.

Peanut Roast

■ 357/Kj 1501 □ 11.5 g

Metric/Imperial

225 g/8 oz peanuts

50 g/2 oz vegetarian fat

2 onions, chopped

2 large tomatoes, skinned and chopped

1 small dessert apple, peeled and diced

25 g/1 oz oatmeal

1 × 5 ml spoon/1 teaspoon chopped sage or pinch of dried sage

salt

pepper

1 egg

little milk

American

1⅛ cups peanuts

¼ cup shortening

2 onions, chopped

2 large tomatoes, skinned and chopped

1 small dessert apple, peeled and cubed

2⅔ tablespoons oatmeal

1 teaspoon chopped sage or pinch of dried sage

salt

pepper

1 egg

little milk

❧Chop, mince or grind the peanuts. Heat the fat and fry the onions, tomatoes and apple until soft. Add the peanuts, oatmeal, sage and salt and pepper to taste. Bind with the egg and just enough milk to give a fairly moist consistency. Press into a greased loaf tin and cover with greased paper. Bake in the centre of a moderate oven (180°C/350°F, Gas Mark 4) for 45 minutes to 1 hour.
To serve: With a green vegetable or salad.
To freeze: This freezes well for up to 6 weeks.
Variations:
1: Use other nuts in place of peanuts. Walnuts, almonds, Brazil nuts and hazelnuts are all suitable.
2: Serve with a sauce made from plain yogurt combined with chopped spring onions (scallions), chopped parsley and sage. Season with salt and pepper.

Rice and Peanut Roast

Use recipe above, but cook 50 g/2 oz/ ⅓ cup brown or white rice; blend with peanuts, etc. before adding the milk. Cook as above, do not turn out of dish.

Stuffed Marrow

■ 257/Kj 1078 □ 17.0 g

Metric/Imperial

1 marrow (450 g/1 lb when prepared)

25 g/1 oz margarine

2 onions, chopped

3 carrots, chopped

2 tomatoes, skinned and chopped

100 g/4 oz mushrooms, sliced

100 g/4 oz Cheddar cheese, grated

salt

pepper

50 g/2 oz fresh wholemeal breadcrumbs

1 × 5 ml spoon/1 teaspoon oil

American

1 squash (1 lb when prepared)

2 tablespoons margarine or shortening

2 onions, chopped

3 carrots, chopped

2 tomatoes, skinned and chopped

1 cup sliced mushrooms

1 cup grated Cheddar cheese

salt

pepper

1 cup soft wholewheat breadcrumbs

1 teaspoon oil

Macaroni and Walnut Casserole

■ 304/Kj 1277 □ 21.1 g

Metric/Imperial
75 g/3 oz macaroni
salt
350 g/12 oz tomatoes, skinned and chopped
pepper
2 × 5 ml spoons/2 teaspoons grated onion
2 bay leaves
50 g/2 oz Cheddar cheese, grated
100 g/4 oz shelled walnuts, chopped

American
¾ cup macaroni
salt
¾ lb tomatoes, skinned and chopped
pepper
2 teaspoons grated onion
2 bay leaves
½ cup grated Cheddar cheese
1 cup shelled chopped walnuts

Put the macaroni into boiling, salted water and cook until just tender. Drain thoroughly. Put the tomatoes into a saucepan with a little salt, pepper, the onion and bay leaves. Cook slowly, stirring several times, until a thick purée is formed. Remove the bay leaves. Grease an ovenproof dish and fill with alternate layers of macaroni, tomato purée, cheese and coarsely chopped nuts, finishing with tomato and cheese. Bake in the centre of a moderately hot oven (200°C/400°F, Gas Mark 6) for approximately 25 minutes until the cheese topping is golden.

To serve: With crisp lettuce.

To freeze: This dish can be frozen for 1 month.

Variation:

Tomato and Walnut Lasagne: Follow the recipe but substitute lasagne for macaroni. Cook 100 g/4 oz/¼ lb lasagne in boiling salted water until tender, drain well. Layer and cook as above. Serve with a green salad.

Above: Peanut Roast. Right: Macaroni and Walnut Casserole

Skin the marrow (squash), cut off one long slice and remove the seeds from the rest of the vegetable. Melt the margarine and fry the chopped vegetables for 5 minutes. Add the mushrooms, half the cheese and salt and pepper to taste. Remove the pan from the heat and stir in the breadcrumbs. Place the vegetable and cheese mixture in the scooped-out marrow (squash). Press down firmly, sprinkle with the rest of the grated cheese. Replace the marrow (squash) top and brush with oil. Put into a floured transparent cook-bag or wrap in oiled foil. Bake in the centre of a moderately hot oven (190°C/375°F, Gas Mark 5) for approximately 1 hour.

To serve: Remove the marrow (squash) lid, cube this neatly and arrange round the marrow (squash). Serve with sliced tomatoes and a parsley topping.

To freeze: This dish should be freshly cooked, but you could use frozen carrots and frozen tomato purée in the stuffing.

Vegetarian Dishes

SAUCES

A sauce can turn a plain dish into a more interesting one. You will often be warned that when slimming you cannot have sauces. This entirely depends upon the **kind** of sauce and slimming routine you are following.

In this chapter are some of the sauces you may well be able to make and they have the advantage that all the family will enjoy them too.

Where a sauce has been referred to in any of the dishes in other sections, calories and carbohydrate content have been calculated on the quantity given in the recipes here, unless stated to the contrary.

SAUCES BASED UPON A ROUX

These sauces are generally made with a fat and flour base (i.e. a roux); but you will see I have used cornflour (cornstarch) instead of flour. The reason is that flour and cornflour (cornstarch) have about the same calorie content, but you need only half the quantity of cornflour (cornstarch) as flour to thicken the liquid, so you halve the calories.

Cornflour (cornstarch) does have a slightly higher carbohydrate content than flour, but nothing like twice as much, so on each type of diet it is a wise choice.

It must be stressed that the calories and carbohydrates given in the recipes are based upon skimmed milk and the low quantity of butter or margarine (a classic white sauce uses 25 g/1 oz/2 tablespoons butter or margarine). Butter is given first, but margarine has slightly fewer calories.

White Sauce

■ 70/Kj 294 □ 6.8 g

Metric/Imperial

15 g/½ oz butter or margarine

15 g/½ oz cornflour

300 ml/½ pint milk

salt

pepper

American

1 tablespoon butter or margarine

2 tablespoons cornstarch

1¼ cups milk

salt

pepper

Heat the butter or margarine, stir in the cornflour (cornstarch). Cook over a low heat for 2 to 3 minutes, stir well, so the mixture does not darken. Remove from the heat and gradually blend in the milk. Bring to the boil, stirring well. Cook until a coating consistency, then add salt and pepper to taste.

BASED ON WHITE SAUCE

If following a low-carbohydrate diet: You can use 25 g/1 oz/2 tablespoons butter or margarine and full-cream milk without altering carbohydrate content.

When making the sauce to serve over vegetables: Use half milk and half vegetable stock; this not only saves calories etc., but gives a better flavour to the sauce.

Anchovy Sauce

Use a few drops of anchovy essence (extract) to flavour the sauce; be sparing with salt.
To serve: With fish dishes.

Béchamel Sauce

Add a piece of carrot, celery and onion to the milk. Heat, leave in a warm place for a time, then strain. Use to make the sauce.
To serve: With most dishes as a more flavoursome variation of white sauce.

Cheese Sauce

Make the white sauce. If you are counting calories very strictly then use only 25 g/1 oz/¼ cup grated Parmesan cheese (this has a stronger flavour than other cheeses for cooking). Add a pinch of mustard too. If using Cheddar or other hard cheese, allow 50 g/2 oz/½ cup grated cheese. Stir the cheese into the hot sauce, do not over-cook once it is added.

As cheese has only a trace of carbohydrate content you can increase these quantities if following a low-carbohydrate diet.

There is a cheese sauce using cottage cheese on page 99.
To serve: With most dishes but excellent with fish, vegetables and hard-boiled (hard-cooked) eggs.

Egg Sauce

Either add a beaten egg or egg yolk or 1 to 2 chopped hard-boiled (hard-cooked) eggs to the sauce.
To serve: With cooked chicken or fish.

Parsley Sauce

Add 1–2 × 15 ml spoons/1–2 tablespoons chopped parsley to the sauce. Cook in the sauce for 2 to 3 minutes if you like a more mellow taste.

Other herbs can be used instead, particularly fennel and tarragon; use more sparingly than parsley.
To serve: With most dishes.

Brown Sauce

■ 51/Kj214 □ 5.4 g

This is made in the same way as the White Sauce, but dripping(s) or fat (shortening) is used instead of butter or margarine and a brown stock, or water and a beef stock (bouillon) cube, instead of milk.

This is, however, a very dull Brown Sauce and you can improve it considerably if you either:

1: Use a *good* 25 g/1 oz/2 tablespoons dripping(s) or fat (shortening) and fry a chopped onion and skinned, chopped tomato in this, then add the cornflour and the liquid and salt and pepper to taste. This sauce can be sieved or puréed in a blender to give a smooth result. As the vegetables help to thicken the sauce, be a little generous with the amount of liquid; OR

2: If you are anxious to avoid using more fat than the 15 g/$\frac{1}{2}$ oz/1 tablespoon then simmer the vegetables in the liquid for about 10 minutes, sieve or purée in the blender to make a smooth thin purée; as the vegetables help to thicken the liquid slightly you can use a little more than the 300 ml/$\frac{1}{2}$ pint/1$\frac{1}{4}$ cups stock.

The calories and carbohydrate content are based upon version 2 above.
To serve: With meat or savoury dishes.

BASED ON BROWN SAUCE

Brown sauce is a basic sauce, and can be varied in a number of ways.
Espagnole Sauce: Follow the directions for versions 1 or 2 above, but add 50 g/2 oz/$\frac{1}{2}$ cup sliced mushrooms. After the sauce has been sieved or puréed, you can add 1 × 15 ml spoon/1 tablespoon sherry when reheating.
To serve: With meat or savoury dishes.
Madeira Sauce: Follow the directions for Espagnole Sauce. Substitute 1 × 15 ml spoon/1 tablespoon madeira for the sherry.
To serve: With meat or savoury dishes.
Note: When adding extra ingredients to either of the basic sauces, you must calculate the difference made in calories etc.

QUICK WAY TO MAKE SAUCES

Although the classic way to make a sauce is based upon preparing the 'roux' first, you can save time if you blend the cornflour (cornstarch) with the liquid, pour this into the pan and add the recommended type of fat. Bring steadily to the boil, stirring well, or whisk briskly as the sauce begins to thicken. Cook slowly for some minutes, so there is no taste of uncooked cornflour.

Far left: Parsley Sauce. Below: Cheese Sauce

FREEZING SAUCES

Sauces prepared with cornflour (cornstarch), rather than flour, tend to separate less in freezing than sauces made with flour. If they have become thinner after thawing and reheating, simply blend a little more cornflour (cornstarch) with extra liquid; stir into the sauce and cook until thickened again.

Use these sauces within a month.

Sauces

*From left: Hollandaise Sauce;
Horseradish Sauce; Tomato Sauce; Oil
and Vinegar Dressing; Yogurt
Dressing; Yogurt Thousand Island
Dressing*

Yogurt Thousand Island Dressing

■ 42/Kj 175 □ 2.1 g

Metric/Imperial

150 ml/¼ pint plain yogurt

1 × 15 ml spoon/1 tablespoon chopped olives or gherkins

2 × 5 ml spoons/2 teaspoons Worcestershire sauce

3 × 15 ml spoons/3 tablespoons finely chopped celery heart

1 hard-boiled egg, finely chopped

1 × 2.5 ml spoon/½ teaspoon finely chopped onion

American

⅔ cup plain yogurt

1 tablespoon chopped olives or sweet dill pickle

2 teaspoons Worcestershire sauce

3 tablespoons finely chopped celery heart

1 hard-cooked egg, finely chopped

½ teaspoon finely chopped onion

❧ Mix all the ingredients together thoroughly and chill before serving.

To serve: Excellent with all salads.

To freeze: Do not freeze.

Yogurt Dressing

■ 69/Kj 292 □ 4.6 g

Metric/Imperial

½ sugar substitute tablet, crushed or few drops liquid sugar substitute

150 ml/¼ pint plain yogurt, chilled

0.5–1 × 15 ml spoon/½–1 tablespoon French mustard

1 × 5 ml spoon/1 teaspoon lemon juice

1 × 15 ml spoon/1 tablespoon finely chopped parsley

1 × 15 ml spoon/1 tablespoon capers or gherkins

American

½ sugar substitute tablet, crushed or few drops liquid sugar substitute

⅔ cup plain yogurt, chilled

½–1 tablespoon French mustard

1 teaspoon lemon juice

1 tablespoon finely chopped parsley

1 tablespoon capers or sweet dill pickle

❧ Add the sugar substitute to the chilled yogurt. Blend well. Add the mustard, lemon juice, parsley and capers or chopped gherkins (dill pickle).

To serve: With a chicken or meat salad.

To freeze: This can be frozen for 2 to 3 weeks, and so can the other yogurt dressings.

Hollandaise Sauce

■ 106/Kj 443 □ Trace

The classic sauce uses a high proportion of butter, which would make it an impossible sauce on a low-calorie diet, but quite acceptable on a low-carbohydrate one. The following is a very appetizing alternative for 'calorie counters'.

❧ Put 2 whole eggs into a basin, add a pinch of salt, pepper and dry mustard. Melt 25 g/1 oz/2 tablespoons butter or margarine; do not allow this to become too hot. Stand the basin over a pan of hot, but not boiling, water. Add 2 tablespoons white wine vinegar or lemon juice and whisk until the sauce becomes thick and creamy. Gradually whisk in the melted butter or margarine.

To serve: Hot with vegetables and fish; this is particularly good on broccoli.

To freeze: Better freshly made.

Variations:

Béarnaise Sauce:

Add a little finely chopped tarragon and shallot to the sauce or infuse in the vinegar or lemon juice, strain and use. Serve with steaks.

Cooked Mayonnaise:

If you whisk the sauce as it cools, then add a little more mustard, sugar substitute and pepper you have a good mayonnaise. The slimmer's adaptation of the classic recipe is on page 164.

Tartare Sauce:
Add a little chopped capers, gherkins (sweet dill pickle) and parsley to the sauce. Serve with fish.

Horseradish Sauce

■ 29/Kj 122 □ 2.4 g

You can add grated fresh horseradish to the White Sauce on page 78, but the best way to make this is to add it to lightly whipped cream (very high in calories, but fairly low in carbohydrates), together with a little lemon juice or white wine vinegar, made (Dijon) mustard and salt and pepper to taste. Add a pinch of sugar or sugar substitute.

A better way to make the sauce for slimmers is to blend the horseradish with plain yogurt, as below.

To each 150 ml/¼ pint/⅔ cup plain yogurt allow 25 g/1 oz/2 tablespoons grated fresh horseradish, 1 × 2.5 ml spoon/½ teaspoon made (Dijon) mustard, 1 × 15 ml spoon/1 tablespoon lemon juice, salt, pepper and sugar substitute to taste. Serve with beef and smoked fish.

Tomato Sauce

■ 27/Kj 113 □ 4.8 g

There are many recipes for tomato sauce, but one of the simplest is to simmer 0.5 kg/1 lb skinned chopped tomatoes with 1 medium chopped onion and 1 to 2 chopped cloves garlic, add a very little water. When a soft purée, sieve or purée in a blender, return to the saucepan with salt, pepper and a pinch of sugar or a very little sugar substitute to taste.

This can be made richer by:
1: Adding a chopped rasher (slice) of bacon or several bacon rinds which naturally must be removed before the sauce is served.
2: Toss the onion and garlic in 25 g/1 oz/2 tablespoons butter or fat (shortening) then add the tomatoes and liquid. Canned plum tomatoes give a very good flavour in a sauce.
3: Emphasize the flavour by adding 1 × 15 ml spoon/1 tablespoon tomato purée (paste) to the ingredients.

The calories etc. given above are calculated on the basic sauce.
To serve: With most foods. Tomato Sauce is particularly good with poached eggs or a small amount of boiled pasta.
To freeze: This freezes well for about 3 months, although the garlic tends to lose flavour. When reheating, add a peeled clove garlic if necessary.

Oil and Vinegar Dressing

■ 76/Kj 319 □ Trace

If you are counting calories the traditional way of making this French (vinaigrette) dressing, with about twice as much oil as vinegar (or lemon juice) is rarely possible.

You will find you get an acceptable dressing by using just 1 × 15 ml spoon/1 tablespoon oil to 3 × 15 ml spoons/3 tablespoons white wine vinegar or lemon juice. Add salt, pepper, a pinch dry mustard, sugar substitute to taste.

Those of you on a low-carbohydrate or less strict diet can increase the amount of oil used, see the Avocado and Bacon Salad on page 98.

For more flavour add chopped fresh herbs or crushed garlic to the dressing.
To serve: With most salads.
To freeze: Do not freeze.

Egg Sauces

Liquid can be thickened with egg, instead of flour or cornflour (cornstarch). See recipe for Egg Custard Sauce.

DESSERTS

Above: Home Made Ice Cream or fresh fruit make a suitable dessert

Practically all desserts contain a high number of calories and some, if not a great amount, of carbohydrate.

Most of us could give up desserts, although it may be difficult if you are used to finishing your meal with a sweet.

This chapter, and other sections of the book, give you a variety of ideas, that are specially selected for slimmers.

Remember where milk is mentioned that you save valuable calories if you choose skimmed milk and you can often use sugar substitute in place of sugar.

USE GELATINE (GELATIN)

Gelatine (gelatin) enables you to make interesting jellies and moulds with fresh fruits and other suitable ingredients.

You can use either fruit juices or a purée made from fruits. As this is somewhat thickened by the fruit itself, you can adjust the amount of gelatine (gelatin) used in proportion to the fruit purée, as given in variation 2 of the recipe below. There will be fruits you can make into purées throughout the year. There are more fruit jellies on page 210.

Prune Mould

■ 149/Kj 626 □ 18.4 g

Metric/Imperial

225 g/8 oz prunes

450 ml/¾ pint water

1 lemon

25 g/1 oz sugar

prune juice, see method

15 g/½ oz powder gelatine

TO DECORATE:

4 × 15 ml spoons/4 tablespoons double cream

25 g/1 oz blanched almonds

American

½ lb prunes

2 cups water

1 lemon

2 tablespoons sugar

prune juice (see method)

2 envelopes powder gelatin

TO DECORATE

¼ cup heavy cream

¼ cup blanched almonds

❦Soak the prunes overnight in the water. Cut very thin strips of the lemon rind, squeeze out the juice. Simmer the prunes in the water in which they were soaked, adding strips of lemon rind to taste (be very careful not to include any of the bitter white pith). Remove the prunes from the liquid, strain, then sieve or stone (pit) and purée in the blender. Add the lemon juice and sugar and measure the pulp. Stir in sufficient prune juice to give 750 ml/1¼ pints/generous 3 cups purée. Soften the gelatine (gelatin) in 2 × 15 ml spoons/2 tablespoons of prune juice, then dissolve over a pan of hot water. Stir into the prune purée. Pour the mixture into a mould, leave until firm. Whip the cream.

To serve: Turn out the prune mould and decorate with the whipped cream and almonds.

To freeze: Open-freeze then wrap and freeze without the decoration.

Variation:

Apricot Mould: Use dried apricots in place of prunes.

Note: Prunes and dried apricots are both good sources of iron.

Orange Mould

■ 65/Kj 273 □ 1.8 g

Metric/Imperial

sugar substitute to taste

450 ml/¾ pint fresh or unsweetened canned orange juice

15 g/½ oz powder gelatine

150 ml/¼ pint plain yogurt

American

sugar substitute to taste

2 cups fresh or unsweetened canned orange juice

2 envelopes powder gelatin

⅔ cup plain yogurt

❦Sweeten the orange juice. Soften the gelatine (gelatin) in 2 × 15 ml spoons/ 2 tablespoons of the cold juice. Heat

150 ml/¼ pint/⅔ cup of the juice, add the gelatine (gelatin), stir until dissolved. Mix with the remainder of the juice, cool, allow to stiffen slightly. Whisk in the yogurt, pour into a rinsed mould. Leave to set.

To serve: With fresh orange segments and more yogurt.

To freeze: Better freshly made.

Variations:

1: Use other fruit juice instead.

2: Use a fruit purée, of a consistency to coat a wooden spoon, instead of juice. In this case use 600 ml/1 pint/2½ cups to the same quantity of gelatine (gelatin).

Apple Mousse

■ 86/Kj 35 g □ 9.5 g

Metric/Imperial
1 lemon
300 ml/½ pint water
350 g/12 oz cooking apples (weight when peeled)
sugar substitute to taste
1 × 7.5 ml spoon/½ tablespoon powder gelatine
2 eggs
few mint leaves

American
1 lemon
1¼ cups water
¾ lb cooking apples (weight when peeled)
1 envelope powder gelatin
2 eggs
few mint leaves

❧ Cut away just the top 'zest' (yellow part of the rind) from the lemon. Put into a saucepan with the water. Squeeze out the juice and put on one side. Slice the apples thinly and simmer in the lemon-flavoured water. Add enough sugar substitute to sweeten the mixture.

Take out a few apple slices when soft, but unbroken; put on one side for decoration. Beat, sieve or liquidize the rest of the apple mixture until a smooth

Above: Apple Mousse; Orange Mould

purée. Return to the saucepan and heat again.

Soften the gelatine (gelatin) in the lemon juice, add to the hot apple purée, stir until dissolved. Separate the egg yolks from the whites. Beat the yolks until they become creamy and thick and then whisk in the apple purée. Leave until cold and beginning to stiffen slightly. Whisk the egg whites until stiff, then fold into the apple mixture.

To serve: Spoon into glasses and top with the apple slices and mint leaves. If preferred, cook all the apple and decorate with unpeeled apple slices.

To freeze: Better freshly made, but an excellent way to use frozen fruit purée.

Variation:

Use other fruits in season; apricots, plums and rhubarb are all suitable.

Desserts

USING SUGAR SUBSTITUTE

There are several kinds of sugar substitute (artificial sweeteners) on the market; these enable you to sweeten desserts without adding calories. Some have a carbohydrate content but one uses so little of the sweetener that this is not a problem.

Sorbitol, used in diabetic diets, is not a perfect choice for slimmers, since it contains some calories. Liquid artificial sweetener is easy to use drop by drop.

When using the artificial sweeteners add sparingly, tasting as you do so, until you have the desired flavour. It is a good thing though to try and educate your palate to enjoy foods that are less sweet in flavour, so that when you have reached your ideal weight you can still select a diet that has fewer calories or carbohydrate content.

Stuffed Peaches

■ 51/Kj214 □ 13.3 g

Metric/Imperial
4 ripe peaches (each about 100 g/4 oz)
juice 1 lemon
175 g/6 oz raspberries
little sugar substitute
American
4 ripe peaches (each about ¼ lb)
juice 1 lemon
generous 1 cup raspberries
little sugar substitute

❧Skin the peaches if desired and halve, remove the stones (pits). Sprinkle the cut surfaces with the lemon juice to prevent them becoming brown. Mash most of the raspberries with a little sugar substitute and spoon into the peach halves. Top with the rest of the raspberries.

To serve: Well chilled with plain yogurt.
To freeze: This must be eaten freshly prepared; but frozen raspberries could be used.
Variation:
Use peeled, halved and cored dessert pears instead of peaches. Fill with the raspberries as above or with apple purée, flavoured with a little sugar substitute and a small amount of ground ginger.

Fresh Fruit Salad

■ 78/Kj328 □ 18.8 g

This can be made with the various fruits in season, so decide on the kind of fruits you would enjoy; check on the weights when prepared, so you know just how many calories your portion will be, and the carbohydrate content.

If using fruits that discolour easily, squeeze out the juice from an orange and ½ lemon *before* preparing apples, pears and bananas (high in calories so use sparingly). Pour this over the fruit as soon as it is sliced and it will then keep a good colour.

The following combination of fruits makes an excellent and colourful fruit salad. The calories are based upon servings for 6 people.

Halve, core and slice 2 dessert apples (each weighing about 100 g/4 oz/¼ lb); 2 dessert pears (each weighing 100 g/4 oz/¼ lb); 1 banana (weighing 100 g/4 oz/¼ lb). Moisten with the juice from 1 large orange and ½ lemon. Add 100 g/4 oz/a generous cup small strawberries; 2 medium sliced oranges and 100 g/4 oz/¼ lb de-seeded grapes.

To serve: Chilled.
To freeze: Can be frozen, but better freshly made.
Variation:
Add a little sugar substitute to the fruit juice if desired.

Fresh Fruit Salad; Melon Basket; Caramelled Oranges

Melon Basket

■ 29/Kj 122 □ 4.4 g

Buy two kinds of melon; it can be a honeydew melon with a golden coloured flesh, and one with a white flesh, or a honeydew melon and a watermelon. The contrast in colour is most appealing. ❧Cut a slice from one of the melons; scoop out all the seeds. Cut away the pulp with a potato baller (generally sold as a vegetable scoop). Halve the other melon and remove the seeds and scoop out the pulp in the same way. If you cannot make balls of the pulp then dice neatly.

Cut the edge of one melon in a Vandyke effect. Spoon the melon balls back into the melon case. There should be plenty of juice, but you could add the juice of a fresh orange and/or lemon or a little sherry blended with a very little ground ginger and sugar substitute.

The calories and carbohydrate content are based upon 675 g/1½ lb melon pulp and the juice of 1 large orange.
To serve: Decorate with sprigs of mint.

Variations:
1: Instead of using two kinds of melon mix the pulp from one melon with other fruits.
2: Choose a pineapple instead of a melon and fill this with the diced pineapple and other fruits.

Caramelled Oranges

■ 101/Kj 424 □ 27.0 g

Metric/Imperial
6 large oranges
300 ml/½ pint water
75 g/3 oz sugar
American
6 large oranges
1¼ cups water
⅜ cup sugar

❧This recipe cannot be made with a sugar substitute, as only sugar or golden (light corn) syrup can be turned into a caramel.

Cut away the peel and pith from the oranges. Lay the peel from two of the oranges on a board with the orange side downwards and cut away any pith. Slice the orange part (the 'zest') into matchstick pieces. Soak the peel in the water for about 30 minutes, then simmer gently for about 20 minutes until softened and the liquid is reduced to approximately 200 ml/8 fl oz/1 cup. Pour into a container. Spoon out 3 × 15 ml spoons/3 tablespoons of the liquid and put into a saucepan with the sugar. Stir until the sugar has dissolved, then allow to boil steadily until a golden caramel. Add the rest of the liquid and the peel and simmer for a few minutes.

Meanwhile slice the oranges into rings, take out any pips, but put the slices together again and secure with a cocktail stick (wooden tooth pick). Pour warm syrup and peel over the oranges.
To serve: Well chilled, on the day the dessert is prepared.
To freeze: Do not freeze.
Variations:
1: Poached apple rings are delicious blended with the orange slices.
2: Use whole peeled tangerines instead of oranges.

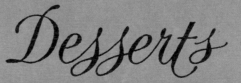
Desserts

FRUIT DESSERTS

The desserts on the previous pages and the recipes on this page are based upon fruits.

Fresh fruit has the advantage that you receive a good amount of roughage which is considered a very important factor in wise feeding today. When serving raw fruits eat the skins where possible of fruits, such as apples and pears, to add to the fibre content of the meal.

Obviously if you are following a low-carbohydrate diet you must check most carefully on the amount of fruit you are having. As you will see from the tables, citrus fruits are the lowest in carbohydrate content. Rhubarb is also a good choice.

Fruit Snow

This is one of the easiest of desserts to make. Choose any fruit that cooks well and forms a smooth purée after cooking.

🍃Simmer the fruit with the minimum of water so it will be a really thick fruit purée. Sieve, mash or purée in a blender. Add a little sugar substitute to taste.

When the fruit is cooked, cool then blend with stiffly whisked egg whites.

Allow 2 egg whites to each 300–450 ml/$\frac{1}{2}$–$\frac{3}{4}$ pint/$1\frac{1}{4}$ to scant 2 cups of the fruit purée.

Fold the egg whites gently and carefully into the fruit purée. Calories, etc. depend upon the fruit used.

To serve: In glasses, well chilled.
To freeze: Do not freeze the completed dish, but this is a good way to use defrosted frozen fruit purée.

Baked apples stuffed with dried fruit and blackberries; Meringue Apples

Baked Apple

■ 84/Kj 353 □ 21.0 g

Metric/Imperial

4 cooking apples (about 200 g/7 oz each)

American

4 cooking apples (nearly $\frac{1}{2}$ lb each)

🍃Core the apples and slit round the skins in the centre; this prevents the pulp breaking through the skin. Put into an ovenproof dish. Add 2 tablespoons water if desired; this helps to stop the fruit sticking to the dish. Bake in the centre of a very moderate oven (160°C/325°F, Gas Mark 3) for about 1–1$\frac{1}{4}$ hours.

To serve: Hot or cold with yogurt or Egg Custard Sauce on page 88.
To freeze: Must be freshly cooked.

Variations:

1: Stuffed Apples Fill the centre of the apples with a little dried fruit; as you will see from the tables this is high in both calories and carbohydrate content; but a good source of natural sugar.

The apples can be filled with crushed blackberries or raspberries, sweetened with a little sugar substitute either before cooking; or remove the apples from the oven when nearly cooked and fill with the other fruit.

2: Meringue Apples Although meringue is better made with sugar than a sugar substitute it is possible to add a little artificial sweetener and still have a good meringue; if served hot.

Bake the apples as the basic recipe or fill with fruit as suggested in variation 1. When cooked remove the skins. Whisk 2 egg whites until stiff; either fold in 50 g/2 oz/¼ cup sugar or sugar substitute to taste. Spread over the apples and return to the oven for a further 10–15 minutes until golden coloured.

3: Citrus Apples Bake the apples as the basic recipe, but pour fresh, unsweetened canned or defrosted frozen orange juice over the fruit before baking. Take the apples out of the oven once or twice during cooking and baste with the fruit juice, this can be sweetened with a little sugar substitute if desired.

The apples absorb the flavour of the orange juice and are absolutely delicious. Decorate with orange segments before serving.

Fruit Fool

This dessert, often called a Fruit Foule, is a pleasant combination of fruit purée and whipped cream or custard. Yogurt can be used.

If you are counting calories then obviously whipped cream is not for you; instead you could use the egg custard sauce on page 88 but use two eggs to the quantity of milk so you have a much thicker custard. You could use custard powder and milk and sweeten this with sugar substitute.

If on the other hand you are on a low-carbohydrate diet then you can have whipped cream.

Low-fat yogurt however is relatively low in both calories and carbohydrate and therefore a good choice on most diets.

♣Cook the fruit with the minimum of water and sugar substitute to taste. Take out a few pieces of cooked fruit for decoration. Sieve or mash the remainder of the fruit or purée in a blender to give a perfectly smooth purée, then cool. Blend with an equal amount of cold custard; whipped cream or yogurt.

If using berry fruits these can be mashed, sieved or liquidized without cooking and it is a good way to use rather small and perhaps less attractive looking fruit.

The calories and carbohydrate content depend upon the fruit used and the food with which it is combined.

To serve: Put into a dish or individual glasses and chill.

To freeze: This does not freeze well when made with custard; but is excellent if using whipped cream and quite satisfactory for a few days if made with yogurt.

Desserts

From left: Strawberry Alaska; fruit Melba; Home Made Ice Cream; Ice Cream Sundaes

USING MILK AND EGGS

Milk and eggs combine to produce both appetizing and delicious desserts. As stated on page 82 most of the desserts in this book, based upon milk, are made with skimmed milk. This gives a good flavour and you save a number of calories, but it does not reduce the carbohydrate content. As there is no fat in the milk take care it does not burn when heated.

The custard sauce below is excellent with all desserts and can be adapted to make a thicker custard by using two, instead of one, egg.

There are recipes for ice creams on these pages so you can produce your own special occasion sundaes and ice cream desserts. The recipe using cream is suitable for a low-carbohydrate diet.

Egg Custard Sauce

■ 73/Kj 307 □ 10.9 g

Metric/Imperial

1 egg

300 ml/½ pint milk

25 g/1 oz sugar

American

1 egg

1¼ cups milk

2 tablespoons sugar

Beat the egg lightly, then add the hot, but not boiling, milk and sugar. Cook in a double saucepan or basin over a pan of hot, but not boiling, water until the custard is thick enough to coat the back of a wooden spoon. At no time should the water in the pan or the custard boil; if it does the custard will curdle.

To serve: Over cooked or fresh fruit or baked apples.

To freeze: Only the uncooked liquid custard can be frozen. Use within a month.

To thaw: In the refrigerator.

Variations:

1: Use sugar substitute instead of sugar.

2: Use full-cream milk instead of skimmed.

Home Made Ice Cream

■ 164/Kj 689 □ 1.3 g

Metric/Imperial

2 eggs

few drops vanilla essence

150 ml/¼ pint double cream

150 ml/¼ pint single cream

sugar substitute to taste

American

2 eggs

few drops vanilla extract

⅔ cup heavy cream

⅔ cup light cream

sugar substitute to taste

Separate the eggs. Whisk the yolks with the vanilla until thick and creamy. Whip the double cream until it just holds its shape, then gradually whisk in the single cream; blend with the egg yolks. Add sugar substitute to taste. Freezing tends to lessen the sweet flavour, so the mixture should be reasonably sweet.

To freeze: Spoon into a freezing tray; freeze on normal setting in a freezer or modern refrigerator with star setting. Turn to the coldest position at least 30 minutes before freezing. Leave the mixture until slightly stiffened. Whisk the egg whites until stiff; fold into the half-frozen cream mixture and continue freezing.

Cover the container and use within 3 months.

To serve: With fruit, or as the suggestions on this page.

Variations:

1: Use 300 ml/½ pint/1¼ cups unsweetened evaporated milk instead of the cream. Place the unopened can in a saucepan of water, boil the water for 15 minutes. Remove the can, cool then chill for some hours in the refrigerator. Open the can, pour the milk into a basin and whisk briskly until thick.

For an even stiffer mixture dissolve 1 × 5 ml spoon/1 teaspoon gelatine (gelatin) in 2 × 15 ml spoons/2 tablespoons water over a pan of boiling water. Open the can of milk *very carefully* after boiling in the water. Pour the hot milk into a basin, add the dissolved gelatine (gelatin) then proceed as above.

2: Make the Egg Custard Sauce, as the recipe on this page. Allow to cool, stirring from time to time to prevent a skin forming. Blend with 300 ml/½ pint/1¼ cups cream, whipped or whipped evaporated milk (see variation 1).

3: Use the basic ice cream recipe or variation 1 or 2 and add strong coffee, chocolate or thick fruit purée to flavour.

Ice Cream Sundaes. Put layers of ice cream, fresh fruit and fresh fruit jelly, as

the recipe on page 210, into tall glasses.

Strawberry Alaska. Form the ice cream into a neat block and put on to an oven-proof plate. Top with sliced fresh strawberries. Whisk 4 egg whites until stiff; add sugar substitute to sweeten the meringue. Spread this over the ice cream and fruit.

Heat for about 3 minutes only in a very hot oven (240°C/475°F, Gas Mark 9) until golden and serve at once.

Snow Eggs

■ 90/Kj 378 □ 7.0 g

Metric/Imperial
2 eggs
600 ml/1 pint milk
few drops vanilla essence or a vanilla pod
sugar substitute to taste

American
2 eggs
2½ cups milk
few drops vanilla extract or a vanilla bean
sugar substitute to taste

☙Separate the eggs and put the yolks into a small basin. Cover with a very little amount of the milk, so they do not dry. Pour the rest of the milk into a deep frying pan, add the vanilla essence or pod. Whisk the egg whites until very stiff, then add sugar substitute to taste.

Bring the milk almost to boiling point and drop spoonfuls of the meringue on top of the milk. Cook steadily for 2 minutes, then put a fish slice or perforated spoon under each meringue and turn over. Cook for the same time on the other side. Lift from the pan and allow to drain in a large sieve (strainer) over a plate.

Strain the milk on to the beaten egg yolks, add a little sugar substitute then cook as the Egg Custard Sauce on the opposite page.

To serve: Pour the custard into a shallow dish, cool then top with the meringues.

To freeze: Must be freshly cooked.

Variations:

1: Omit the vanilla essence or pod and flavour the milk with finely grated lemon or orange rind; a little rum or brandy or a pinch of ground cinnamon, allspice or cocoa powder.

2: Instead of adding spoonfuls of the meringue mixture, pipe from a bag into star or other shapes. Cook for approximately the same length of time as the basic meringue mixture.

3: For those members of the family not dieting, use sugar instead of the sugar substitute for making the meringue and custard.

Note: When the milk is strained over the egg yolks rinse the vanilla pod (bean) in cold water and return to the container or cut into two halves and place these in a jar of sugar. This flavours the sugar.

Desserts

SNACKS

Often it is 'that little snack' that proves more disastrous than a sustaining main meal. Many of the foods served for savouries and snacks have a surprisingly generous calorific value and some have a high carbohydrate content too.

What then are the best foods to choose for that light supper, lunch or high tea? This chapter outlines some interesting and wisely chosen snacks, including ingredients on toast.

SERVE IT ON TOAST

You may be told you cannot eat bread on a slimming diet; this advice is generally given only if a diet is a very strict one, for bread provides a certain amount of protein, is a source of the B group of vitamins and is a satisfying food.

What is undoubtedly true is that you must *restrict* your intake of bread. A diet sheet may suggest one or two slices a day; if it does then you can use it as the basis of toasted snacks.

If a definite weight of bread is given then cut a slice, weigh it, note the thickness, so you can make your calculations easily.

The calorie and carbohydrate content below are based on one large thin slice or a smaller and slightly thicker slice, weighing 25 g/1 oz. If you buy low-calorie (often called slimming) bread, the figures will be slightly less, consult the tables on pages 212 to 220. The calorie and carbohydrate content is based on this slice before it is toasted, and is calculated on white bread; wholemeal (wholewheat) bread has slightly lower figures, see pages 212 to 220.
■ 70/Kj294 □14.9 g

If you add 15 g/½ oz/1 tablespoon margarine you will then have total figures as below. Butter would be slightly higher in calories and low-calorie spread would reduce this.
■ 110/Kj462 □14.9 g

Toasted Snacks

Toast the bread, spread with margarine or butter (if you omit this then you lower the calories). The figures given though assume you have spread the toast with margarine.

Angels on Horseback

Sprinkle 2 oysters, weighing about 40 g/1½ oz each, with a very little pepper and a squeeze of lemon juice. De-rind and stretch a long rasher (slice) of streaky bacon (about 25 g/1 oz) and halve. Wrap round the oysters, roll, secure with wooden cocktail sticks (toothpicks) and grill (broil), turning several times, until the bacon is crisp. Garnish with lemon.
■ 373/Kj1567 □15.0 g

Beans on Toast

Heat 50 g/2 oz canned haricot (navy) beans in tomato sauce and spoon on to the toast.
■ 232/Kj974 □24.7 g

Cheese on Toast

Cut a slice of Edam cheese, weighing 50 g/2 oz (Edam is one of the lower-caloried hard cheeses). Place on the hot toast, spread with margarine and put under the grill (broiler) for a few minutes until the cheese begins to melt. Garnish with a medium halved grilled tomato. You can spread the toast with a little made mustard before adding the cheese, if desired.
■ 376/Kj1579 □18.1 g

Devils on Horseback

This is made just like the Angels on Horseback, but using prunes (cooked without sugar) instead of oysters. The figures allow 100 g/4 oz/¼ lb prunes (weight with stones).
■ 479/Kj2011 □52.9 g

Mushrooms on Toast

Simmer 100 g/4 oz/1 cup mushrooms in a little stock. If you fry them the calories must include those of the fat (shortening). Drain and put on the toast, garnish with parsley.
■ 188/Kj790 □14.9 g

Peanut Butter on Toast

Peanut butter is an excellent source of protein, and liked by most children, as well as adults. The figures allow for 15 g/½ oz peanut butter *instead of the margarine or spread*. Toast the bread and spread with the peanut butter. This does vary in carbohydrates, but the average is given. It can be topped with a few chopped nuts, but they have not been counted in the figures.
■ 157/Kj659 □17.9 g

Poached Egg on Toast

Top the toast with an egg, poached as page 92.

■ 260/Kj 1092 □ 14.9 g

Prawns on Toast

Drop 50 g/2 oz shelled prawns (shrimp) into a small quantity of boiling water to heat; drain. Put on the toast and garnish with a slice of lemon.

■ 240/Kj 1008 □ 14.9 g

Roes on Toast

Place 100 g/4 oz/¼ lb soft herring roes on a plate, top with 2×15 ml spoons/2 tablespoons skimmed milk, add salt and pepper to taste. Cover with a second plate and steam over boiling water for 10 minutes, or until tender. Spoon on to the toast. Garnish with cayenne pepper or paprika and a sprig of parsley.

■ 370/Kj 1554 □ 18.4 g

Sardines on Toast

A large sardine weighs about 25 g/1 oz, so only 50 g/2 oz have been allowed. Put on to the hot toast. If you mash the sardines you make them look rather more, as they cover the toast. The figures are for sardines in tomato sauce, not in oil.

■ 348/Kj 1462 □ 15.7 g

Scotch Woodcock

Scramble the eggs as below, then garnish with 2 anchovy fillets.

■ 310/Kj 1302 □ 15.6 g

Scrambled Eggs on Toast

Blend 2 eggs with 1×15 ml spoon/1 tablespoon skimmed milk, salt and pepper to taste. Heat 15 g/½ oz/1 tablespoon margarine in a pan and scramble the eggs slowly, stirring gently until as firm as desired. Spoon on to the hot toast, as soon as cooked.

If you use a non-stick pan you can omit the margarine in cooking, but the figures below are based on using this, with NO margarine spread on the toast.

■ 270/Kj 1134 □ 15.6 g

Tomatoes on Toast

Halve 2 medium tomatoes, sprinkle with a little salt and pepper and grill (broil). Serve on the toast and garnish with chopped parsley or basil.

■ 212/Kj 890 □ 21.3 g

Snacks on toast, from bottom left: Poached Egg; Roes; Prawns; Scotch Woodcock; Tomatoes; Mushrooms

Snacks

Boiled Eggs

A boiled egg provides one of the best ways of eating protein without adding many calories and no carbohydrate content.

Devilled Cottage Eggs

■ 155/Kj646 □4.8 g

Metric/Imperial

4 hard-boiled eggs

1 × 1.25 ml spoon/¼ teaspoon dry mustard

2 × 5 ml spoons/2 teaspoons vinegar

1 × 15 ml spoon/1 tablespoon chutney or diced pickles or relish

225 g/8 oz cottage or cream cheese, see note

1 × 1.25 ml spoon/¼ teaspoon salt

pinch cayenne pepper or paprika

1 × 5 ml spoon/1 teaspoon chopped chives

TO GARNISH:

1 × 2.5 ml spoon/½ teaspoon chopped parsley

lettuce

American

4 hard-cooked eggs

¼ teaspoon dry mustard

2 teaspoons vinegar

1 tablespoon chutney or diced pickles or relish

1 cup cottage or cream cheese, see note

¼ teaspoon salt

pinch cayenne pepper or paprika

1 teaspoon chopped chives

TO GARNISH:

½ teaspoon chopped parsley

lettuce

Shell the eggs and cut in half lengthways, remove the yolks. Mash the yolks with the mustard, vinegar and chutney or diced pickles or relish. Add the cheese and mix well, season with salt and pepper or paprika and add the chives. Fill the egg whites with the mixture, piling it high. Decorate with parsley.

To serve: In lettuce 'cups'.

To freeze: Do not freeze.

Note: Cream cheese would give three times as many calories but *slightly* less carbohydrate content.

Baked Eggs

It is wise to invest in small oven-proof dishes, so you cook and serve in the same container.

Grease the bottom of the dish with a little butter, break in an egg, add salt and pepper, 1 × 15 ml spoon/1 tablespoon milk, plus a very little butter on top. You can omit the butter if counting calories. Bake for 10–12 minutes in a moderately hot oven.

You can add grated cheese, cooked diced chicken, ham, asparagus tips or fish to the egg. Calories and carbohydrates depend on additions to the egg.

Poached Eggs

If you are on a calorie-controlled diet poach eggs in water. If you are on a low-carbohydrate diet then you can use this method, or a heated, buttered metal cup in an egg poacher.

Half fill a frying pan with water, if you are poaching several eggs, or use a saucepan for one egg. Add a pinch of salt, bring the water to boiling point. Break the eggs in one at a time and cook **steadily** for about 3 minutes. Lift out with a fish slice, drain and serve.

Mushroom and Egg Ragoût

■ 85/Kj356 □Trace

Metric/Imperial

175 g/6 oz small button mushrooms

150 ml/¼ pint white stock

salt

pepper

1 × 15 ml spoon/1 tablespoon chopped parsley

4 eggs

American

1½ cups small mushrooms

⅔ cup white stock

salt

pepper

1 tablespoon chopped parsley

4 eggs

Wash but do not peel the mushrooms. Simmer in the stock for 5 minutes, add salt and pepper to taste. Do not cover the pan so the liquid evaporates during cooking. Add the parsley at the last minute. Meanwhile, poach the eggs and put each egg into an individual dish.

To serve: Top with the mushroom mixture and serve at once. This is easier to eat with a spoon.

To freeze: Not suitable for freezing.

Variations:

1: Add 1 to 2 crushed cloves of garlic or a little chopped onion to the mushrooms before cooking in the white stock.

2: Put a slice of lean ham under each poached egg then top with the hot mushroom mixture.

Scrambled Eggs

The slimmer's way of scrambling eggs is given on page 91. This can be varied, as in the recipe below or you could add chopped cooked chicken, ham or fish.

Mushroom Scramble

■ 233/Kj979 □0.99 g

Metric/Imperial

100 g/4 oz button mushrooms

25 g/1 oz butter

4 × 15 ml spoons/4 tablespoons milk

8 eggs

salt

pepper

toast or crispbread

American

1 cup mushrooms

2 tablespoons butter

¼ cup milk

8 eggs

salt

pepper

toast or crispbread

Leave 4 mushrooms whole, chop the rest. Melt 15 g/½ oz/1 tablespoon butter and fry the whole and the chopped mushrooms. Melt the remaining butter in another pan, add the milk. Beat the eggs lightly, add salt and pepper, pour into the butter and milk and cook over a gentle heat, stirring constantly. Add the chopped mushrooms when the eggs start to set and continue stirring. Put into a shallow dish and garnish with the whole mushrooms.

To serve: On hot plates garnished with triangles of toast or crispbread round the edge. The calories etc. *exclude* the toast or crispbread.

To freeze: Do not freeze.

Variation:

Piperade: Peel and chop 1 to 2 onions, 1 to 2 cloves of garlic and 2 to 3 tomatoes. Discard the core and seeds of a green pepper and dice. Cook in the butter until soft then scramble the eggs as in the recipe above, but omit the milk.

From rear: Devilled Cottage Eggs; Mushroom and Egg Ragoût; Mushroom Scramble

Vegetable Garnishes

These enhance the look of dishes without appreciably adding to the calorie or carbohydrate content.

Lemon Twists Cut moderately thin slices of lemon; remove any pips. Make a cut at one side, twist the slice. Cucumber can be cut and twisted in the same way as a lemon slice.

Celery Curls Cut thin strips of celery, put in ice-cold water for several hours, drain well. They will then have formed attractive curls. If preferred, make cuts in the short strips of celery, reaching two-thirds down the strip. Put in ice-cold water when they will open out rather like a fan. If you cut the green stems of spring onions (scallions) in the same way they will open out in ice-cold water.

Tomato Water Lilies Choose firm tomatoes. Insert the tip of a knife in the centre and cut in a Vandyke fashion; each time feel the point of the knife going into the centre of the tomato. Gently pull the halves apart. Radishes can be cut in the same way or you can make cuts halfway down radishes (as described under celery). Put into ice-cold water for an hour, drain and you have attractive 'flowers'.

Gherkin Fans Drain good-sized gherkins (sweet dill pickles); make several cuts as shown below. Pull open the slices to form a 'fan'.

Apple Avocado Salad

■ 218/Kj916 □ 15.6 g

Metric/Imperial
4 dessert apples
2 avocados
juice of 2 lemons
1 × 15 ml spoon/1 tablespoon salad oil
50 g/2 oz salted mixed nuts
watercress

American
4 dessert apples
2 avocados
juice of 2 lemons
1 tablespoon salad oil
½ cup salted mixed nuts
watercress

The smooth, creamy texture of avocado contrasts with the crispness of the apples and is a good source of protein. Core the apples but do not peel. Cut into 4 mm/⅛ inch slices. Halve the avocados, remove the stones (pits) and skin. Cut into slices about 7 mm/¼ inch thick. Cover apple and avocado slices with lemon juice to prevent browning. Just before serving, add the oil and the salted nuts.

To serve: On a bed of watercress.

Variation:

Chicken Salad: To make a more satisfying meal, add about 225 g/8 oz/½ lb cooked chicken, cut into neat slices.

Golden Salad

■ 193/Kj767 □28.9 g

Metric/Imperial
4 medium oranges
4 hard-boiled eggs
175 g/6 oz cooked sweetcorn
50 g/2 oz watercress
1 lemon, cut into wedges
4 thin rings fresh pineapple
4 medium carrots, grated

American
4 medium oranges
4 hard-cooked eggs
1 cup cooked sweetcorn
2 oz watercress
1 lemon, cut into wedges
4 thin rings fresh pineapple
4 medium carrots, grated

❧ Cut away the skin and pith from the oranges and slice the fruit. Shell the eggs, halve, remove the yolks, then halve these. Chop the whites, add to the sweetcorn.

To serve: Arrange a bed of watercress on a dish with the sweetcorn in the centre bordered by orange, lemon, the pineapple rings and grated carrots. Place two halved egg yolks on each slice of pineapple.

Left: Golden Salad; Below: Apple Avocado Salad

Vegetable garnishes, from left: Tomato Water Lilies; Celery curls and fans; Cucumber twists; Gherkin Fans; Radish Water Lilies; Spring onion (scallion) fans; Lemon twists

Snacks

PICNICS

The golden rule when planning a picnic, and following a slimming routine, is to plan a satisfying main dish, rather than a selection of sandwiches, pasties and similar high-carbohydrate and high-calorie foods.

Modern insulated carrying boxes make it easier to transport hot or cold foods; these are described in greater detail on page 102. The recipes in this section can be carried without this type of equipment.

Suggestions for serving the various dishes are given in each recipe as the dishes are equally suitable for serving at home.

Below from front: Orange Tomato Soup; Chicken Chowder; mixed salad; Egg and Ham Cutlets. Far right: Egg and Ham Cutlets

CARRYING THE FOOD

Thermos flasks are equally useful for carrying cold, as well as hot, food. If purchasing a new thermos choose a wide-necked type so that you can put in it meat stews, sauces, soups, like the Chicken Chowder, with a variety of chopped foods; fruit salad or other prepared fruits, and still use the thermos flask on another occasion for drinks.

Salads and savoury dishes can be placed in polythene (styrofoam) boxes so that they keep fresh and unspoiled; separate dressings in screw-topped jars.

Remember many foods used in salads are highly perishable, such as in the Fish Salad, page 98, and must be kept cool. If you want to carry just one substantial dish a chowder, as the recipe right shows, is a good choice, particularly on a chilly day.

The Orange Tomato Soup is most refreshing.

Orange Tomato Soup

■ 55/Kj230 □7.2 g

Metric/Imperial

1 small onion, chopped

15 g/½ oz butter or margarine

600 ml/1 pint water

3 large oranges

450 g/1 lb tomatoes, chopped

2 × 5 ml spoons/2 teaspoons chopped basil or chives

salt

pepper

TO GARNISH:
little chopped parsley

1 small orange, sliced

American

1 small onion, chopped

1 tablespoon butter or margarine

2½ cups water

3 large oranges

1 lb tomatoes, chopped

2 teaspoons chopped basil or chives

salt

pepper

TO GARNISH:
little chopped parsley

1 small orange, sliced

Toss the onion in the hot butter or margarine for 2 to 3 minutes, add the water and simmer for 5 minutes. Grate the peel from the oranges, be careful to grate just the yellow 'zest' and none of the bitter white pith. Add to the water, together with the tomatoes, herbs and a little salt and pepper. Cover the saucepan and simmer for 10 minutes. Sieve the mixture or purée in a blender.

To serve: As a hot soup: Return to the saucepan with the orange pulp cut into small pieces and reheat for 1 to 2 minutes only, to retain the vitamin C content of the fruit. As a cold soup: Chill thoroughly then add the orange pieces. Spoon into hot or cold soup cups and garnish with chopped parsley and orange slices.

To freeze: This soup does not freeze well.

Chicken Chowder

■ 145/Kj 608 □ 7.1 g

Metric/Imperial

1 or 2 lean bacon rashers

600 ml/1 pint chicken stock or water and 1 chicken stock cube

1 large onion, chopped

1 medium carrot, diced

2–3 sticks celery, chopped

225 g/8 oz uncooked chicken, diced

salt

pepper

1 green pepper, de-seeded and chopped

1 red pepper, de-seeded and chopped

squeeze of lemon juice

1 × 15 ml spoon/1 tablespoon chopped parsley

1 small can sweetcorn or 75–100 g/3–4 oz cooked sweetcorn

American

1 or 2 lean bacon slices

2½ cups chicken stock or water and 2 chicken bouillon cubes

1 large onion, chopped

1 medium carrot, diced

2–3 sticks celery, chopped

½ lb uncooked chicken, diced

salt

pepper

1 green capsicum, de-seeded and chopped

1 red capsicum, de-seeded and chopped

squeeze of lemon juice

1 tablespoon chopped parsley

1 small can corn kernels or 3–4 oz cooked corn

De-rind the bacon, cut into thin strips and fry for 2 to 3 minutes. Pour the stock, or water and stock cube(s), into the saucepan, add the onion, carrot, celery and chicken, together with salt and pepper to taste. Cover the saucepan and simmer for 10 minutes, add the peppers (capsicums) and continue cooking for another 10 minutes. Stir in the lemon juice, parsley and corn.

To serve: Hot with toasted croûtons, see page 30 under Creamed Liver Soup.

To freeze: This soup freezes well for 2 months. Do not overcook the ingredients before freezing.

To thaw: Place in the refrigerator for several hours.

Variation:
Fish Chowder: Add diced raw fish, instead of chicken.

Egg and Ham Cutlets

■ 259/Kj 1083 □ 10.3 g

Metric/Imperial

150 ml/¼ pint white sauce, as page 78

4 hard-boiled eggs, finely chopped

100 g/4 oz lean cooked ham, finely chopped

1 × 5 ml spoon/1 teaspoon chopped chives

1 × 5 ml spoon/1 teaspoon chopped parsley

few drops Worcestershire sauce

salt

pepper

TO COAT:
1 egg, beaten

25 g/1 oz crisp breadcrumbs

TO GARNISH:
4–6 pieces macaroni

few lettuce leaves

2 medium tomatoes

American

⅔ cup white sauce, as page 78

4 hard-boiled eggs, finely chopped

¼ lb lean cured ham, finely chopped

1 teaspoon chopped chives

1 teaspoon chopped parsley

few drops Worcestershire sauce

salt

pepper

TO COAT:
1 egg, beaten

¼ cup crisp breadcrumbs

TO GARNISH:
4–6 pieces macaroni

few lettuce leaves

2 medium tomatoes

Remove the sauce from the heat, add the remaining cutlet ingredients. Divide the mixture into 4 portions and place in a cool place until sufficiently firm to handle. Form the mixture into 4 cutlet shapes. Coat the cutlets with the egg and breadcrumbs. Insert the pieces of macaroni to look like meat bones. Grease and heat a flat baking tray for 5 minutes in a hot oven (220°C/425°F, Gas Mark 7) then place the cutlets in this and cook for 10 minutes. Garnish with lettuce and 'water-lilies' of tomato, see page 94.

To serve: Hot with tomato sauce, as page 81, or cold with a mixed salad.

To freeze: The hard-boiled eggs make this unsuitable for freezing.

Variations:

1: Herbed Cutlets: To reduce the calorie and carbohydrate content of these cutlets, form into cutlet shapes but omit the coating; place on the serving dish, top with finely chopped parsley and chives.

2: Egg and Crab Cutlets: Use flaked crabmeat in place of the ham.

3: Egg and Vegetable Cutlets: Use diced cooked vegetables in place of the ham.

4: If you are on a low-carbohydrate diet you can fry the cutlets.

Picnics

Fish Salad

■ 157/Kj657 □7.0 g

Metric/Imperial

450 g/1 lb cod or other white fish

salt

pepper

2 hard-boiled eggs, chopped

¼ medium cucumber, peeled and diced

2 medium carrots, grated

2 medium tomatoes, skinned and sliced

2 × 15 ml spoons/2 tablespoons chopped fennel root

2 × 5 ml spoons/2 teaspoons chopped fennel leaves

2 × 5 ml spoons/2 teaspoons chopped parsley

1 × 15 ml spoon/1 tablespoon lemon juice

150 ml/¼ pint plain yogurt

lettuce

1 lemon, thinly sliced

American

1 lb cod or other lean fish

salt

pepper

2 hard-boiled eggs, chopped

¼ medium cucumber, peeled and diced

2 medium carrots, grated

2 medium tomatoes, skinned and sliced

2 tablespoons chopped fennel root

2 teaspoons chopped fennel leaves

2 teaspoons chopped parsley

1 tablespoon lemon juice

⅔ cup plain yogurt

lettuce

1 lemon, thinly sliced

🍃Poach the fish in a little water with salt and pepper to taste, do not overcook. Drain and blend with the other ingredients, except the lettuce and lemon, while still warm. Add just enough yogurt to bind. Put into a bowl or mould and leave until the fish and eggs are cold, and the salad chilled.

To serve: Turn out onto a bed of lettuce, top with the remaining yogurt and with the thin slices of lemon arranged around the edge of the mould.

To freeze: An excellent way to use frozen fish, but do not freeze the salad.

Variations:

1: Use any mixture of fish.

2: Be sparing with the salt and pepper and flavour the plain yogurt with anchovy essence (paste) or with curry powder.

98

Chicken and Bean Salad

■ 212/Kj895 □ 7.0 g

Metric/Imperial

450 g/1 lb French beans

salt

pepper

4 × 15 ml spoons/4 tablespoons oil and vinegar dressing, see page 81

100 g/4 oz cold cooked chicken

100 g/4 oz cooked lean ham

3 × 15 ml spoons/3 tablespoons single or double cream

½ cucumber

2 × 15 ml spoons/2 tablespoons chopped spring onions or chives

American

1 lb green beans

salt

pepper

¼ cup oil and vinegar dressing, see page 81

¼ lb cold cooked chicken

¼ lb cooked lean ham

3 tablespoons light or heavy cream

½ cucumber

2 tablespoons chopped scallions or chives

🍃Cut the ends from the beans and any sides if they seem tough, but leave the beans whole. Cook in boiling salted water until just tender. Drain and chop, toss in the dressing while hot, cool. Dice the chicken and ham finely, season well with salt and pepper and fold into the cream; chill.

To serve: Surround the chicken mixture with the bean mixture and sliced cucumber. Sprinkle with finely chopped spring onions (scallions) or chives.

To freeze: This, like other salads, cannot be frozen.

Avocado and Bacon Salad

■ 249/Kj1044 □7.4 g

Metric/Imperial

4 rashers lean bacon

3 hard-boiled eggs

about 8 spring onions

about 8 green or black olives

1 small lettuce

bunch watercress

FOR THE DRESSING:

3 × 15 ml spoons/3 tablespoons oil

2 × 15 ml spoons/2 tablespoons lemon juice

salt

pepper

few drops Tabasco sauce

2 ripe *firm* avocados

4 large tomatoes, skinned and sliced

American

4 slices lean bacon

3 hard-boiled eggs

about 8 scallions

about 8 green or black olives

1 small head lettuce

bunch watercress

FOR THE DRESSING:

3 tablespoons oil

2 tablespoons lemon juice

salt

pepper

few drops Tabasco sauce

2 ripe *firm* avocados

4 large tomatoes, skinned and sliced

Avocado and Bacon Salad; Chicken and Bean Salad; Fish Salad

❧Grill (broil or fry) the bacon until crisp. Shell and cut the eggs into quarters and dice the bacon. Chop the spring onions (scallions), include some of the green stalks, and chop the olives, discard the stones (pits). Wash the lettuce and watercress well, shake dry. Sprig the watercress. Place the lettuce and watercress on a flat dish.

Blend the oil, lemon juice, salt, pepper and Tabasco sauce together, add the chopped bacon, spring onions (scallions) and olives. Halve, skin and slice the avocados, mix with the bacon dressing *at once* so they do not discolour.

To serve: Pile onto the bed of lettuce and watercress and arrange the eggs and tomatoes round the dish.

To freeze: This salad is not suitable for freezing.

Eggs in Cheese Sauce

This is a simple and delicious dish which takes very little time to prepare. Cook 8 eggs in simmering water until hard-boiled. Shell, halve and serve with:

Cottage Cheese Sauce: Either sieve 225 g/ 8 oz/1 cup cottage cheese and blend with 4 × 15 ml spoons/4 tablespoons milk or put the cheese with the milk into the blender and blend together until smooth, add a small amount of chopped chives, salt and pepper to taste.

To serve: Place the eggs on a bed of crisp lettuce and cover the eggs with the sauce.

■ 220/Kj925 □ 2.1 g

Refreshing Drinks

Some of the fresh fruit drinks given on page 145 are a good choice. Iced Tea, i.e.

well-strained Indian or China tea, can be carried in the thermos flask with *crushed* ice plus a sprig of mint. Always crush the ice so it cannot harm the inside of the thermos.

Iced coffee is another excellent cold drink and if the coffee is not too strong, you will not need to carry milk.

Well-chilled white or rosé wine or cider are an excellent choice in warm weather, but remember you must consider the calorie and carbohydrate content of any alcoholic drink served as well as of the food.

Desserts

Nothing is more refreshing for a picnic than a fresh fruit salad and you will find a variety of suggestions on page 84.

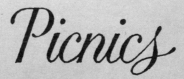

Menus for Slimming

Menus for Slimming

The menus given on the following pages cover several job situations and the needs of different people. Both low-calorie and low-carbohydrate menus are given, so either can be chosen to suit your individual life-style. There are menus for those who like three meals a day; are vegetarians; and for those who hold a sedentary or active job.

Packed Meals

With a little thought, you can devise a great variety of interesting dishes which are quite easy to carry and which are relatively low in either calories or carbohydrates, depending on the diet you have chosen.

If you intend to take sandwiches then follow the Scandinavian routine of having only a bottom slice of thin bread. Each open sandwich must be topped by a neat square of greaseproof (wax) paper instead of the second slice of bread.

Modern insulated boxes and bags are not unduly expensive and it would be worthwhile purchasing one if you know you have to follow a slimming routine.

You have a variety of menus on this and the following page, some based upon low-calorie foods, others on a low-carbohydrate content.

LOW-CALORIE OPEN SANDWICHES

All these sandwiches give a *total* calorific value of approximately 200 calories, i.e. 420 Kilojoules. Consult the tables, starting on page 212, to enable you to select exactly the right amount of the various basic foods used for toppings.

Breads vary a little in their calorific value but not enough to spoil your diet.

The figures are based on a 25 g/1 oz slice bread. Consult the tables, starting on page 212 for the calories and grammes of different breads.

Spread the bread with just under 15 g/½ oz/1 tablespoon low-calorie spread (no carbohydrate value) then several crisp lettuce leaves and one of the following toppings, which will give the total value of about 200 calories. The carbohydrate value of the topping will be small in most cases.

1: A slice of underdone beef, a little horseradish sauce, with gherkins, olives and sliced raw mushrooms.

2: Cottage cheese blended with diced red pepper (capsicum) and diced cooked tongue.

3: Part of a smoked trout, 50 g/2 oz edible weight,

Day 1
- melon balls
- grapefruit
- smoked trout open sandwich

Day 2
- Ham and Egg cutlets
- lettuce
- tomato

Day 3
- Chicken and Bean Salad
- cottage cheese
- crispbread
- iced coffee

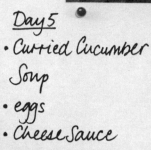

Day 4
- Tomato Soup
- Edam cheese
- lettuce
- green pepper
- watercress

Day 5
- Curried Cucumber Soup
- eggs
- Cheese Sauce
- chicory
- grapes

Day 6
- orange juice
- Potted Meat
- crispbreads
- tomato

topped with 25 g/1 oz/⅛ cup cottage cheese flavoured with horseradish cream.

4: Medium portion Fish Pâté, see recipe page 26, with sliced cucumber and lemon.

5: Scrambled egg and cottage cheese blended with chopped green pepper (capsicum).

6: Sliced cooked chicken with rings of green pepper (capsicum) and a very little mayonnaise to moisten.

7: Small portion Slimmer's Liver Pâté, see recipe page 25, with sliced cucumber.

8: Thinly sliced Edam cheese, topped with seasoned cottage cheese.

Fitting Your Packed Lunches into the Day's Menus

When you consider the menu for a packed meal think of the day as a whole and allocate the calories and carbohydrates to each meal. Ensure a good balance of textures, flavours and nutrients.

Never take highly perishable fish, for example, for a packed meal unless you have a cool storage place for your packed meal, or you have an insulated carrying box or bag.

Any milk you take for coffee or tea should be from a daily allowance of 300 ml/ ½ pint/1¼ cups.

Day One

Pack 75 g/3 oz of melon balls and 75 g/3 oz of grapefruit segments into a polythene (plastic) container or vacuum flask (thermos bottle) and place the smoked trout open sandwich in a rigid container.

■ 217/Kj 911 □ 7.8 g

Day Two

Carry the ham and egg cutlets (see recipe on page 97) in a covered foil dish and the lettuce and one tomato in a polythene (plastic) container.

■ 285/Kj 1197 □ 14.0 g

Day Three

Carry the chicken and bean salad (see recipe on page 98) in a polythene (plastic) container; the cottage cheese in a screw-topped jar with the crispbread wrapped in foil and the iced coffee in a chilled vacuum flask (thermos bottle).

■ 263/Kj 1105 □ 11.7 g

Day Four

Carry hot tomato soup in a vacuum flask (thermos bottle) and a salad of 50 g/2 oz Edam cheese, lettuce, half a green pepper and watercress in a polythene container.

■ 316/Kj 1327 □ 6.7 g

Day Five

Carry the curried cucumber soup (see recipe on page 33) in a vacuum flask (thermos bottle), the eggs and cheese sauce (see recipe for sauce on page 78) separately; the chicory (endive) in a polythene (plastic) bag and 50 g/2 oz/½ cup grapes in a polythene (plastic) container. This menu is high in carbohydrates so check carefully when selecting other meals.

■ 342/Kj 1436 □ 21.7 g

Day Six

Carry 150 ml/¼ pint/⅔ cup of orange juice in a vacuum flask (thermos bottle). The home-made potted meat (see recipe on page 165) can be carried in a polythene (plastic) container with the two crispbreads and one large tomato individually wrapped in foil.

■ 293/Kj 1231 □ 25.7 g

Menus

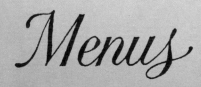

Meals for the Nibbler

These meals come within the 1,200 calorie or 60 gramme carbohydrate allowance. You can combine two small meals into one more substantial one if preferred without affecting the diet.

The Nibbler

If you have always been a 'nibbler', this could well account for the fact you are over-weight.

Do not try to change your complete pattern of eating. It would be far better to continue with more meals, each of which is smaller in content.

The between-meal 'nibbles' you must banish on either a low-calorie or low-carbo-hydrate diet are biscuits – sweet or plain (cookies or crackers), cakes of every kind, sugary and milky tea or coffee, for when milk and sugar are added to beverages they become a food, rather than a drink.

If you plan your meals wisely you *can* have a drink, but it means you may have to go without some food.

Low-Calorie Meals for the Nibbler

The calorie allowance covers 300 ml/½ pint/1¼ cups of skimmed milk each day, to add to tea or coffee or use in cooking and approximately 15 g/½ oz/1 tablespoon butter or margarine or double this amount of low-calorie spread.

Tea and coffee are not given in the menus, but you can have as much of these as desired, so long as you do not add sugar or extra milk. Low-calorie soft drinks can be included, where they have almost no calorific value, but check on this most carefully, for other soft drinks are surprisingly high in calories.

Day One

☐ On awaking you can have half a grapefruit.
☐ For breakfast allow yourself one poached egg on a 25 g/1 oz slice of toast.
☐ As a mid-morning nibble you can have one slice of crispbread spread with yeast extract.
☐ For lunch you can have Chicken chowder (see recipe on page 97) and one fresh peach.
☐ At tea-time serve Mushrooms on toast (see recipe on page 90).
☐ For dinner, serve one grilled (broiled) lamb chop (cutlet) with speedy tomato sauce (see recipe on page 165), a portion of cauliflower and Apple mousse (see recipe on page 83).
☐ Later in the evening you can have a slice of crispbread with 25 g/1 oz/⅛ cup of cottage cheese.

Day Two

☐ Allow yourself one crispbread spread with part of the day's allowance of butter, margarine or low calorie spread on awaking.
☐ For breakfast serve one orange with one jugged kipper made by placing a 100 g/4 oz kipper in a jug or thermos flask and covering with boiling water, leave for ten minutes then drain and serve with a 25 g/1 oz slice of bread spread with the remaining daily allowance of butter, margarine or low calorie spread.
☐ For a mid-morning snack have one apple.
☐ At lunch time have a health salad (see recipe on page 209).
☐ For a tea-time nibble, have one slice of crispbread spread with yeast extract.
☐ At dinner time, serve Steak and kidney ragoût (see recipe on page 175) with Courgettes (zucchini) Lyonnaise (see recipe on page 179).
☐ Later in the evening you can have a 75 g/3 oz slice of melon, edible weight.

Day Three

☐ On awaking you can have one cream cracker.
☐ For breakfast, allow yourself 25 g/1 oz/1 cup of cornflakes with milk from your daily allowance and one orange.
☐ One apple will provide a mid-morning snack.
☐ For lunch have a Piquant shrimp cocktail (see recipe on opposite page).
☐ At tea-time have one crispbread with half of the day's butter, margarine or low calorie spread allowance.
☐ For dinner, serve Beef with sour cream sauce (see recipe on page 52) and brussels sprouts.
☐ Later on in the evening you can allow yourself one large grilled (broiled) tomato on a 15 g/½ oz piece of toast spread with the remainder of the daily allowance of butter, margarine or low calorie spread or a 75 ml/3 fl oz glass of red Burgundy.

Low-Carbohydrate Meals for the Nibbler

Do not think you can have unlimited fruit, for most fruit is high in carbohydrate content.

Instead you will see that nuts, fingers of cheese or cottage cheese are often suggested in this and other low-carbohydrate menus.

Each day the 60 grammes include 300 ml/½ pint/1¼ cups of milk, either skimmed or full cream to add to drinks or use in cooking. There is no need to ration butter or other fat.

Day One

☐ On awaking have a finger of hard cheese.

☐ For breakfast you can have one grilled (broiled) rasher (slice) of bacon with one tomato and a 50 g/2 oz sausage, unless you know that they have a very high meat content. Carbohydrate value does vary.

☐ As a mid-morning snack you can allow yourself a 15 g/½ oz slice of buttered wholemeal (wholewheat) bread.

☐ At lunch time, serve Chicken dolmas (see recipe on page 175) with broccoli and hollandaise sauce (see recipe on page 80).

☐ Allow yourself one pear for tea-time.

☐ For dinner have 50 ml/2 fl oz/⅓ cup of dry sherry followed by Sole Meunière

(see page 37) served with one 75 g/3 oz boiled potato.

☐ Later in the evening you can have Home-made ice cream (see recipe on page 88) with 50 g/2 oz blackcurrants cooked with sugar substitute.

Day Two

☐ On awaking serve fresh grapefruit segments, allowing 75 g/3 oz which is approximately half a good-sized grapefruit.

☐ For breakfast serve fish cakes with 1 fried tomato.

☐ A finger of Cheddar or other hard cheese can be eaten as a mid-morning snack.

☐ At lunch time you can have roast beef with a salad of lettuce, watercress, green pepper (capsicum) and sliced raw mushrooms.

☐ For tea-time, allow yourself one 25 g/1 oz slice of bread and butter.

☐ For dinner you can have grilled (broiled) liver and bacon with creamed spinach made by mixing together 100 g/4 oz/½ cup of chopped

spinach and 25 ml/1 fl oz/2 tablespoons double (heavy) cream. Finish off with a fruit soufflé omelette (see recipe on page 191).

☐ Later in the evening you can have one whisky and soda with 25 g/1 oz/¼ cup of peanuts.

Day Three

☐ When you wake up you can have one slice of bran crispbread spread with butter.

☐ For breakfast you can have 100 g/4 oz/¼ lb edible weight of orange and a Swiss omelette (see recipe on page 75).

☐ Mid-morning you can have one 50 g/2 oz peach.

☐ For lunch serve 175 g/6 oz of fried cod's roe with mushrooms.

☐ For a tea-time snack you may have a finger of hard cheese.

☐ At dinner time, serve Roast duck with Orange sauce (see recipe on page 165) with 100 g/4 oz/¼ lb edible weight of green beans.

☐ Later in the evening you can have a finger of hard cheese.

Piquant Shrimp Cocktail

■ 130/Kj 544 ☐ 1.9 g

Metric/Imperial

3 × 15 ml spoons/
3 tablespoons mayonnaise

1 × 5 ml spoon/1 teaspoon
French mustard

3 × 15 ml spoons/
3 tablespoons plain yogurt

2 × 5 ml spoons/2 teaspoons
tomato purée

few drops Worcestershire
sauce

1 2 × 5 ml spoons/
1–2 teaspoons chopped
parsley

350 g/12 oz shelled shrimps

½ small lettuce, shredded

TO GARNISH:
1 lemon, cut in wedges

1 × 15 ml spoon/1 tablespoon
chopped parsley

American

3 tablespoons mayonnaise

1–2 teaspoons Dijon mustard

3 tablespoons plain yogurt

2 teaspoons tomato paste

few drops Worcestershire
sauce

1–2 teaspoons chopped
parsley

¾ lb shelled shrimp

½ small head lettuce, shredded

TO GARNISH:
1 lemon, cut in wedges

1 tablespoon chopped parsley

Blend the mayonnaise, mustard, yogurt, tomato purée (paste), sauce and parsley. Add the shrimp. Leave for 1 hour so the shrimp absorb the flavour of the sauce. Divide the lettuce between individual glasses. Top with the shrimp mixture. Garnish with lemon and chopped parsley.

To serve: Freshly made.
To freeze: Not suitable for freezing.

Variation:
Stuffed Tomatoes: Cut a slice from the stem end of four large tomatoes. Scoop out the seeds and some of the flesh. Add the flesh to the mayonnaise mixture in place of the tomato purée (paste). Stuff the tomatoes with the shrimp mixture and finish as above. Cooled, cooked globe artichokes are good served with the shrimp filling.

Menus

The Three Meal Family

The suggestions on these pages will give an idea of just how you will plan *either* your low calorie *or* low carbohydrate diets.

As the recipes throughout the book give both calories and carbohydrates this will enable you to choose your dishes within the restrictions of the particular diet.

Low-Calorie Meals

Based on a daily calorie count of approximately 1,200 calories, the number on which most women achieve a steady weight loss. If a 1,000 calorie diet is recommended reduce the portions or omit one item of about 200 calories. Most men will probably be able to increase the amounts of food slightly.

Allow 300 ml/½ pint/ 1¼ cups skimmed milk, plus 15 g/½ oz/1 tablespoon butter or margarine or 25 g/1 oz/ 2 tablespoons low-calorie spread each day, which can be used on the toast.

The allowance for butter or margarine each day is 130 calories. Allow 130 calories if using a low-calorie spread.

Obviously you can replace either bread or toast with crispbread. The tables will give you the calorific value of this; also the carbohydrate content, should you be following this type of diet.

Day One

☐For breakfast, serve one orange, 1 boiled egg and a 25 g/1 oz slice of toast with tea or coffee using some of the day's milk allowance.
☐For lunch serve a Cottage Cheese Salad, including for each portion, 50 g/2 oz/¼ cup cottage cheese topped with 3 sliced olives, 1 small carrot cut into sticks or grated, 25 g/

1 oz/¼ cup shrimp, a small piece of cucumber or half a green pepper, 1 medium tomato, a few onion rings, a good portion of lettuce and a small apple, diced (cubed). (Non slimming members of the family can include potato salad or, if you are losing weight on a slightly higher calorie allowance potato salad can be added.) A 25 g/ 1 oz slice of bread can be eaten with this using some of your daily allowance of butter, margarine or low calorie spread.
☐Dinner could consist of Curried Chicken Kebabs (see recipe on page 55), cauliflower, a fresh fruit salad and 150 ml/¼ pint/⅔ cup plain yogurt. Allow 70 calories per portion of fresh fruit salad and choose types and quantities of fruit accordingly.

Day Two

☐For breakfast you can have half a grapefruit followed by one grilled (broiled) rasher (slice) of bacon weighing 25 g/1 oz with two grilled (broiled) tomatoes and 1 slice of bread weighing 25 g/1 oz. Spread the bread with yeast extract as the day's allowance of butter, margarine or low

calorie spread is used up at lunch or dinner.
☐Lunch could consist of Queen Soup (see recipe on page 29), followed by Herb Omelette (see recipe on page 183), a Green salad consisting of lettuce, a little cucumber and a small piece of green pepper (capsicum) and one 25 g/1 oz slice of bread. Use two eggs for the Herb Omelette and cook it in half the daily allowance of butter, margarine or low calorie spread.
☐ For dinner you can have a portion of Slimmers' Liver Pâté (see recipe on page 25),

1 grilled (broiled) plaice (flounder) weighing 100 g/ 4 oz/¼ lb with spinach or broccoli and one boiled potato. Use the remainder of your daily allowance of butter, margarine or low calorie spread to cook the fish. Finish off with Orange Mould (see recipe on page 82).

Day Three

☐For breakfast you can have one orange, a portion of smoked haddock weighing 50 g/2 oz and 1 slice of bread. Use half your allowance of butter, margarine or low

DAY ONE
Orange, egg, toast,
tea or coffee
-o-
Cottage Cheese Salad
bread
-o-
Curried Chicken Kebabs
cauliflower
Fresh Fruit Salad
plain yogurt

DAY TWO
grapefruit
bacon, tomatoes
bread
-o-
Queen Soup
Herb Omelette
green salad, bread
-o-
Slimmer's Liver Pâté
fish
spinach or broccoli
potato
Orange Mould

DAY THREE
orange, smoked haddock
bread
-o-
Onion Soup
Cheese on Toast, tomato
-o-
Lamb Cutlets in Herb Sauce
cauliflower
brussels sprouts

Low carbohydrate

DAY ONE
orange juice
bacon, kidney
bread
-o-
avocado
Cheese Omelette, tomato
-o-
Tomato Soup
lamb chops, mushrooms
broccoli
apricots and cream

DAY TWO
tomato juice, cereal
-o-
Hamburger, mushrooms
watercress
orange
-o-
Citrus Chicken Espagnole
spinach
cheese, celery
whisky and soda, peanuts

DAY THREE
grapefruit
eggs, bread
-o-
sherry
ham
lettuce, tomato, cucumber
cheese, digestive biscuit
-o-
Horseradish and Liver Pâté
Meat Loaf
Scalloped Celeriac
brussels sprouts
Snow Eggs, Burgundy

calorie spread melted over the haddock and the other half on the bread.

☐ For lunch serve Onion soup (see recipe on page 125), followed by Cheese on toast and 1 grilled (broiled) tomato.

☐ For dinner you can serve Lamb Cutlets in Herb sauce (see recipe on page 48) with a portion of cauliflower and brussels sprouts.

Low Carbohydrate Meals
These diets are based on a daily carbohydrate allowance of 60 grammes. Each day allow 300 ml/½ pint/1¼ cups milk; this can be full cream or skimmed since the carbohydrate content is the same. You can have butter or other fat as desired.

Day One
☐ For breakfast you can have 150 ml/¼ pint/⅔ cup orange juice followed by grilled (broiled) bacon and kidney and one slice of bread weighing 25 g/1 oz. Use your daily allowance of butter, margarine or low calorie spread on the bread.

☐ For lunch choose half an avocado filled with prawns (shrimp) mixed with real mayonnaise. Follow this with a cheese omelette (see recipe on page 183) and one tomato.

☐ For dinner have tomato soup (see recipe on page 32), grilled (broiled) lamb chops (cutlets) with grilled (broiled) mushrooms and a portion of broccoli. For dessert, serve 100 g/4 oz/¼ lb apricots cooked with sugar substitute to sweeten and served with 25 ml/1 fl oz/2 tablespoons single (thin) cream.

Day Two
☐ At breakfast time you can have 150 ml/¼ pint/⅔ cup of tomato juice followed by 25 g/1 oz/1 cup cornflakes.

☐ At lunchtime have a hamburger (see recipe on page 45) with grilled (broiled) mushrooms and a good portion of watercress. You can have one orange, 100 g/4 oz/¼ lb of edible weight.

☐ Dinner could consist of Citrus chicken Espagnole (see recipe on page 54), a portion of leaf spinach and cheese and celery. Allow yourself a whisky and soda and 15 g/½ oz/scant tablespoon of peanuts.

Day Three
☐ At breakfast time have 75 g/3 oz grapefruit segments. Follow with a portion of scrambled eggs cooked in butter and one slice of bread weighing 15 g/½ oz.

☐ For lunch allow 50 ml/2 fl oz/⅓ cup sherry, ham and lettuce and half a medium-sized tomato, 25 g/1 oz/1 tablespoon diced (cubed) cucumber, and cheese with 1 digestive biscuit (Graham cracker).

☐ Dinner can consist of horseradish and liver pâté followed by a portion of Meat loaf (see recipe on page 45), scalloped celeriac (see recipe on page 63) and 50 g/2 oz brussels sprouts. Finish with snow eggs (see recipe on page 89) and a 150 ml/¼ pint/⅔ cup glass of red Burgundy wine. Allow ⅙ of the total recipe of meat loaf and pâté.

Menus

Low calorie meals

```
    Low calorie meals
         Day 1
   muesli, strawberries
          +++
     smoked trout
 lettuce, tomato, bread
     cottage cheese
          +++
     Mushroom Soup
 pork sausages, tomato
 crispbread, white wine
```

```
         Day 2
     Orange Starter
          +++
      Health Salad
       bread, figs
          +++
         avocado
   ox tongue, broccoli
```

```
         Day 3
       grapefruit
  Frankfurter sausages
         toast
          +++
       Hamburgers
          +++
     tomatoes, peas
          +++
  canned salmon, lettuce
     tomato, cucumber
         peach
```

The Non-Cook

If you haven't the time, opportunity or desire to cook, there are still many ways by which you can slim.

Nowadays there are many excellent cooked meat and delicatessen counters that sell a selection of cooked meats, salads, etc. Shop wisely: avoid the salads with rich dressings, the pastries and pies. Instead base your diet on cooked meat, canned fish, fruit and the vegetables which need little if any cooking.

Low-Calorie Foods to Buy

Look carefully at labels and see you are buying low-calorie as opposed to the ordinary foods.

The allowance of 1,200 calories includes 300 ml/ ½ pint/1¼ cups skimmed milk and 15 g/½ oz/1 tablespoon butter or margarine or 25 g/ 1 oz/2 tablespoons low-calorie spread. Page 106 gives more information about this.

Day One

☐For breakfast allow 50 g/ 2 oz muesli-type cereal, topped with 50 g/2 oz/scant ½ cup fresh strawberries or other low calorie fruit.
☐For lunch serve smoked trout allowing 175 g/6 oz edible weight with 2 × 5 ml

spoons/2 teaspoons horseradish cream, lettuce and one medium-sized tomato, one 25 g/1 oz slice of bread spread with half the daily allowance of butter, margarine or low calorie spread and 25 g/1 oz/⅛ cup of cottage cheese seasoned with salt and freshly ground pepper.
☐For dinner you can have 150 ml/¼ pint/⅔ cup of canned cream of mushroom soup, grilled pork sausages, allowing 100 g/4 oz/¼ lb which is approximately two sausages and a medium-sized grilled (broiled) tomato. You may also have one crispbread spread with the remainder of your daily allowance of butter, margarine or low calorie spread and a 150 ml/ ¼ pint/⅔ cup glass of dry white wine.

Day Two

☐Serve orange starter (see recipe on page 195) for breakfast.
☐At lunch time, serve health salad (see recipe on page 209) with a 25 g/1 oz slice of wholemeal (wholewheat) bread spread with half your daily allowance of butter, margarine or low calorie spread followed by 100 g/ 4 oz/¼ lb edible weight of fresh figs.

☐For dinner you can have 100 g/4 oz/¼ lb edible weight of avocado sprinkled with lemon juice. Follow with 100 g/4 oz/¼ lb cooked ox (beef) tongue which can be heated in 3 × 15 ml spoons/ 3 tablespoons of Madeira and served with 100 g/4 oz/¼ lb of broccoli topped with the remainder of your daily allowance of butter, margarine or low calorie spread.

Day Three

☐At breakfast, serve 75 g/ 3 oz fresh or unsweetened canned grapefruit segments followed by 100 g/4 oz/¼ lb of Frankfurter sausages and one slice of toast spread with your daily allowance of butter, margarine or low calorie spread.

☐For lunch you can have 100 g/4 oz/¼ lb hamburgers with two medium-sized tomatoes and 50 g/2 oz/⅜ cup of frozen peas.
☐At dinner time, allow yourself 75 g/3 oz edible weight of canned salmon served with a salad of lettuce, one medium-sized tomato and a small piece of cucumber tossed in lemon dressing (see page 111) plus one small peach.

Low-Carbohydrate Foods to Buy

Consult pages 20 and 21 for information on the difference between a calorie and carbohydrate diet. Your daily 300 ml/½ pint/1¼ cups milk can be skimmed or full-cream.

There is no need to restrict

Low carbohydrate meals
Day 1
orange juice
eggs, bread
+++
Herbed Chicken
+++
sherry
asparagus soup
Ham and Avocado Rolls
cheese, celery

Day 2
grapefruit
fish fingers
+++
tomato juice
salami, lettuce, bread
+++
melon
steak
tomato, carrots

Day 3
Sardines on Toast
orange
+++
consomme
Beef and Horseradish
salad
+++
fish
ratatouille

your fat intake on this diet, unless you have been advised to do so.

Day One

☐At breakfast time allow 150 ml/¼ pint/⅔ cup of fresh or canned orange juice with one or two boiled eggs and one 25 g/1 oz slice of bread spread with butter, margarine or low calorie spread.

☐For lunch serve herbed chicken, made by jointing a cooked chicken into portions then brushing them with melted butter and sprinkling with chopped fresh or dried herbs to taste before heating through under the grill (broiler).

☐At dinner time have one 75 g/3 fl oz/generous ⅓ cup glass of dry sherry followed by 150 ml/¼ pint/⅔ cup of

cream of asparagus soup, ham and avocado rolls (see recipe right), a portion of cheese and 75 g/3 oz of celery.

Day Two

For breakfast allow 75 g/3 oz fresh or unsweetened canned grapefruit segments followed by 75 g/3 oz fish fingers (sticks) which you can fry in butter or margarine.

☐Lunch can consist of 150 ml/¼ pint/⅔ cup of tomato juice then 100 g/4 oz/¼ lb sliced salami with a little lettuce and one 25 g/1 oz slice of wholemeal (wholewheat) bread spread with butter, margarine or low calorie spread.

☐For dinner serve 100 g/4 oz/¼ lb of melon then grilled (broiled) steak, a

small tomato and 50 g/2 oz fresh or canned carrots.

Day Three

☐For breakfast serve sardines on toast (see recipe on page 91) and 100 g/4 oz/¼ lb edible weight of orange.

☐Lunch can consist of canned consommé, beef and horseradish salad (see recipe on page 146).

☐ For dinner serve fried fish in batter allowing 100 g/4 oz/¼ lb. Serve with 75 g/3 oz canned ratatouille.

Ham and Avocado Rolls

■ 489/Kj 2054 ☐2.8 g

Metric/Imperial
1 green pepper
4 tomatoes, skinned
3 sticks celery, chopped
1 × 15 ml spoon/1 tablespoon mayonnaise
1 avocado, 125 g/5 oz in weight
1 × 15 ml spoon/1 tablespoon lemon juice
salt
pepper
8 slices lean cooked ham, each 40 g/1½ oz

TO GARNISH:

1 × 15 ml spoon/1 tablespoon chopped parsley

American
1 green pepper
4 tomatoes, skinned
3 celery stalks, chopped
1 tablespoon mayonnaise
1 avocado, 5 oz in weight
1 tablespoon lemon juice
salt
pepper
8 slices lean cooked ham, each 1½ oz

TO GARNISH:
1 tablespoon chopped parsley

❧Blanch the pepper in boiling water for 5 minutes to soften, drain and chop the pulp (discard the core and seeds). Cut the tomatoes into narrow strips. Mix the pepper, most of the tomato and celery with the mayonnaise. Halve the avocado, stone and skin, cut the flesh into strips, moisten with the lemon juice. Blend most of the avocado with the rest of the vegetables, mayonnaise, salt and pepper. Divide the mixture between the slices of ham and roll up.

To serve: Garnish with parsley and the remaining avocado and tomato strips.

To freeze: Do not freeze.

Menus

Vegetarian Menus

The menus given here provide a choice of a low-calorie or a low-carbohydrate slimming routine. The total daily calories are 1,200 and the daily carbohydrate content 60.0 grammes.

The Vegetarian

The vegetarian will probably be wiser to choose a low-carbohydrate, rather than a low-calorie diet, especially if he is a sufficiently strict vegetarian not to eat fish, in addition to not eating meat.

Eggs are relatively low in calories and have no carbohydrate content; cheese and nuts are both relatively high in calories but have very little carbohydrate value.

The pulses – beans, lentils and peas – contain starch and must therefore be eaten sparingly on any form of slimming diet.

Do not try to reduce the protein content if you are following a slimming diet for any length of time, for this is the nutrient which is so important.

The vegetable 'crash diet' on pages 124–125 would give some ideas for serving vegetables as the basis for your eating programme over three days, but remember this *is* a 'crash' and not a proper long-term slimming routine and should therefore be followed only for three days. You could include an egg or small piece of hard cheese or cottage cheese for breakfast; add nuts to a salad; a cheese dish, or sauce, to a selection of vegetables and immediately you change the food into ideal fare for slimming on a long-term basis.

A vegetarian slimming routine can be successful, appetizing and interesting and certainly comparatively inexpensive.

Low-Calorie Meals

Each day the calories include 300 ml/½ pint/1¼ cups skimmed milk to use in beverages and cooking. If, as a vegetarian, you omit milk from your diet, then you can use the extra 100 calories on other foods.

The daily allowance for margarine or oil or a vegetarian spread is 130 calories.

Day One

☐ For breakfast, allow 150 ml/¼ pint/⅔ cup of yogurt and one 15 g/½ oz slice of wholemeal (wholewheat) bread spread with yeast extract.

☐ At lunch time you can have cheese pudding (see recipe on page 135) with coleslaw and lemon dressing (see recipe on opposite page).

☐ Dinner can consist of half a portion of nut coleslaw and carrot ring.

Day Two

☐ For breakfast serve boiled eggs with one slice of wholemeal (wholewheat) bread spread with butter, margarine or low calorie spread.

☐ At lunch time you can have gazpacho, 50 g/2 oz of cheese with lettuce, 25 g/1 oz of chopped almonds and one slice of wholemeal (wholewheat) bread spread with butter, margarine or low calorie spread.

☐ Dinner can consist of carrot and yogurt bake (see recipe on page 62) and fennel and cauliflower salad (see recipe on page 64).

Day Three

☐ Allow yourself 150 ml/ ¼ pint/⅔ cup of yogurt and one 25 g/1 oz slice of wholemeal (wholewheat) bread spread with yeast extract for breakfast.

☐ For lunch serve avocado cream followed by asparagus and egg salad.

☐ At dinner time you can serve peanut roast (see recipe on page 76) with 100 g/4 oz/ ¼ lb broccoli followed by mock syllabub (see recipe on page 157).

Low-Carbohydrate Meals

If you include milk in your diet, then allow yourself 300 ml/½ pint/1¼ cups skimmed or full-cream milk. This has been allowed in the daily 60.0 grammes of carbohydrate. Care must be taken that the fruits eaten do not exceed the weight or quantity suggested, as most of these are fairly high in carbohydrate content. This is why the weight is always given on this diet, but rarely on the low-calorie diet, when the few extra calories are relatively unimportant.

Low calorie meals

Day 1
yogurt, bread

Cheese Pudding
Coleslaw
Lemon Dressing

Nut Coleslaw
Carrot Ring

Day 2
eggs, bread

Gazpacho
cheese, lettuce
almonds, bread

carrot and yogurt
bake
Fennel and
cauliflower salad

Day 3
yogurt, bread

Avocado Cream
asparagus and
egg salad

Peanut Roast
broccoli
Mock Syllabub

Low carbohydrate meals

Day 1
grapefruit, egg

Peanut Roast
vegetables
apples

soup
Cottage Cheese
Pudding
Coleslaw
Lemon Water Ice

Day 2
muesli, apple
yogurt

Tomato Ice
Cheese Omelette
spinach, bread

Health Salad
Stuffed Peaches

Day 3
Orange Starter
bread

Aubergine and
Tomato Bake
cheese salad

Mushroom Soup
Bird in the Nest
fresh fruit salad

Day One

☐ For breakfast you can have half a grapefruit followed by one poached egg and one 25 g/1 oz slice of wholemeal (wholewheat) bread.

☐ For lunch, serve peanut roast (see recipe on page 76) with 100 g/4 oz/¼ lb of brussels sprouts and 100 g/4 oz/¼ lb of bamboo shoots. Finish off with one apple.

☐ Dinner can consist of curried cucumber soup (see recipe on page 33), cheese pudding (see recipe on page 135) with coleslaw and lemon dressing (see recipe on this page). Follow with lemon water ice (see recipe on page 141).

Day Two

☐ At breakfast time allow 50 g/2 oz muesli mixed with one diced (cubed) apple and 150 ml/¼ pint/⅔ cup of yogurt.

☐ For lunch you can serve tomato ice followed by cheese omelette (see recipe on page 183) using some of the day's butter, margarine or vegetarian fat to cook the omelette and serve with spinach, allowing 100 g/4 oz/¼ lb. You can also have one 25 g/1 oz slice wholemeal (wholewheat) bread

☐ Dinner can consist of health salad (see recipe on page 209) and stuffed peaches (see recipe on page 84).

Day Three

☐ For breakfast you can have orange starter (see recipe on page 195) with one 25 g/1 oz slice wholemeal (wholewheat) bread spread with yeast extract.

☐ At lunch time serve aubergine (eggplant) and tomato bake (see recipe on page 61) with a cheese salad consisting of 75 g/3 oz Edam cheese and a mixed salad. The cheese will be 264 calories so allow yourself 60 calories for the salad. Serve with one 25 g/1 oz slice of wholemeal (wholewheat) bread.

☐ For dinner serve mushroom soup (see recipe on page 198), bird in the nest and fresh fruit salad, allowing 60 calories for the fruit.

Coleslaw

This is best made with Dutch white cabbage, but when this is not available then use the heart of a cabbage.

Wash in cold water, dry then shred this very finely. Coleslaw can be blended with many dressings; the Lemon Dressing on this page is particularly good.

The calorific value and carbohydrate content will depend on the dressing, but the figures for raw cabbage are given below. This is for each 25 g/1 oz/⅜ cup.

To serve: With hot or cold dishes.

To freeze: Must be freshly prepared.

Variations:

1: Add grated raw carrot.

2: Add finely chopped apple.

3: Add chopped nuts, chopped celery and chopped green pepper, discard the core and seeds.

■ 5/Kj21 ☐ 0.9 g–1.1 g

Lemon Dressing

■ 41/Kj172 ☐ 4.1 g

Metric/Imperial

grated rind and juice of 1 lemon

300 ml/½ pint yogurt

1 × 5 ml spoon/1 teaspoon Dijon mustard

pinch saffron powder

American

grated rind and juice of 1 lemon

1¼ cups yogurt

1 teaspoon Dijon mustard

pinch saffron powder

Blend all the ingredients together. The saffron gives the dressing a very pleasant golden colour.

To serve: With any salads, but particularly good over cucumber and pepper salad or a coleslaw.

To freeze: This dressing is better freshly made.

Variation:

Add finely chopped herbs or chopped gherkins (sweet dill pickles) and capers.

Menus

The Sedentary Job

If you lead the kind of life where you expend little energy in physical activities then you may well have put on an appreciable amount of weight and find it difficult to lose weight.

A few examples of how many calories physical energy will consume is given below.

If you walk briskly for an hour, not stopping to rest, you will use up about 180 calories. Very few of us keep up a brisk pace in walking for an hour.

If you play a *vigorous* game of tennis or golf for an hour you may well 'burn up' 200–300 calories, so you see exercise is of a certain value and will enable you to lose weight on a slightly more generous calorie allowance.

Let us put it the other way round then:

If your job or profession or way of life means you have little time or opportunity for physical activities *then* your diet must be planned accordingly. This is why the basic calorie controlled diet in this group is based on 1,000 calories only. This should give you an average *weekly* weight loss of a kilogramme or 2 lb. If the loss is much greater then you can raise it to about 1,200 calories and check again.

In the low-carbohydrate diet you have once again a slightly lower content, i.e. 53 instead of 60 grammes.

It is, however, up to you to check upon your progress in slimming and adjust the food intake accordingly.

Low-Calorie Diet

Although this diet is based on 1,000 calories only, it does provide a good balance of foods and nutrients.

Do not try to cut down on any of the essential foods, for 1,000 calories is not over-generous and if you keep to this allowance you should lose weight steadily.

Check with your medical adviser that it is in order for you to follow a slimming routine.

In addition to the foods given in the menus, the 1,000 calories also includes 300 ml/ ½ pint/1¼ cups of skimmed milk (100 calories) and approximately 15 g/½ oz/ 1 tablespoon butter or margarine or 25 g/1 oz/ 2 tablespoons low-calorie spread; 130 calories have been allowed for this.

Day One

☐ Breakfast can consist of half a grapefruit, one boiled egg and a slice of bread weighing 25 g/1 oz.

☐ For lunch serve tomato soup (see recipe on page 32) followed by fish Florentine (page 135) and one orange.

☐ At dinner time you can have savoury beef (see recipe on page 47) with courgettes (zucchini) Lyonnaise (see recipe on page 179) and one medium-sized pear.

Day Two

☐ Breakfast can consist of 50 g/2 oz of muesli and 150 ml/¼ pint/⅔ cup of yogurt.

☐ For lunch have half a grapefruit and one hard boiled egg, a mixed salad and cottage cheese dressing (see

```
Low calorie
meals
Day 1

grapefruit
egg, bread
***
Tomato Soup
Fish Florentine
orange
***
Savoury Beef
Courgettes
 Lyonnaise
pear
```

recipe on page 146). Allow 50 calories for the salad.

☐ For dinner have a grilled lamb chop allowing 100 g/4 oz/¼ lb edible weight with 1 grilled (broiled) medium tomato. Have 75 g/3 oz edible weight of spinach and 1 small orange.

Day Three

☐ For breakfast allow 75 g/3 oz/1 cup of bran flakes and a 25 g/1 oz slice of toast spread with yeast extract.

☐ At lunch time start with a 50 ml/1 fl oz/scant ⅓ cup glass of dry sherry followed by 100 g/4 oz/¼ lb edible weight of roast chicken and 75 g/3 oz edible weight of brussels sprouts. Finish with

apple mousse (see page 83).

☐ For dinner serve nut coleslaw and one small pear.

Low-Carbohydrate Diet

The daily 56 grammes of carbohydrate includes 14 grammes for the 300 ml/½ pint/1¼ cups of milk.

Day One

☐ For breakfast you can have grilled (broiled) bacon allowing 50 g/2 oz edible weight per serving. Also serve 150 ml/¼ pint/⅔ cup yogurt.

☐ At lunch time serve herb cocottes (see recipe on page 149) with a 25 g/1 oz slice of bread with butter and cheese.

☐ For dinner serve 75 g/3 oz grapefruit segments, grilled

(broiled) steak with mushrooms, followed by 75 g/3 oz of cheese and celery.

Day Two

☐ You can have low-calorie grapefruit juice for breakfast with scrambled eggs and one 25 g/1 oz slice of wholemeal (wholewheat) bread.

☐ At lunch time serve roes on toast (see recipe on page 91) with 50 g/2 oz edible weight of watercress.

☐ For dinner you can have roast lamb with 100 g/4 oz edible weight of cauliflower and 75 g/3 oz edible weight of carrots. Accompany with 50 g/2 oz rhubarb cooked with sugar substitute and

home-made ice cream.

Day Three

☐ For breakfast you can allow 150 ml/¼ pint/⅔ cup of orange juice with smoked haddock and a 15 g/½ oz slice of wholemeal bread.

☐ For lunch you can allow 100 g/4 oz/¼ lb of ham with one tomato and a slice of wholemeal (wholewheat) bread weighing 25 g/1 oz with butter and cheese.

☐ At dinner time serve grilled veal chops (cutlets) with grilled mushrooms and 75 g/3 oz of spinach followed by rhubarb sorbet and half a glass of white wine.

Day 2
muesli, yogurt
***
grapefruit, egg
mixed salad
Cottage Cheese
 Dressing
***
lamb chops
tomato, spinach
orange

Day 3
cereal, toast
***
sherry
roast chicken
brussels sprouts
Apple Mousse
***
Nut Coleslaw
pear

Low carbohydrate
meals
Day 1
bacon, yogurt
***
Herb Cocottes
bread, cheese
***
grapefruit
steak, mushrooms.
cheese, celery

Day 3
orange juice
smoked haddock
bread
***
ham, tomato,
bread, cheese
***
veal chops
mushrooms
spinach
Rhubarb Sorbet
white wine

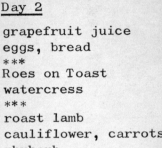

Day 2
grapefruit juice
eggs, bread
***
Roes on Toast
watercress
***
roast lamb
cauliflower, carrots
rhubarb
Home Made Ice Cream

Menus

Low calorie meals
Day 1
* cereal, milk, orange
* bread, cottage cheese
* Stuffed Tomato,
  Bird in the Nest
* Beef Mould, mixed salad
  Rice and Apple Mould
  cheese, watercress

Low carbohydrate meals
Day 1
* orange juice, bacon, egg, toast
* pear
* Lamb chops, tomato
* yogurt
* fish, mushrooms,
  Home Made Ice Cream

Day 2
* tomato juice, eggs, bread
* apples, yogurt
* roast chicken, mixed salad
  potatoes, Caramelled Oranges
* bread, cottage cheese
* Steak Niçoise
  Mock Syllabub

Day 2
* grapefruit, kippers, bread
* yogurt
* Hamburgers, lettuce, green
  pepper, Fruit Soufflé Omelette
* bread, cheese
* cold meat, tomato and
  mushroom salad

Day 3
* muesli, yogurt
* bread
* Macaroni and Walnut
  casserole, mixed salad
* apples
* Crab and Avocado Pâté
  Chicken in Lemon and
  Tarragon, peas, beer

Day 3
* orange, bread
* crispbread
* Curried Kidneys, rice
* cheese
* Brown Fish Soup, beef
  pickled red cabbage
  Fresh Lemon Jelly

Active Jobs

It is extremely difficult to diagnose just how to adjust the calorie and carbohydrate content of an active job, without knowing just *how* energetic this may be.

Pages 112–113 give two examples of leisure activity which will result in the 'burning up' of some calories but if the whole of one's working day is spent in really prolonged and hard physical activity, then undoubtedly you will be able to have a higher basic diet and still continue to lose weight.

The calories allowed on the diet are 1,500, instead of the more usual 1,200 or 1,000 for the sedentary way of life (see pages 112–113) and 64 instead of the standard 60 grammes of carbohydrate.

Low-Calorie Diet for an Active Life

Pages 112–113 emphasise that exercise and physical activity play their part in keeping one slim, but if you need to lose weight then undoubtedly you will need to restrict your intake of food and follow a diet low in calories or carbohydrates.

Each day's calories allow 300 ml/½ pint/1¼ cups skimmed milk (100 calories) plus 130 calories for butter or other fat, this is discussed more fully on pages 104–105.

Day One

☐ At breakfast time allow 50 g/2 oz/2 cups of corn-flakes with 150 ml/¼ pint/⅔ cup of skimmed milk over and the daily allowance plus one orange.

☐ For a mid-morning snack you can have a 25 g/1 oz slice of bread made into a sandwich with 25 g/1 oz of cottage cheese.

☐ At lunch time you can have a stuffed tomato (see recipe on page 151) and Bird in the Nest (see recipe on page 151).

☐ For a tea-time nibble have a 25 g/1 oz slice of wholemeal (wholewheat) bread with some of the day's allowance of butter and yeast extract.

☐ Serve Beef mould (see recipe on page 138) for dinner with a mixed salad of no more than 50 calories. Follow with Rice and apple mousse (see recipe on page 137), 25 g/1 oz of Edam cheese and a little watercress.

Day Two

☐ At breakfast time allow 150 ml/¼ pint/⅔ cup of tomato juice with two boiled eggs and a 25 g/1 oz slice of wholemeal (wholewheat) bread with yeast extract.

☐ Mid-morning you can allow one to two apples as long as you have 100 g/4 oz edible weight and 150 ml/¼ pint/⅔ cup of yogurt.

☐ For lunch serve 100 g/4 oz/¼ lb of cold roast chicken with a mixed salad of no more than 50 calories. Serve with 100 g/4 oz/¼ lb of boiled potatoes and follow with Caramelled oranges (see recipe on page 85).

☐ At tea-time make a sandwich of one 25 g/1 oz slice of bread with a filling of 25 g/1 oz of cottage cheese.

☐ For dinner you can have Steak Niçoise (see recipe on page 205) followed by Mock Syllabub (see recipe on page 157).

Day Three

☐ For breakfast allow one orange, 50 g/2 oz of muesli and 150 ml/¼ pint/⅔ cup of yogurt.

☐ For a mid-morning snack have a 25 g/1 oz slice of bread with yeast extract.

☐ At lunch time have a small portion of Macaroni and Walnut casserole (see recipe on page 77) with a mixed salad of no more than 50 calories.

☐ Tea-time can consist of one to two apples weighing no more than 100 g/4 oz/¼ lb edible weight.

☐ Serve Crab and avocado pâté for dinner followed by Chicken in lemon and tarragon (see recipe on page 175) with 100 g/4 oz/¼ lb of peas and a glass of beer measuring 300 ml/½ pint/1¼ cups.

Low-Carbohydrate Diet for an Active Life

The advantage of a low-carbohydrate diet for busy and energetic people is that it enables you to have generous amounts of meat and fish, cheese, eggs and nuts, all excellent sources of protein.

Milk is also a protein food and 14.0 grammes each day are allocated for 300 ml/½ pint/1¼ cups skimmed or full-cream milk.

Day One

☐ For breakfast you can have 150 ml/¼ pint/⅔ cup of orange juice followed by grilled or fried bacon, one egg and one 25 g/1 oz slice of toast.

☐ Mid-morning you can have 50 g/2 oz edible weight of pear.

☐ At lunch time serve two lamb chops allowing 100 g/4 oz/¼ lb and one tomato.

☐ At tea-time you can have 150 ml/¼ pint/⅔ cup of yogurt.

☐ For dinner serve baked or grilled (broiled) white (lean) fish with mushrooms followed by Home-made ice cream (see recipe on page 88).

Day Two

☐ Have a breakfast of half a grapefruit, weighing 75 g/3 oz followed by grilled kippers and one 25 g/1 oz slice of bread.

☐ Mid-morning allow 150 ml/¼ pint/⅔ cup of yogurt.

☐ For lunch you can have hamburgers (see recipe on page 45) and allow yourself a generous portion if desired as they have no carbohydrate content. Serve with a little lettuce and a green pepper followed by fruit soufflé omelette (see recipe on page 191).

☐ At tea-time have one 25 g/1 oz slice of bread with cheese.

☐ At dinner time serve a plate of mixed cold meats with a tomato and raw mushroom salad, allowing 100 g/4 oz of tomato.

Day Three

☐ At breakfast time you can have 100 g/4 oz/¼ lb edible weight of orange with a 15 g/½ oz slice of wholemeal (wholewheat) bread.

☐ Allow yourself one slice of crispbread spread with yeast extract mid-morning.

☐ For lunch serve curried kidneys (see recipe on page 53) and 25 g/1 oz/⅙ cup cooked rice.

☐ A finger of cheese will serve as a tea-time bite.

☐ For dinner you can have Brown fish soup (see recipe on page 30) followed by cold slices beef and pickled red cabbage and Fresh lemon jelly for dessert (see recipe on page 210) using sugar substitute instead of sugar.

Menus

Crash & Short-Term Diets

Crash & Short-Term Diets

Frequently the very circumstances that impel us
to diet make us impatient for results.
To this end there are 'crash diets' which
really should last for only a few days and
'short term diets' which may last for
about 10 days, but no longer.
There are times when results are urgent;
maybe for professional reasons, such as going
for a special interview, or for very important
private occasions, a prospective bride
wants to look lovelier on her wedding day,
perhaps there is a special dinner or dance
and the zip on an evening dress or the buttons
on a dinner suit will not meet and the garment
is uncomfortably tight.

FOLLOWING A CRASH DIET

In order to go on a crash diet you need to be very strong-willed and very fit. It is a good idea to do it over a weekend or a time of greater leisure so that you are not expending extra energy on working.

Most doctors and nutritionists dislike this form of dieting for two very important reasons.

It is apt to lead to loss of energy, one could feel weak or 'nervy', have a headache or even feel sick and dizzy. It is therefore very important that you do not try and carry on as normal when you are following this short and very unnatural form of dieting. It is better to avoid driving or anything where your reactions have to be very sharp. If you can treat it as a complete time of relaxation rather than a normal period, you will feel appreciably better at the end of the period and you will also have lost a good amount of weight.

The second reason that this form of dieting is unpopular is that it does not establish a sensible slimming routine. You really will have learned very little about the kind of foods to choose and those to avoid.

How much weight does one lose on a crash diet? This is very difficult to assess. If you are badly overweight, your loss could be really quite amazing. You could lose probably more than 0.5 kg/ 1 lb a day.

If you are almost at a normal weight, it will not be quite as much but, in most cases, it will be appreciably more than the usual 1 kg/2 lb average a week that you can hope to lose on most sensible slimming routines.

FOLLOWING A SHORT TERM DIET

The 'short term' diets provide a very much better balanced form of eating than a 'crash diet' but they are still very low in the total intake of food. Many of the comments given under 'crash diets' apply here, although most people find they can follow a normal, but not too energetic, routine while on this strict routine.

The workings of both the 'crash' and 'short term' diets must be obvious but briefly they are as follows:

Instead of counting calories or carbohydrates in food you follow a routine of eating foods that are very much below the normal dietary needs and which are low in either calories or carbohydrates, and possibly in both; in fact you are, in some cases, *approaching* almost a starvation level. This sounds alarming, but in the civilised world, where we tend to eat too much anyway, it will not matter *for a short period*.

As explained on pages 20 and 21, if you eat less than your body needs in energy and are a reasonably healthy person, you are bound to lose some weight.

Because the 'short term' diet gives you more of the foods needed to maintain good health you can continue this for a longer period than the 'crash diet', but it cannot in any way be called a permanent slimming routine.

The weight loss will be less each day than that lost on the 'crash diet', but you probably will be following the routine for a longer period so the *total* weight lost could be similar.

Crash Diets

100
calorie diet

A daily intake of only 100 calories is, of course, *very severe* and it should be followed for two consecutive days only. Its virtue is that it is often a good starting point for people who have problems in losing weight within the first few days of an ordinary slimming diet; so you could follow this for two days then start your proper slimming routine. It will enable you to lose the first encouraging 1 kg/2 lb.

Often when you have been steadfastly eating a slimming diet for a considerable period, in order to achieve an ideal weight, there comes a time when you seem to stay at a certain weight. This can be very frustrating and it could be the time when you might weaken and give up your diet because 'it only works to start with'. It often helps to transfer to this 'crash' diet for *two days only*; then return once more to your planned and well balanced slimming meals. Then you generally find the regular, if comparatively small loss of weight, will start again and continue. It is almost as though your body needed shock treatment.

How will you expend your 100 calories? Here are some suggestions:
1. 300 ml/½ pint/1¼ cups skimmed milk to add to tea and coffee *or*
2. 150 ml/¼ pint/⅔ cup low fat plain yogurt, 25 g/1 oz/⅛ cup cottage cheese and a small piece of cucumber *or*
3. 25 g/1 oz Edam cheese and 1 medium tomato *or*
4. White fish poached in fish stock, see page 35. Allow 100 g/4 oz edible weight, topped with 2 × 15 ml spoons/2 tablespoons plain yogurt blended with a little chopped parsley or dill *or*
5. 1 egg, poached or boiled and a medium tomato *or*
6. Boiled chicken, served hot or cold. Allow just 100 g/4 oz edible weight *or*
7. A 25 g/1 oz slice bread, toasted, spread with yeast extract and topped with 100 g/4 oz/1 cup mushrooms, simmered in a little water

From right: A selection of food from the 100-calorie diet. Suggestions 4; 8; 2; 7

with salt and pepper to taste and a small orange, allow 75 g/3 oz edible weight, *or*

8. 2 medium tomatoes, ¼ medium cucumber, 50 g/ 2 oz/¼ cup cottage cheese, 1 head chicory (endive) about 75 g/3 oz in weight *or*

9. 3 to 4 oranges, giving a *total* edible weight of 300 g/ 11 oz *or*

10. 1 to 2 bananas giving an edible weight of 115 g/4½ oz.

You can have cups of tea or coffee, but do not add milk unless you have chosen (1) as your 100 calorie allowance. You can also include drinks made with yeast extract and water.

INCREASING CALORIES

The 100 calorie unit is a good starting point for 'crash diets'. You can work out a number of permutations from this.

If you want to increase the daily intake to 200 calories you could choose the milk *plus* one of the other 100 calorie portions or you could omit the milk and select two 100 calorie units or allow yourself a double quantity of one of these.

A 400 calorie intake would enable you to have the milk and three other 100 calorie units, so you could have one each of these for breakfast, lunch and dinner.

Food for the Banana and Milk Diet.

This diet was very popular many years ago and seemed to have been successful.

Because bananas are satisfying, people tended to feel better fed than on many 'crash' diets. You have a total of 6 bananas and 600 ml/ 1 pint/2⅔ cups milk, which can be full cream, during a day and you divide the bananas and milk into three or six portions. If you do not like milk, then you can substitute 300 ml/½ pint/ 1¼ cups plain yogurt for half the milk and 100 g/4 oz/ ½ cup cottage cheese for the rest of the milk.

Follow this diet for 3 days only.

Crash Diets

WHY CRASH DIETS AND SHORT TERM DIETS ARE LESS ADVISABLE

It is sad to relate that the faster weight is lost, the faster it is likely to be regained. Diets which induce a loss of more than 1 kg/2 lb a week must, of necessity, be so extreme that they cannot be of long duration. It means that your body has not had time to accustom itself to a new routine of feeding.

It often happens that those who have been on such a diet will compensate for the deprivation they feel they endured by eating injudiciously when the diet ends. They often hoodwink themselves into thinking that just *one* cocktail, *one* ice cream, a *few* potatoes or *one* portion of a rich dessert can do no harm. This, needless to say, has an insidious way of being the first step back to the unfortunate eating pattern that made the diet advisable in the first place.

If you treat a 'crash' or 'short term' diet as the first step to 'get you going' on a routine either to lose weight or to maintain an ideal weight, then there is a place for these various ways of eating.

Do not assure yourself that you can 'eat what you please' for a time, then lose that weight by returning to the strict diet that lost that extra weight so quickly – what you are establishing is a pattern of overeating, followed by undereating, and that uneven method of feeding cannot but have an adverse effect on both your health and your looks.

VITAMINS ON CRASH DIETS

Because you are *not* having a well balanced diet when following one of the 'crash' or 'short term' diets, it is worthwhile considering taking vitamin tablets. Choose multi-vitamins which will help to compensate for the lack of vitamins A and D, normally obtained from butter and margarine, see page 11, also the B group of vitamins from wheatgerm in bread, plus vitamin C (ascorbic acid). This is particularly important if your diet does not include citrus fruit. You could also add a little wheatgerm to the soups in the Vegetable Diet on pages 124 and 125.

Right: Vitamin tablets and wheatgerm are sensible additives when following a crash diet

2 DAY fruit diet

This diet will suit those people who usually eat a fairly generous amount of fruit, but it may cause upset stomachs if you only eat a limited amount of fruit under normal conditions.

You can have some fruit and some whole fruit, or just whole fruit, or just fruit juice, whichever you prefer. Keep your daily calorie intake to around 250 and follow this diet for two days only.

Your plan of campaign on each day could be:

Fruit to be eaten on Day 1 of the Two Day fruit Diet.

DAY 1

Breakfast
½ grapefruit
1 apple
Tea with a slice of lemon

Mid-morning
Drink made from yeast extract and water or tea with a slice of lemon

Lunch or Dinner
½ grapefruit
1 banana

Teatime
Tea with a slice of lemon

Dinner or Lunch
1 peach or 1 pear
100 g/4 oz/scant cup strawberries

DAY 2

Breakfast
150 ml/¼ pint/⅔ cup fresh orange juice
Tea with a slice of lemon

Mid-morning
as Day 1

Lunch or Dinner
3 dessert plums
100 g/4 oz/1 cup grapes

Teatime
as Day 1

Dinner or Lunch
150 ml/¼ pint/⅔ cup fresh orange juice

Crash Diets

3
DAY
vegetable diet

During the three days only vegetables are served; but you can have an infinite variety. Do not, however, include beans, lentils, peas, potatoes or beetroot but as much of the other vegetables as desired.

The suggestions below need not be followed exactly, you can replace cooked dishes with raw salads and omit the soups but these all help to add interest to the menus.

Do not add anything in the way of eggs, cheese, meat, fish, sauce, butter or margarine but you can have 300 ml/½ pint/1¼ cups skimmed milk each day, which you can add to tea and coffee or use in the soups, but do not exceed this allowance.

The yeast extract used for drinks, or in soups, is an excellent source of the B group of vitamins and should be included.

Serve the cooked vegetables the moment they are ready and make them look interesting by topping them with chopped herbs.

DAY 1

Breakfast
½ grapefruit
Grilled (broiled) tomatoes on 15 g/½ oz bread, toasted and spread with yeast extract. Do not use fat (shortening) in cooking the tomatoes.
Tea or coffee with some of the day's milk allowance.

Mid-morning
Drink made with yeast extract and water

Lunch or Dinner
Onion soup, see recipe on the opposite page
Raw vegetable salad. Mix as many vegetables as you like, except those given in the introduction.

Teatime
Tea with milk from the daily allowance

Dinner or Lunch
A plate of mixed cooked vegetables, include those that give variation of texture,

colour and flavour, such as Brussels sprouts, carrots and leeks.

DAY 2

Breakfast
½ grapefruit
Sliced raw tomatoes with sliced raw mushrooms and a slice of crispbread
Tea or coffee with some of the day's milk allowance

Mid-morning
as Day 1

Lunch or Dinner
Courgettes (zucchini) with Sanfayna, see opposite page

Teatime
as Day 1

Dinner or Lunch
Fennel and cucumber soup
Raw vegetable salad

DAY 3

Breakfast
1 orange
Mushrooms, cooked in a little water, with yeast extract, salt and pepper to flavour; drained and served on a 15 g/½ oz slice of toast
Tea or coffee with some of the day's milk allowance

Raw vegetable salad; a plate of mixed cooked vegetables

Fennel and Cucumber Soup
Right: Onion Soup

Mid-morning

as Day 1

Lunch or Dinner

Cauliflower with celeriac and onion purée, see this page
Sliced green pepper (capsicum)

Teatime

as Day 1

Dinner or Lunch

Aubergine Pâté, see recipe page 25 with mixed salad

Onion Soup

Peel and chop, or slice, 225 g/ 8 oz/½ lb onions and 1 garlic clove. Simmer in 750 ml/ 1¼ pints/3⅓ cups water or vegetable stock for 10 minutes.

Add 2–4 × 5 ml spoons/ 2–4 teaspoons yeast extract, salt and pepper and continue simmering until the onions are quite tender.
To serve: Hot, topped with plenty of chopped parsley.
Variations:
1: Sieve or purée in a blender after cooking.
2: Use beef stock as the liquid.
3: French Onion Soup. Cut the onions into slices, then separate into rings. Fry with the garlic in 50 g/2 oz/¼ cup butter, then add the beef stock, a little yeast extract (this improves the flavour), salt and pepper.
■ 14/Kj59 □ 2.7 g

Celeriac and Onion Purée

Peel and dice a small celeriac root, together with an onion. Cook the vegetables in the minimum of water, with salt, garlic salt and a good pinch of black pepper. Sieve or purée in a blender. For extra colour you could add a skinned tomato when cooking.
To serve: Over vegetables or fish.
■ 14/Kj59 □ 2.7 g

Sanfayna

This is a well known Spanish sauce. The version given has a good flavour, but the food is cooked differently for this vegetable diet.

Skin and chop 4 medium tomatoes, 2 medium onions, 2 red peppers (capsicums), discard core and seeds, 1 small courgette (zucchini), 1 garlic clove.

Put the ingredients into a saucepan with 2–3 × 15 ml spoons/2–3 tablespoons water, salt and pepper to taste.

Simmer until a soft mixture is formed.
To serve: Over cooked fish or vegetables.
Variation:
The classic way to cook the vegetables is to fry them in a little oil.
■ 36/Kj150 □ 4.6 g

Fennel and Cucumber Soup

Dice a root of fennel and a peeled cucumber. Simmer in 900 ml/1½ pints/4 cups stock left from cooking other vegetables with salt and pepper to taste until just tender.

To serve: Top with the chopped fennel leaves.
■ 13/Kj54 □ 2.1 g

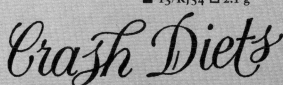
Crash Diets

10

DAY
diet
mainly eggs

A slimming diet that has proved to be very effective for many people is one based primarily on eggs, spinach and grapefruit. It has the advantage in that people who have followed this diet seem to feel extremely well-fed.

There are however disadvantages about this routine.

Many doctors feel that *too many eggs are not good* and you certainly cannot follow this diet if you have been warned to reduce your intake of cholesterol.

If you decide to try this diet you must not follow it for more than 10 days.

You can eat more than one egg at each meal if you wish and you can add more grapefruit too, but the basic principles must be followed. You can drink as much tea or coffee as you wish but *without* milk. Do not have fruit drinks, soft drinks or alcohol on this particular diet.

This diet was originally given to me as having eggs at all three meals on the first, fourth, seventh and tenth days, but I have found the variations more palatable and as successful in leading to weight loss.

When serving steak, chops (cutlets) or chicken allow only 75 g/3 oz edible weight.

When serving white (lean) fish allow only 100 g/4 oz edible weight. In order to avoid using fat in cooking the fish, poach in a little fish stock. To make a good *fish stock* simmer the bones and skin of fish in water with a squeeze of lemon juice, salt, pepper and a sprig of parsley.

DAY 1

Breakfast

Grapefruit
Boiled or Poached Egg
1 thin slice of toast, without butter

Lunch or Dinner

Grapefruit
An omelette (omelet) cooked with the minimum of butter or a poached egg
1 tomato
Cooked spinach

Dinner or Lunch

Grapefruit
1 or 2 grilled (broiled) lamb chops (cutlets), with courgettes (zucchini) and spinach

DAY 2

Breakfast

as Day 1

Lunch or Dinner

Grapefruit
Cottage cheese with lettuce, watercress, raw mushrooms, green pepper (capsicum)

Dinner or Lunch

Grapefruit
1 portion of chicken, free from fat with spinach and a side salad of sliced cucumber with lemon juice

DAY 3

Breakfast

as Day 1

Lunch or Dinner

as Day 1

Dinner or Lunch

Grapefruit
Portion of white (lean) fish, steamed or grilled (broiled) with lemon juice, but the absolute minimum of fat
Sliced cucumber and spinach

DAY 4

Breakfast

as Day 1

Lunch or Dinner

Grapefruit
Grilled (broiled) steak with mushrooms, cooked with little if any butter
Spinach

Dinner or Lunch

Grapefruit
Raw vegetable salad with a hard-boiled egg, choose only shredded cabbage, watercress, cucumber

DAY 5

Breakfast

as Day 1

Lunch or Dinner

Grapefruit
1 or 2 grilled (broiled) lamb chops (cutlets) with spinach and a salad of cucumber

Dinner or Lunch

Grapefruit
Cottage cheese salad
see Day 2

DAY 6

Breakfast

as Day 1

Lunch or Dinner

Grapefruit
Baked white (lean) fish with a tomato and cucumber salad

Inset left: Lamb chops; spinach; cucumber salad
Inset right: Steak, tomatoes; spinach

Dinner or Lunch

Grapefruit
Omelette (omelet) cooked in the minimum of butter
Spinach

DAY 7

Breakfast

as Day 1

Lunch or Dinner

as Day 1

Dinner or Lunch

as Day 1

DAY 8

Breakfast

as Day 1

Lunch or Dinner

Grapefruit
Grilled (broiled) steak with sliced raw or cooked tomatoes and spinach

Dinner or Lunch

Grapefruit
Poached egg on spinach

DAY 9

Breakfast

as Day 1

Lunch or Dinner

as Day 2

Dinner or Lunch

as Day 2

DAY 10

Breakfast

as Day 1

Lunch or Dinner

as Day 4

Dinner or Lunch

as Day 4

Crash Diets

Diets for Special Needs

Special Needs

Throughout this book are recipes and hints on choosing
foods and cooking dishes to enable you to lose weight
and remain well and full of energy. There is also a section
which gives advice and recipes on maintaining your
ideal weight.

In this section the theme is continued, but with a somewhat
different emphasis. The pages that follow are devoted to
groups of people who have special needs. There are
recipes for people of all ages who have been advised to
follow a low-cholesterol or a low-fat diet.

There are recipes to appeal to overweight children, of
which there are a disturbing number, together with
suggestions for their parents to help make the child's diet as
pleasant as possible.

Elderly people who are overweight may need special
recipes and these are given on pages 156–159. They also
will find many other recipes interesting.

It may seem disturbing to need both a
slimming *and* a special diet combined.
However, this need not be unduly worry-
ing or difficult to follow if you assess the
dietary requirements in a *positive manner*.

Assure yourself that the diet *will*
succeed; maybe you have tried to follow
diets before and failed. Ask yourself why.
Was it that the diet was over-difficult or
dull? The latter is unnecessary; if a diet
lacks interest the chances of it succeeding
are not very high. I hope you will agree
that the dishes in this book are interesting
and easy to prepare.

Check on the foods to *avoid*; that can
be a little depressing if the list includes
many of your favourite dishes, but then
it is more important to recognize, and
appreciate, the variety of foods you *can*
eat. In most cases it will be a relatively
long list and it will include a variety of
nutritious and pleasant ingredients. Plan
a few days' menus, or look through the
balanced menus on pages 103, 104 and
106, and convince yourself that you *will*
enjoy this new way of eating. It is the
first few days that may prove difficult to
follow, after all you could be changing
the culinary habits of a lifetime. Keep on
convincing yourself that you *like* this
new pattern of eating, and as the days
pass you may well find you are not only
following a diet which is highly successful, but at the same time you really are
enjoying your completely new cuisine.

Throughout this book it has been
stressed that strict slimming diets must
only be followed under doctor's orders.
It is even more important to receive, and
adhere to, medical advice before you
embark on any other specialist diet; do
not prescribe for yourself.

Families and friends can help to make
dieting successful. Do not keep sympa-
thizing with the person who is trying to
follow a pretty strict routine. It is far
better to be encouraging, or to behave as
though it were a perfectly normal routine.
If family meals can be as similar as
possible that is helpful, both for the cook
and for the person dieting. Low-cholesterol diets are often sensible precaution-
ary measures and even the low-fat diet is
one that may prove beneficial to all the
family for a time.

Do not try and persuade people to waiver from their diet; it is quite amazing how often friends try to 'sabotage' a diet. You can do this by offering foods that have no place in the particular diet, on the pretext that one sweet (candy) or a single biscuit (cookie) could not matter. Slimming, and any form of dieting, means not only limiting your intake of particular foods, but educating your palate to like the right things; that odd sweetmeat (candy) could so easily re-create a longing for sweet foods with disastrous results.

The same thing applies to a low-cholesterol or low-fat diet; all the time one is educating taste buds to become familiar with a different routine and per-haps even *new* flavours. It is essential, therefore, not to be tempted to break the rules. People are dieting for the good of their health and that is a very precious thing.

Do not make fun of people when they are either overweight or dieting to get rid of that surplus weight; laughing about a fat person may seem a good way to encourage people to do something about dieting, but it can have the oppo-site effect, especially with children; they may well feel they are a 'figure of fun', they are destined to be fat and it is not worth trying to be anything different.

ENTERTAINING

It is very important when you are on a diet to continue to lead as normal a social life as possible. If your diet is strict, as in the case of a low-fat or low-cholesterol diet, it is probably kinder to let your host or hostess know, so they can have suit-able foods.

If you are entertaining yourself, then it is a challenge to produce a super spread with the kind of foods that are permitted on your diet, plus a few lavish extras.

One of the best dishes for informal entertaining is a dip.

Piquant Cheese Dip

Blend 450 g/1 lb sieved cottage cheese

Piquant Cheese Dip

with the sieved pulp of two tomatoes, a little made (Dijon) mustard, salt, pepper and enough plain yogurt to give the consistency of a thick cream.

To serve: Put the dip in a bowl on a big tray with cauliflower florets, sticks of young carrot or cucumber and tiny spring onions (scallions) around.

To freeze: A dip will freeze for a few days only.

Variations:

1: Blend it with the pulp of two avocados or shrimps (shelled shrimp); not for people on a low-cholesterol diet.

2: You can add Worcestershire or Tabasco sauce to give a hotter taste.

■ 77/Kj 323 □ 3.9 g

Special Needs

What is a low-cholesterol diet?

This diet is very often recommended to people who are recovering from a heart attack, or where a doctor feels the diet could be a helpful factor in preventing heart and coronary troubles.

Some people have a high cholesterol level in their blood and, in the opinion of many medical experts, are far more likely to have a heart attack than people with a lower level. If the blood cholesterol rises, so does the risk of coronary diseases. That is why it makes sense to reduce the cholesterol level in the blood stream if you are advised to do so.

Another contributing factor to heart trouble is overweight, and frequently one is advised to follow both a low-cholesterol *and* a slimming routine. The former advice means you can reduce the cholesterol in the blood stream if you avoid those foods high in this; these are outlined in the following column. Most doctors then advise slimming by reducing the carbohydrate content of the diet, with particular emphasis on cutting down on sugar.

Do not let the words 'low-cholesterol' alarm you, as you will agree it is not an impossible diet to follow and by adhering to this you could make an important contribution to good health.

Obviously diet in relation to heart disease is not the only consideration; you may be advised to give up smoking, for this is known to raise the cholesterol levels. You may also be advised to take more exercise, to worry less and relax more. All these points will be discussed with you by your medical adviser.

FOODS TO AVOID

One does not need to avoid fats (shortenings), although these must be used sparingly if on a low-cholesterol diet, but rather to choose them carefully.

There are several brands of soft margarine which will be labelled quite clearly 'Polyunsaturated' and these can be used as a spread or in cooking.

Then there are the plant oils, such as corn oil, cotton seed oil and sunflower seed oil; olive oil is less suitable on this particular diet.

Peanut butter also can be included as this is a good source of protein and very popular with children.

You should avoid the hard fats – cooking fats, lard, hard margarines, suet and coconut oil and omit butter or eat it very sparingly.

Choose meats carefully; lean chicken and turkey, lean beef and game such as pheasant are the best choice, but you could have lean lamb. It is quite simple to cut away the fat. You would be wise to limit, or omit, pork and bacon, and products made from these from your

Left: Foods to avoid on a low-cholesterol diet
Right: Foods encouraged on a low-cholesterol diet

diet, and the richer poultry like duck and goose. Unfortunately offal (variety meats), such as heart, liver, kidney and brains, are high in cholesterol, so must be avoided.

You have a wide choice of white (lean) *fish* and oily fish, such as herrings, for these are low in cholesterol. Avoid shell-fish and fish roes.

Most *nuts* are high in 'polyunsaturated' fat so you can use these in dishes, although they are high in calories too, so slimmers must be aware of this; the exceptions are cashew nuts and coconut; avoid these.

Choose skimmed, rather than full-cream, *milk*, and buy or make low-fat plain yogurt. Low-fat cottage or curd *cheese* can be included in your diet (rather than hard or creamy cheese) and fortunately these fit well into a slimming routine. Do not include *cream*.

Egg yolks cannot be eaten too generously, medical opinion advises 2 to 3 only each week. The egg whites pose no problems. There are ways of using the whites on pages 136 and 137.

FOODS TO ENJOY

As explained, a low-cholesterol diet means certain changes in the normal diet, but as you will be aware it still leaves many foods to enjoy.

Maybe you are a cheese lover; it is important to restrict cheeses with a full-fat content, or even avoid them altogether. You can have cheese though, in the form of the cottage variety, given more flavour by interesting additions, as the recipe that follows illustrates.

Cottage Cheese Fondue

■ 88/Kj 371 □ 4.6 g

Metric/Imperial

25 g/1 oz polyunsaturated margarine

15 g/½ oz cornflour

300 ml/½ pint skimmed milk

salt

pepper

1 × 5 ml spoon/1 teaspoon made mustard

1 garlic clove, peeled

350 g/12 oz cottage cheese, sieved

American

2 tablespoons polyunsaturated margarine

2 tablespoons cornstarch

1¼ cups skimmed milk

salt

pepper

1 teaspoon Dijon mustard

1 garlic clove, peeled

1½ cups cottage cheese, sieved

Heat the margarine in a saucepan, stir in the cornflour (cornstarch), then gradually blend in the milk. As skimmed milk is used stir carefully and keep the heat low, so you make certain that the sauce does not burn. Add the salt, pepper, mustard and peeled, whole garlic clove. Transfer to a bowl over a fondue heater or into an attractive bowl or casserole and stand over a saucepan of hot, but not boiling, water. Remove the garlic clove. Blend in the cottage cheese and keep just warm.

To serve: As a dip with florets of cauli-flower, pieces of carrot or celery.

To freeze: A fondue will not freeze well and is better when freshly prepared.

Variation:

Add chopped fresh herbs: chives, oregano, parsley, tarragon, to the mixture, or shelled prawns (shrimp) or shrimps (but not on a low-cholesterol diet).

Special Needs

133

The dishes on these pages give plenty of variety and fit comfortably into a low-cholesterol diet.

Peppers (Capsicums) with Rice

■ 121/Kj 509 □ 10.0 g

Metric/Imperial

2 large green peppers

salt

pepper

1 × 15 ml spoon/1 tablespoon corn oil

1 large onion, chopped

1 garlic clove

2 large tomatoes, skinned and chopped

4 olives, sliced

75 g/3 oz cooked rice

TO GARNISH:
the whites of 2 hard-boiled eggs, chopped

1 × 15 ml spoon/1 tablespoon chopped parsley

American

2 large green capsicums

salt

pepper

1 tablespoon corn oil

1 large onion, chopped

1 garlic clove

2 large tomatoes, skinned and chopped

4 olives, sliced

generous $\frac{1}{2}$ cup cooked rice

TO GARNISH:
the whites of 2 hard-cooked eggs, chopped

1 tablespoon chopped parsley

❧ Cut the peppers (capsicums) into halves. Take out the centre cores and discard the seeds. Put the peppers (capsicums) into boiling water with salt and pepper to taste. Cook for 5 minutes, drain. Heat the oil, fry the onion, garlic, tomatoes, olives and when soft, mix with the rice and salt and pepper. Spoon into the 4 pepper halves. Put into the centre of a moderately hot oven (190°C/375°F, Gas Mark 5) and bake for 25 minutes.

To serve: Top with the chopped egg white and parsley.

To freeze: Egg whites will not freeze, but the peppers (capsicums) freeze for 2 months.

Left: Fish Florentine; Peppers (Capsicums) with Rice

Fish Florentine

■ 176/Kj 738 □ 5.3 g

Metric/Imperial
450 g/1 lb fresh or frozen spinach

salt

pepper

4 portions white fish, each 100 g/4 oz

25 g/1 oz polyunsaturated margarine

150 ml/¼ pint plain yogurt

1 × 15 ml spoon/1 tablespoon lemon juice

50 g/2 oz cottage cheese

TO GARNISH:
2 tomatoes, sliced

few watercress sprigs

American
1 lb fresh or frozen spinach

salt

pepper

4 portions lean fish, each ¼ lb

2 tablespoons polyunsaturated margarine

⅔ cup plain yogurt

1 tablespoon lemon juice

¼ cup cottage cheese

TO GARNISH:
2 tomatoes, sliced

few watercress sprigs

❧Cook the spinach in the minimum of water with a little salt and pepper. Strain carefully and chop or sieve to give a smooth purée. Put into an ovenproof dish and place the uncooked fish portions on top. Spread these with half the margarine and a light dusting of salt and pepper. Cover the dish with aluminium foil and bake in the centre of a moderately hot oven (190°C/375°F, Gas Mark 5) for approximately 20 minutes.

Blend the remainder of the margarine with the yogurt, lemon juice, and the cheese. This mixture could be put into the blender to give a very smooth sauce. Remove the foil, spread the sauce over the fish and spinach and return to the oven for a further 8 to 10 minutes.

To serve: Top with the tomato slices and watercress.

To freeze: Better freshly made, but an excellent method of using both frozen spinach and frozen fish, after defrosting completely.

Variations:

1: Substitute orange juice for the lemon juice and add a little grated orange rind.
2: Add herbs such as dill, parsley or fennel to the yogurt mixture.

Cheese Pudding

■ 176/Kj 738 □ 5.3 g

Metric/Imperial
300 ml/½ pint skimmed milk

50 g/2 oz fresh breadcrumbs

salt

pepper

25 g/1 oz polyunsaturated margarine

350 g/12 oz cottage cheese, sieved

1 × 15 ml spoon/1 tablespoon grated onion or chopped chives

1 × 15 ml spoon/1 tablespoon chopped parsley

2 egg whites

American
1¼ cups skimmed milk

1 cup fresh breadcrumbs

salt

pepper

2 tablespoons polyunsaturated margarine

1½ cups cottage cheese, sieved

1 tablespoon grated onion or chopped chives

1 tablespoon chopped parsley

2 egg whites

❧Warm the milk in a saucepan, remove from the heat and add the breadcrumbs, salt, pepper and margarine. Allow to stand for 15 minutes to soften the breadcrumbs. Stir in the cheese, the herbs and lastly fold in the egg whites, which should be stiffly whisked.

Spoon into a pie dish, brushed with a little margarine or corn oil and bake in the centre of a moderately hot oven (200°C/400°F, Gas Mark 6) for approximately 25 minutes until well risen and golden coloured.

Lower the heat slightly after 15 minutes if the pudding seems to be darkening too much.

To serve: As soon as cooked.
To freeze: Unsuitable for freezing.
Variations:

1: Add a little finely chopped lean ham and blend a little mustard powder with the milk.
2: Use half the amount of cheese and add about 100 g/4 oz/¼ lb flaked cooked white (lean) fish.
3: Use tomato juice in place of milk.

Cheese Pudding

Special Needs

COOKING WITHOUT EGGS

Mix pancake and fritter batters with milk only or better still use, as the Dutch do, beer for the batter (omit the egg in both cases). If you are experienced in using yeast in cooking, use the yeast pancake batter. Mix stuffings with stock, tomato juice or skimmed milk instead of using eggs. When coating fish, or other food, such as rissoles, etc. coat with a layer of seasoned flour, then with skimmed milk or egg white and breadcrumbs. For deep frying use a batter, as suggested above. Breakfast-time can be a problem, particularly if you have to give up eggs, after eating them for some time. Substitute fish of all kinds, grilled (broiled) white (lean) fish makes an excellent breakfast dish, and grilled (broiled) lean bacon with tomatoes, mushrooms and apple rings.

Yeast Pancakes

■ 175/Kj734 □ 26.0 g

Metric/Imperial

1.5 × 5 ml spoons/1½ teaspoons dried yeast or 7 g/¼ oz fresh yeast
1 × 5 ml spoon/1 teaspoon sugar
600 ml/1 pint skimmed milk, warmed
225 g/8 oz strong or plain flour
pinch salt
25 g/1 oz polyunsaturated margarine, melted
FOR FRYING: corn oil

American

1½ teaspoons dried yeast or ¼ cake of compressed yeast
1 teaspoon sugar
2½ cups skimmed milk, warmed
2 cups strong or all-purpose flour
pinch salt
2 tablespoons polyunsaturated margarine, melted
FOR FRYING: corn oil

🐾 If using dried yeast dissolve the sugar in the warm milk, sprinkle the yeast on top, leave for 10 minutes in a warm place until frothy then proceed as if using fresh yeast. With fresh yeast, cream with the sugar and then add the warm milk.

Sieve the flour and salt into a warm mixing bowl, add the yeast liquid, the melted margarine and whisk briskly.

Put a cloth or sheet of polythene (styrofoam) over the bowl; leave in a warm, but not too hot, place, until the surface is covered with bubbles. Whisk again. The mixture is then ready to cook.

Heat just enough corn oil in a pancake pan or frying pan (skillet) to give a greasy layer. Pour in just sufficient batter to give a thin layer. Cook steadily until golden on the bottom side, then toss or turn and cook on the second side.

As each pancake is cooked put onto a large plate over a saucepan of hot water. **To serve:** These pancakes can be filled with cooked fruit, sweetened with a sugar substitute or with raw fruit, or just served with lemon or orange juice. They are equally good filled with a vegetable, fruit and cheese mixture (a pleasant combination of sweet and savoury ingredients) or with meat or fish. The figures given only cover the pancakes and 25 g/1 oz/2 tablespoons corn oil.

To freeze: These freeze well; separate each pancake with a square of waxed (wax) paper, then put into a polythene (styrofoam) container or wrap in aluminium (aluminum) foil. This enables you to peel off the required number of pancakes and reheat them.

To use Egg Whites: The two recipes that follow are an indication of the way in which egg whites can be used, without the yolks, to coat a mixture before frying, this is a recipe for a time when you can relax your diet slightly, or in a dessert.

Turkey Cutlets

■ 463/Kj 1944 □ 25.0 g

Metric/Imperial

450 g/1 lb cooked turkey (light and dark meat)

2 medium onions, chopped

50 g/2 oz polyunsaturated margarine

15 g/½ oz cornflour

150 ml/¼ pint turkey stock

50 g/2 oz fresh breadcrumbs

½ teaspoon chopped lemon thyme or pinch dried thyme

2 × 15 ml spoons/2 tablespoons plain yogurt

salt

pepper

TO COAT:
1 egg white

50 g/2 oz crisp breadcrumbs (raspings)

TO FRY:
25 g/1 oz corn oil

Left : Yeast Pancakes

American

1 lb cooked turkey (light and dark meat)

2 medium onions, chopped

¼ cup polyunsaturated margarine

2 tablespoons cornstarch

1¼ cups turkey stock

1 cup fresh breadcrumbs

½ teaspoon chopped lemon thyme or pinch dried thyme

2 tablespoons plain yogurt

salt

pepper

TO COAT:
1 egg white

½ cup crisp breadcrumbs

TO FRY:
2 tablespoons corn oil

❧ Mince (grind) all the turkey meat, or mince (grind) the dark meat and dice the breast meat finely to give a variation in texture. Fry the onions in the hot margarine for 3 minutes, stir in the cornflour (cornstarch) and blend well. Add the stock, bring to the boil, stir over a moderate heat until a thick sauce. Add the breadcrumbs, thyme, yogurt, turkey meat, with salt and pepper to taste. Allow the mixture to become quite cold and firm. Form into 8 cutlet shapes. Brush with the lightly beaten egg white and coat in crisp breadcrumbs. Heat the oil and fry the cutlets on both sides until golden brown. Drain on kitchen paper.
To serve: Hot or cold with tomato sauce, see page 81.
To freeze: Open-freeze after cooking, then wrap. Use within 3 months.
Variations:
1: Flavour the mixture with a little curry

Turkey Cutlets
Below left : Rice and Apple Mousse

powder or grated lemon rind.
2: Use tomato juice in place of stock and flavour with tomato purée (paste).
3: Crisp the cutlets on a greased and heated baking sheet (cookie sheet) in a moderate oven for about 15 minutes.

Rice and Apple Mousse

■ 79/Kj 331 □ 15.3 g

Metric/Imperial

40 g/1½ oz round grain rice

300 ml/½ pint skimmed milk

sugar substitute

300 ml/½ pint *thick* apple purée

2 egg whites

American

2 tablespoons short grain rice

1¼ cups skimmed milk

sugar substitute

1¼ cups *thick* apple purée

2 egg whites

❧ Put the rice, milk and sugar substitute into a bowl over hot water or in the top of a double saucepan. This prevents the possibility of the milk burning. When soft add the apple purée and sugar substitute to taste. Allow to cool. Beat the egg whites until very stiff, fold into the rice and apple mixture. Chill.
To freeze: This freezes moderately well. The rice tends to lose its texture. Keep for only 3 to 4 weeks.
Variation:
Use other fruit purées in exactly the same way. Plums, greengages, apricots are particularly good.

Special Needs

To Serve Meat: It is important to avoid animal fats and this beef mould gives one way of serving leftover meat in an unusual way that fits into the diet.

Beef Mould

■ 250/Kj 1052 □ 4.6 g

Metric/Imperial

350 g/12 oz cooked lean beef, minced

1 × 15 ml spoon/½ oz powder gelatine

450 ml/¾ pint tomato juice

salt

pepper

1 × 5 ml spoon/1 teaspoon Worcestershire sauce

TO GARNISH:
lettuce and radishes

American

¾ lb cooked lean beef, ground

2 envelopes powder gelatin

scant 2 cups tomato juice

salt

pepper

1 teaspoon Worcestershire sauce

TO GARNISH:
lettuce and radishes

❧Put the minced (ground) beef into a bowl or mould. Soften the gelatine in a little cold tomato juice, heat the rest of the juice, pour over the gelatine mixture and stir until dissolved. Pour over the beef while hot, this softens the meat. Stir in the rest of the ingredients, except the garnish. Allow to set.

To serve: Put the lettuce and radishes onto a serving dish and invert the mould onto this.

To freeze: This freezes well for up to 2 months.

Variations:

1: Use chicken or turkey meat instead of beef.

2: Use stock in place of tomato juice.

3: Omit a little tomato juice and add the same amount of tomato purée (paste) instead.

4: Flavour the liquid with a generous amount of French (Dijon) mustard.

Making Shortcrust Pastry

Although this recipe may not be used while slimming it is useful for the days ahead when you have lost weight.

Pastry can be made with either polyunsaturated margarine or with corn oil with excellent results.

As the margarine is so soft you can make the pastry very quickly, by a One-stage method as given below.

Metric/Imperial

225 g/8 oz plain flour

pinch salt

125 g/5 oz polyunsaturated margarine

2 × 15 ml spoons/2 tablespoons water

American

2 cups all-purpose flour

pinch salt

⅝ cup polyunsaturated margarine

2 tablespoons water

❧Put all ingredients in a mixing bowl, stir briskly. Knead firmly, but gently.

It is essential to use the margarine from the refrigerator or a cool larder, for if it becomes too soft the pastry will be extremely difficult to handle.

To use: As ordinary shortcrust pastry.

Variation:

Use just 100 g/4 oz/½ cup of the margarine, and add a little extra water.

Above: Corn Oil Sponge
Left: Beef Mould

Using Corn Oil

Blend 110 ml/4 fl oz (8 tablespoons) corn oil with a scant 3 × 15 ml spoons/3 tablespoons cold water in a mixing bowl. Sieve 225 g/8 oz (2 cups) plain (all-purpose) flour with a pinch of salt into the corn oil and water. Blend well, then knead gently. Roll out between two sheets of greaseproof (wax) paper.

To use: As ordinary shortcrust pastry. Calories and carbohydrate content have not been given for the pastries as they will vary so much with the dish.

Corn Oil Sponge

■ 346/Kj 1452 □ 47.4 g

Metric/Imperial
100 ml/3½ fl oz corn oil
100 ml/3½ fl oz water
125 g/5 oz plain flour
25 g/1 oz cornflour
125 g/5 oz caster sugar
2 × 5 ml spoons/2 teaspoons baking powder
2 egg whites

American
½ cup corn oil (scant measure)
½ cup water (scant measure)
1¼ cups all-purpose flour
2 tablespoons cornstarch
⅝ cup sugar
2 teaspoons baking powder
2 egg whites

❧ Blend the oil and water together. Sift the flour, cornflour (cornstarch), sugar and baking powder into a mixing bowl. Add the oil and water and beat briskly until a smooth batter. Whisk the egg whites in a separate bowl, then fold gently and carefully into the batter. Prepare two 18 cm/7 inch tins (baking pans) and spoon in the mixture. Bake for approximately 20 minutes, or until firm to the touch, just above the centre of a moderate oven (180°C/350°F, Gas Mark 4). Cool on a wire rack.

To serve: As an ordinary sponge.

To freeze: Freeze for up to 3 months.

Variation:

A nice filling can be made by creaming 225 g/8 oz/½ lb curd cheese with the grated rind and juice of 1 lemon. Add 75 g/3 oz/½ cup chopped walnuts. Sandwich together and decorate as liked.

Special Needs

Low-fat diets

Fats of all kinds are high in calories and must be eaten very sparingly on a low-calorie diet. They do *not* add to the carbohydrate content of a dish.

It may seem difficult to change long established habits and cook with little, if any, fat. The recipes and suggestions in this section are designed to give satisfactory results without fat.

Modern developments make this easier; you can put meat, fish and vegetables in special polythene bags or aluminium foil or cook in 'non stick' saucepans and frying pans (skillets). These not only prevent food sticking but enable you to reduce fat to an absolute minimum. Brush the frying pan (skillet) with a few drops of oil or rub with enough fat to give a greasy surface; heat the pan and fry steadily.

It is essential to recognize the foods with a fat content. These are outlined on the right of this column.

HIGH-FAT FOODS

Obviously one must avoid using butter, margarine, cooking fats and oil of any kind on a low-fat diet together with the fat from meat and poultry and nuts, which contain oil.

Choose white (lean) or shell fish, although the latter group of fish must be omitted on a low-cholesterol diet.

A food that one cannot eat on a low-fat diet is a whole egg; it is the yolk which is the source of fat; although you can eat the egg white quite happily.

A low-fat diet means making good use of cereals, such as wheat and rice, and of fruit and vegetables.

Include low-fat plain yogurt, cottage cheese and skimmed milk in limited quantities, if these are permitted.

If all this sounds depressing, your loss of weight should bring you considerable encouragement. Remember one gramme of fat produces more than twice the calories of one gramme of protein or carbohydrate, so, when you reduce your fat intake drastically, you will probably lose weight without difficulty. Spoil yourself with delicious fish, low-fat meat, together with interesting vegetable dishes. You will find a good selection throughout this book and many of the recipes suggested for a low-cholesterol diet will be helpful (see pages 132–141).

Make a speciality of interesting fruit desserts, some of which follow.

Hot Fruit Soufflé

Cook enough fruit, with little if any water to produce a really thick purée, or sieve or put soft ripe fruit in a blender, without cooking.

Measure out just over 150 ml/¼ pint/⅔ cup; add sugar substitute to taste. Whip the whites of 4 eggs and fold into the fruit purée slowly and carefully to produce a light fluffy mixture. Spoon into a soufflé dish and bake for about 25 minutes in the centre of a moderately hot oven (190°C/375°F, Gas Mark 5).

To serve: As soon as cooked; although soufflés made with egg whites only, fall less than when whole eggs are used.

Note: The figures will vary according to the particular fruit used; those given are based upon raw blackcurrants.

To freeze: An excellent way of using frozen fruit purées, which have been thawed.

■ 28/Kj 116 □ 2.8 g

Above right:
Orange, Lemon and Blackcurrant
Water Ices; Hot Fruit Soufflé

Water Ices

This is a form of dessert that all the family, young and old, will enjoy. A Water Ice is simply fruit in season, sugar substitute to sweeten and a little extra flavouring, if you feel this compliments the flavour of the fruit.

The method of making is simply to sieve or purée in a blender, ripe fresh fruit, or to cook harder fruits with the minimum quantity of water, then to sieve or put in a blender to produce a smooth purée. Add sufficient sweetening to give a good taste and flavouring if required.

Pour the mixture into a freezing tray, ovenproof or flameproof dish (both are suitable for use in a freezer) and freeze *lightly*. Water Ices are spoiled if they are too solidly frozen, so it is advisable to bring them from the freezer or freezing compartment of a refrigerator a little while before the meal.

You can make large quantities of the dessert to store in the freezer; it keeps well for up to 4 months. In this case pack in small amounts and use a little gelatine (gelatin), as suggested when making a Sorbet. The recipe for Sorbets and advice on using gelatine are to be found on pages 82 and 196.

Listed below are suggestions for flavouring and serving fruits in the form of Water Ices.

Sundaes

Spoon several different kinds of ices into tall sundae glasses and serve; or you may like to freeze one kind of purée, then add a second kind and finally a third variety to the freezing container.

APPLES: Cook with a little lemon juice and colour with a few drops of green food colouring.

AVOCADOS: Sieve or put in a blender the avocado pulp with lemon juice to keep a good colour. The purée can be mixed

with either a little salt and pepper for a savoury ice or with sugar substitute for a sweet one.

BLACKBERRIES, BLUEBERRIES, RED AND BLACKCURRANTS, RASPBERRIES AND OTHER BERRY FRUITS are nicer if uncooked purée is prepared. It can be diluted with a little water, or lemon juice and water if desired.

DAMSONS, GREENGAGES AND ALL TYPES OF PLUMS can be cooked then sieved. Choose a cooking plum with plenty of flavour.

GOOSEBERRIES: Choose a sharp cooking variety rather than dessert fruit.

MELONS: Every type of melon makes a good ice. Sieve the pulp or put this into the blender and blend with a very little lemon or orange juice. If rather colourless, add a few drops of green food colouring. Watermelon is particularly good when the pulp is frozen.

ORANGES, LEMONS, GRAPEFRUIT and other citrus fruit pulp or strained fruit juice make excellent ices. For a more economical recipe simmer the peel with

a little water for several minutes, strain and blend the liquid with the pulp or juice. Instead of freezing the mixture in a container you can spoon this into hollowed-out orange or lemon cases.

■ Calories etc., depend upon the type of fruit used.

No-fat 'Cream'

If you feel the loss of cream badly and become tired of substituting yogurt, this mixture is very pleasant on fruit. Naturally the syrup does add to the calorie and carbohydrate content of the dish.

Weigh out 50 g/2 oz/3 tablespoons golden (light corn) syrup into a saucepan and warm this gently; do not allow to become too hot. Whisk 2 egg whites until very stiff, then gradually whisk in the syrup.

To serve: At once or stand for a time.

To freeze: This does not freeze.

Variation:

Use jelly or sieved jam instead of the syrup.

■ 47.5/Kj 200 □ 11.2 g

Special Needs

Over-weight children

It was once considered quite unnecessary to worry about overweight children. Parents and friends would console themselves with the fact that it was 'puppy-fat' that would disappear as the child got older; in some cases it did go when the child became a young adult, but in others the overweight child developed into an overweight adult.

Nowadays we *are* concerned if a child *is* overweight, for in many cases it has a serious effect upon the mental and physical well-being of the child.

Most overweight children find it difficult to participate in games, and physical recreation. They tire easily, can become short of breath, are slower in movement and it is quite usual for the child to withdraw from these activities and become a 'loner' so they lose much of the enjoyment of participating in various activities.

The health problems of overweight children are similar to those experienced by the overweight man and woman. The excess weight can make them more susceptible to colds and puts a strain on their heart. How then is the problem of losing weight to be tackled?

Children vary considerably in their attitude to being overweight. Some may not *appear* to mind the fact that they are fat and will make little, if any effort, at self-discipline in the way they eat and their choice of foods; other children will follow with great willingness, a pretty strict diet.

Suggestions for helping the co-operative child are given on the right and hints on helping those boys and girls who are unwilling to diet on page 144.

Remember that you must not put any child of any age on a strict diet, and help them towards losing an appreciable amount of weight *without* medical advice.

I AM WILLING TO TRY

You may well find that children are keen, in fact over anxious sometimes, to lose weight. It is very important that adults keep a sense of proportion about this matter. While appreciating that overweight children have a problem, do not make it so important that the dieting and losing weight becomes an obsession, for you may find the child continues to diet stringently even after the required weight has been established. This can lead to that very serious condition known as Anorexia Nervosa.

Discuss the kind of food the child has been eating so far. Point out the ones that may well be causing overweight, i.e. those foods high in carbohydrates (starches and sugars) plus an excess of fat. Work out how you can substitute other food. If your child is a big milk drinker, then it may well be necessary to cut down on the quantity. You will be able to substitute skimmed milk in place of full cream. If fresh skimmed milk is difficult to obtain then use the dried variety, which is perfectly adequate in cooking as well as in drinks. Use plain yogurt with fruit instead of cream.

Devise various 'treats' for the child. They may like a special kind of fruit which is too expensive for family fare. This could be their treat instead of a popular pudding. Appreciate the dishes a child likes and do not cut these out from the diet completely. Reduce the quantity and see if this is the way towards losing weight. It is important that a growing child has a diet high in protein foods and other important nutrients and it may just be their rather over large appetites that has caused the extra weight. Salads and most vegetables have a great ability to make one feel 'full of food', and do not add greatly to the carbohydrate content of the meal, so serve these as often as possible, not forgetting winter salads, see pages 146–147. Potatoes are so popular with children and an important food that it is better to reduce the quantity, rather than omit them altogether, cook them by baking rather than frying or roasting. The same rule applies to bread and pasta – reduce, rather than completely omit, for a growing child needs some form of carbohydrate and wheat is a nutritious source of this food.

Remove temptation as much as you can; tins of sweets (candies) or biscuits (cookies) should be hidden and devise ways of keeping the children particularly interested during their period of losing weight.

Right: Foods which over-weight children should avoid. Far right: Foods which over-weight children should be encouraged to eat

Special Needs

I DON'T WANT TO DIET!!

Dieting is a challenge to most of us and not one that is particularly enjoyable. In many cases it means going without many of the foods we enjoy and have always eaten. If adults find this difficult, then one must appreciate the unwillingness of many children to forgo most of those pleasant foods that probably made them fat. It is, therefore, a job for parents to work out just how to tackle the problem. You may find that after a few weeks of careful meal planning the child realises he or she *is* losing weight and will then begin to take an interest in the improved appearance, and change from an un-co-operative to a willing partner in the slimming campaign.

Work out the most 'offending' foods in the diet:
Is he in the habit of eating many sweet-meats (candies), ice cream, lollies?

If this is the case then replace these with fruit. This is a source of natural sugar, but is much lower in calories and carbohydrate than sweetmeats (candies).

Iced lollies can be made with fresh fruits and a recipe is on page 153.

What kind of breakfast does he eat?

Perhaps he eats little food at breakfast time; the chances are that if this is the case he will eat fattening snacks mid-morning. Get him up about 10 minutes earlier in the morning so he has time to have a more satisfactory breakfast. He could have an egg, cooked in one of a variety of ways, or grilled (broiled) bacon, sausages (although most sausages do have a carbohydrate content), cooked fish, see page 34. If, as a family, you do not eat breakfast, it would be a help to your child if you all changed your eating habits and ate the same food at this time.

If he would rather have a cereal buy the lower calorie variety and use only a little sugar on top. You could add fruit as well as milk.

Avoid too much toast, butter and marmalade.

Be sparing with sugar in drinks (as well as cooking) and you may like to use skimmed milk instead of the full cream

variety; the former is an excellent source of protein, but much lower in calories. Does he generally take a snack to school? Halve the amount or substitute fresh fruit.

Midday meals at school may present problems, as you, the parent, will not be there. Many schools offer salads as an alternative to cooked meals. Try and persuade him to have this and avoid too many chips (French fries) or other fried foods. Suggest he takes extra fresh fruit to eat instead of a pudding. If he takes a packed lunch to school or comes home, then you can plan a meal in accordance with the recipes in this chapter and throughout the book.

Tea and/or supper or an evening dinner, depending upon the age of the child, will fit in with family meals, and dishes low in carbohydrate content should be planned.

Many children are nibblers and want odd snacks between meals, plus soft drinks. As you will see from the tables, biscuits (cookies), cakes, sweetmeats (candies) and sweetened fruit cordials and squashes are extraordinarily high in both calories and carbohydrate content.

Replace the biscuits (cookies), cake or chocolate with crisp celery, carrot or fruit and the cordial or squash with

homemade fruit drinks and fruit juice, recipes are in this section. Make fruit sorbets and fruit lollies for treats and take pleasure in making the slimming dishes look particularly interesting and appetizing.

Do not nag your child about the kind of foods he *should* eat, present the dishes, and make them appear as much like the usual fare as possible.

YOUNG CHILDREN

This book does not set out to deal with feeding young children, but it should be remembered that incorrect feeding often begins with the baby or toddler. Over-sweetened baby foods are given, so that the child develops a liking only for sweet tastes and avoids savoury dishes. Prevention is always preferable to a cure so start on wise feeding from the earliest stage. This means avoiding too much sugar; giving a wide and wise selection of main dishes, although new tastes and textures must be introduced gradually.

As the baby grows into a toddler avoid giving him sweetmeats (candies), sweet biscuits (cookies) or cakes, especially between meals. Most young children have relatively small appetites which are easily spoiled by sweet between-meal nibbles.

Milk Shakes

Milk is an important food for growing children, although modern medical opinion inclines to the view that if a child eats plenty of protein foods there is no need to insist on a high amount of milk or milky foods.

One of the enjoyable ways to have milk is in a hot or cold milk shake. Avoid the rather highly sweetened commercial fruit-flavoured syrups sold to add to milk, but use fresh fruits instead. The lightest milk shakes are made in a blender.

To make two drinks allow just over 300 ml/½ pint/1¼ cups milk (choose skimmed milk for lower calories), the selected fruit, this could be raspberries, strawberries, blackcurrants, an orange or tangerine, plus a little crushed ice for a cold milk shake. Prepare the fruit, allow 2–3 × 15 ml spoons/2–3 tablespoons soft fruit, but the figures given include a medium orange.

If using this fruit cut away the peel and pith, then cut the orange into segments, discarding pips (seeds) and skin.

Put into the blender with the crushed ice and milk. Switch on until the fruit is blended with the milk and you have a light fluffy drink.

To serve: Pour into tall glasses.

Variations:

1: Omit the ice, use a little more milk and heat this. Serve as soon as the drink is prepared, for the fruit and hot milk mixture could separate with standing.

2: Savoury milk shake. Use beef or yeast extract instead of fruit.

■ 68/Kj286 ☐ 16.8 g

Above: Milk Shakes. Left: A slimming lunch for a child at school could consist of a grilled (broiled) chicken drumstick, mixed salad and an apple. Far left: Fruit-flavoured lollies

Special Needs

CHILDREN'S SALADS

Children differ considerably in the kind of flavours they enjoy. Some children have very adult tastes and prefer a subtle blending of savoury ingredients, while other children prefer bland flavours.

Fortunately one can combine such a variety of ingredients in a salad so it is possible to cater for all tastes.

On the whole children find a salad easier to eat if all the ingredients are chopped or diced and mixed together rather than having slices of meat or cheese plus a salad.

The Cottage Cheese Dressing adds flavour and protein to green or mixed salads.

Cottage Cheese Dressing

■ 73/Kj 305 □ 4.8 g

Metric/Imperial

1 × 3.75 ml spoon/¾ teaspoon mustard powder

150 ml/¼ pint white wine vinegar

1 × 2.5 ml spoon/½ teaspoon salt

pinch paprika

pinch black pepper

150 ml/¼ pint unsweetened evaporated milk

50 g/2 oz cottage or cream cheese or grated cheese

American

¾ teaspoon mustard powder

⅔ cup white wine vinegar

½ teaspoon salt

pinch paprika

pinch black pepper

⅔ cup unsweetened evaporated milk

¼ cup cottage or cream cheese or grated cheese.

❧Blend the mustard with the vinegar, salt and peppers. Add the evaporated milk. Beat the cheese into the mixture and continue beating until smooth. Store in a screw-top jar in a refrigerator. Shake before using.

Beef and Horseradish Salad; Toadstool Salad; Nutty Banana and Cheese Salad

To serve: With hot or cold vegetables or salads.

To freeze: Do not freeze.

Beef and Horseradish Salad

■ 423/Kj 1776 □ 5.5 g

Metric/Imperial

450 g/1 lb cooked lean beef

2 × 15 ml spoons/2 tablespoons pickled onions, chopped

4 × 15 ml spoons/4 tablespoons pickled red cabbage

1 red pepper, de-seeded and diced

salt

pepper

50 g/2 oz raw mushrooms, sliced

300 ml/½ pint plain yogurt

2 × 15 ml spoons/2 tablespoons horseradish cream

1–2 × 5 ml spoons/1–2 teaspoons made mustard

lettuce

TO GARNISH:
pickled gherkins

American

1 lb cooked lean beef

2 tablespoons pickled onions, chopped

4 tablespoons pickled red cabbage

1 red capsicum, de-seeded and diced

salt

pepper

2 oz raw mushrooms, sliced

1¼ cups plain yogurt

2 tablespoons horseradish cream

1–2 teaspoons Dijon mustard

lettuce

TO GARNISH:
small sweet dill pickles

❧Cut the meat into neat strips. Mix with all the other ingredients and allow to stand for about 1 hour.

To serve: On a bed of lettuce; garnish with gherkin 'fans'.

To freeze: This salad should not be frozen.

Variations:

1: Add a few chopped nuts.

2: Add cooked chopped prunes to the sauce and omit the pickled cabbage.

Nutty Banana and Cheese Salad

■ 369/Kj 1550 □19.1 g

Metric/Imperial

225 g/8 oz cream cheese

2 × 5 ml spoons/2 teaspoons honey

1 × 15 ml spoon/1 tablespoon double cream

4 bananas, peeled

150 ml/¼ pint plain yogurt

50 g/2 oz walnuts, finely chopped

TO GARNISH:

lettuce

50 g/2 oz grapes or seasonal fruit

American

1 cup cream cheese

2 teaspoons honey

1 tablespoon heavy cream

4 bananas, peeled

⅔ cup plain yogurt

½ cup finely chopped walnuts

TO GARNISH:

lettuce

2 oz grapes or seasonal fruit

♣ Mash the cream cheese with the honey and cream. Cut the bananas into 1-cm/½-inch pieces and sandwich together with the cheese mixture. Dip in the yogurt then roll in the finely chopped walnuts. Arrange on a bed of lettuce. Garnish with grapes or with seasonal fruit.

To serve: Top the banana mixture with any remaining yogurt and walnuts.

To freeze: Not suitable for freezing.

Variation:

Apricot and Cheese Salad: This is a delicious variation when fresh apricots are in season. Plunge the apricots into boiling water for 10 seconds, then into iced water. Ease the skins off. Halve and stone (pit), then sandwich together with the cream cheese mixture. Finish and serve as above.

Other fruits and nuts can be used. Peaches, apples or pears are all good substitutes. Different nuts may be used for the walnuts.

Toadstool Salad

■ 114/Kj 477 □2.7 g

Metric/Imperial

4 hard-boiled eggs

2 large tomatoes

lettuce

¼ cucumber, peeled and sliced

2 × 15 ml spoons/2 tablespoons low-calorie mayonnaise

American

4 hard-boiled eggs

2 large tomatoes

lettuce

¼ cucumber, peeled and sliced

2 tablespoons low-calorie mayonnaise

♣ Shell the eggs and cut a slice from each end, so they stand firmly. Cut the tomatoes into halves across the centre. Arrange a bed of shredded lettuce and sliced cucumber. Top with the slices removed from the eggs. Place the eggs on the green salad. Balance the halved tomatoes on these.

To serve: Put small spots of the salad dressing on the tomatoes to look like the marks on a toadstool. Spoon the rest of the dressing on the lettuce.

To freeze: Not suitable for freezing.

Special Needs

INTERESTING SAVOURY DISHES

There are many savoury dishes throughout this book which would be appealing to children for high tea or supper, especially in the section beginning on page 146.

Most children enjoy Fish Cakes and Hamburgers. You will find the first recipe on the right and Hamburgers on page 45. The former recipe traditionally uses an equal amount of mashed potato and fish, but the recipe that follows has reduced the potato content. This means it is rather more fragile to handle than the usual recipe; this is why baking, rather than frying, is a good method of cooking. Also the dish is not so high in calories as it is when fried.

Fish Cakes

Fish Cakes

■ 163/Kj686 □ 13.7 g

Metric/Imperial

450 g/1 lb white fish (weight without skin and bone)

salt

pepper

175 g/6 oz boiled potatoes

1 egg

1 × 15 ml spoons/1 tablespoon chopped parsley (optional)

25 g/1 oz crisp breadcrumbs (raspings)

American

1 lb lean fish (weight without skin and bone)

salt

pepper

6 oz boiled potatoes

1 egg

1 tablespoon chopped parsley (optional)

¼ cup crisp breadcrumbs

❧ Put the fish on a greased plate, sprinkle with a little salt and pepper. Cover the plate with greased foil and steam over a saucepan of gently boiling water until just tender. By cooking in this way you keep the fish firm and not over moist. Lift the fish from the plate, break into small flakes and blend with the potato. Mash together until smooth. Separate the egg, add the yolk to the fish mixture together with the parsley, if used, and a little more salt and pepper. Allow to cool, then form the mixture into 8 round cakes. Brush each with the egg white and coat with the breadcrumbs; the amount allowed gives only a thin coating but is adequate for baking. Put a greased baking tray into the oven to get really hot. This prevents the mixture sticking to the tin. Remove and place the fish cakes on the hot tray. Bake and crisp towards the top of a moderately hot oven (190°C/375°F, Gas Mark 5) for approximately 15 minutes.

To serve: Hot with vegetables or a salad.

Variation:

You can use leftover mashed potato, but if this has been creamed with milk and butter you add to the calorie and carbohydrate content of the dish.

Herb Cocottes

■ 130/Kj 537 □ 4.3 g

Metric/Imperial

225 g/8 oz cottage cheese, sieved

3 hard-boiled eggs, chopped

2–3 spring onions, chopped

1 × 15 ml spoon/1 tablespoon chopped parsley

2 × 5 ml spoons/2 teaspoons chopped chives

a few drops Tabasco sauce

little milk

salt

pepper

TO GARNISH:

2 medium tomatoes, skinned and chopped

1 lemon, sliced

American

½ lb cottage cheese, sieved

3 hard-boiled eggs, chopped

2–3 scallions, chopped

1 tablespoon chopped parsley

2 teaspoons chopped chives

a few drops Tabasco sauce

little milk

salt

pepper

Herb Cocottes

TO GARNISH:

2 medium tomatoes, skinned and chopped

1 lemon, sliced

❧ Mix all the ingredients (except garnish) together, adding enough milk to make a consistency resembling whipped cream. Spoon into small individual dishes. Mix the chopped tomatoes with a little salt and pepper. Spoon into the centre of the cheese and egg mixture. Garnish with the lemon slices.

To serve: With a little crisp toast (this is not included in the calories etc.).

To freeze: Unsuitable for freezing.

Variation:

This makes an excellent party dip. Put the mixture into a bowl and place this on a tray or dish. Arrange small florets of raw cauliflower, fingers of carrot and cucumber, green pepper (capsicum) strips and lengths of celery around.

THE VALUE OF CHEESE

Cheese is one of the important foods for children, for it is an excellent source of protein and calcium. Cottage or curd cheese are very much lower in calories than any other varieties as you will see in the tables on pages 112 to 120.

Children generally prefer a hard cheese and most Dutch cheeses are a good choice for they are mild in flavour and low in fat, compared with many other cheeses, and have, therefore, a lower calorie content than most other cheeses. They can be used in salads or for cooking.

Sometimes children do not appear to enjoy cheese. You may well find, in this case, that they will eat a processed or a cream cheese. The latter is high in calories but may be a good introduction to this important food. As the child appears to like this flavour more you can create your own kind of cream cheese by blending grated hard cheese with a little milk or plain yogurt.

Special Needs

A SENSIBLE APPROACH TO CALORIES

It would be almost impossible to ask children to count calories and to keep an account of these when they are at school during the day. That is why it is, on the whole, better to cut down on the carbohydrate content of their dishes so their whole diet is less fattening and probably more health giving.

You may, however, get older children somewhat interested in the effect of reducing certain foods with high calorie and carbohydrate content; for example if one spoonful of sugar was left out of each drink during a day you may well save the total of 25 g/1 oz/2 firmly packed tablespoons, i.e. 112 calories and 29.7 g of carbohydrate.

Stuffed Potatoes

If a potato is baked in its 'jacket' it can be used as a basis for interesting savoury dishes. Potatoes cooked in their skins have an advantage over the other methods of cooking this vegetable; there is no wastage in preparation; you keep in all the flavour of the vegetable and if you eat the skin you are adding important fibre to your diet and the potato seems more satisfying. Two easy supper dishes, based on jacket potatoes, follow. In each case the term 'medium' potato means one weighing 225 g/8 oz/½ lb and the calories and carbohydrate are based on this amount.

Above: Stuffed Tomatoes
Below from left: Bird in the Nest;
Beans au Gratin; Baked Soufflé
Potatoes

Bird in the Nest

■ 276/Kj 1158 □ 45.3 g

Metric/Imperial

4 medium potatoes

salt

pepper

2 × 15 ml spoons/2 tablespoons milk

4 eggs

American

4 medium potatoes

salt

pepper

2 tablespoons milk

4 eggs

❧ Prepare and bake the potatoes as the recipe that follows. Cut a slice from the top of each potato, scoop out the pulp and mash until soft adding a little salt, pepper and milk. Return the pulp back to the potato cases to make a nest shape; leave a good space in the centre of each potato for an egg. Put into an ovenproof dish. Break an egg carefully into the space in each potato, return to a moderately hot oven (200°C/400°F, Gas Mark 6) and bake for about 10 minutes until the egg is set.

To serve: As soon as the egg is set.

To freeze: Not suitable for freezing.

Variations:

1: Add a little grated cheese to the mashed potato.

2: Put a little chopped ham or chicken in the potato 'nest' before adding the egg.

Baked Soufflé Potatoes

■ 258/Kj 1082 □ 46.4 g

Metric/Imperial

4 medium potatoes

2 eggs

2 × 15 ml spoons/2 tablespoons single cream

salt

pepper

TO GARNISH:
2 tomatoes, sliced

American

4 medium potatoes

2 eggs

2 tablespoons light cream

salt

pepper

TO GARNISH:
2 tomatoes, sliced

❧ Wash the potatoes, prick and bake for 1 hour in a moderate oven (180°C/350°F, Gas Mark 4). Cut a slice from the top of each potato, scoop out the pulp and mash until soft. Separate the eggs. Add the egg yolks and cream to the potato mixture, with salt and pepper to taste. Whisk the egg whites and gently fold into the mixture. Pile back into the potato cases and cook for 15 minutes in a moderately hot oven (190°C/375°F, Gas Mark 5) until just pale golden brown.

To serve: As soon as cooked, garnished with tomato.

To freeze: Not suitable for freezing.

Variation:

Add 50 g/2 oz/½ cup grated cheese or a little diced lean ham to the mashed potato before adding the eggs.

Stuffed Tomatoes

■ 70/Kj 293 □ 3.8 g

Metric/Imperial

5 large tomatoes

50 g/2 oz Edam cheese, grated

125 g/5 oz prawns

little lettuce

small portion of cucumber, diced

1 × 15 ml spoon/1 tablespoon chopped chives

salt

pepper

American

5 large tomatoes

½ cup Edam cheese, grated

5 oz shrimp

little lettuce

small portion of cucumber, diced

1 tablespoon chopped chives

salt

pepper

❧ Wipe the tomatoes and cut a slice from the top of each. Scoop out the centre pulp with a spoon, chop it finely and put into a bowl. Add some of the cheese.

Peel all the prawns (shrimp), except five, chop and blend with the tomato pulp, together with a little lettuce, which should be shredded, save some leaves whole and place these on the serving dish.

Add the cucumber, chives and a little salt and pepper to the tomato pulp. Spoon into the tomato cases. Top with the remaining cheese and the unpeeled prawns (shrimp) and stand on the lettuce.

To serve: When freshly prepared.

To freeze: Unsuitable for freezing, although completely thawed prawns (shrimp) could be used.

Variation:

A medium melon can be substituted for the tomatoes. Cut in half and scoop out the seeds (pits). Dice the flesh and continue as above. Cut the melon shells in half to serve.

Beans au Gratin

■ 235/Kj 989 □ 22.9 g

Metric/Imperial

3 tomatoes, skinned and chopped

salt

pepper

1 × 220 g/7¾ oz can baked haricot beans in tomato sauce

50 g/2 oz Cheddar cheese, grated

American

3 tomatoes, skinned and chopped

salt

pepper

1 × 7¾ oz can baked navy beans in tomato sauce

½ cup Cheddar cheese, grated

❧ Blend the chopped tomatoes with a little salt and pepper. Blend the beans with half the cheese, put into an ovenproof dish. Top with the tomato mixture and the remainder of the cheese. Bake in the centre of a moderately hot oven (190°C/375°F, Gas Mark 5) for 25 to 30 minutes.

To serve: Hot with a green salad.

To freeze: Better freshly cooked.

Note: Baked (navy) beans are a favourite with most children and a good source of protein although relatively high in calories and carbohydrate content. This method of serving avoids too much bread and adds extra protein in the form of cheese.

Variation:

Use other kinds of cheese.

Special Needs

151

USING SOYA FOR CHILDREN

Many children are used to soya products often known as Textured Vegetable Protein (T.V.P.) as they have dishes based on this excellent food at school.

There are various ways of buying T.V.P.; it can be as an extender to meat, the dehydrated product is blended with liquid and added to raw minced (ground) beef and used in a variety of ways.

Other forms of T.V.P. are sold in cans as ready-to-use foods. They are available as a mince product, or diced, to resemble stewed steak. The following recipe is based on canned soya mince. This can be served in a variety of ways as the suggestions that follow.

Soya products are quite low in calories but most people find them more palatable when combined with other savoury ingredients which naturally add to both the calorie and carbohydrate content.

Savoury Mince

■ 168/Kj 706 ☐ 15.7 g

Metric/Imperial

1 medium onion, chopped

50 g/2 oz mushrooms, sliced

1 × 226 g/8 oz can plum tomatoes

1 × 15 ml spoon/1 tablespoon tomato purée

1 × 425 g/15 oz can soya mince

salt

pepper

1 × 15 ml spoon/1 tablespoon chopped parsley

American

1 medium onion, chopped

½ cup mushrooms, sliced

1 × 8 oz can plum tomatoes

1 tablespoon tomato paste

1 × 15 oz can soya mince

salt

pepper

1 tablespoon chopped parsley

❧Put the onion, mushrooms, canned tomatoes, with the liquid from the can, and tomato purée (paste) into a saucepan. Heat gently until the onion is tender, then add the rest of the ingredients and heat thoroughly.

To serve: With various vegetables or as one of the variations below.

To freeze: This will freeze well for up to 3 months.

Variations:

1: With spaghetti: Serve with cooked spaghetti; remember 25 g/1 oz dry spaghetti yields a much higher amount when cooked and would *add* 104 calories; Kj 437 and a carbohydrate content of 23.9 g.

2: Shepherd's Pie: Put the mixture into an ovenproof dish, top with 225 g/8 oz/1 cup mashed potatoes, brown and crisp in the oven. The potatoes *add* 68 calories; Kj 286 and a carbohydrate content of 10.2 g per portion.

3: Golden Shepherd's Pie: Put the mixture into an ovenproof dish. Cover with foil and heat thoroughly. Beat 2 eggs with a pinch of salt and shake of pepper, pour over the savoury mince and return to the oven for 10 to 15 minutes to set the egg topping. This *adds* 40 calories; Kj 168 per portion but no extra carbohydrate content.

4: Slimmers' Moussaka: Add 225 g/8 oz sliced courgettes (½ lb sliced zucchini) to the tomato mixture and simmer until tender, then add the soya mince. Put into an ovenproof dish, heat thoroughly. Top with 150 ml/¼ pint/⅔ cup plain yogurt and 25 g/1 oz/¼ cup Cheddar cheese, grated, and heat for a few minutes only. This variation *adds* 52 calories; Kj 218 and 2.8 g of carbohydrate to each portion.

Below: Savoury Mince with spaghetti; different types of Textured Vegetable Protein (dehydrated and reconstituted)

Make a Batter

Most children enjoy a crisp batter and this is a useful dish, which is not too high in calories or carbohydrate content and yet provides the child with protein in the form of flour, milk and egg.

Blend 100 g/4 oz plain flour (1 cup all-purpose flour) with a pinch of salt, an egg and 300 ml/½ pint/1¼ cups skimmed milk. Heat 15 g/½ oz/1 tablespoon fat (shortening) in an ovenproof dish or tin and bake for approximately 35 minutes towards the top of a hot oven (220°C/425°F, Gas Mark 7), reduce the heat slightly after 15 minutes.

To serve: As soon as cooked, with meat or as the variations below.

To freeze: You can freeze containers of uncooked batter. Use within a month.

Variations:

1: Toad in the Hole: Heat 225 g/8 oz to 450 g/1 lb sausages in the fat for 10 minutes. Add the batter and continue cooking.

2: Norfolk Pudding: Heat 225 g/8 oz sliced apples plus a tablespoon black treacle (molasses) or sugar in the fat. Add the batter and cook as the basic recipe.

■ 173/Kj 725 ☐ 25.5 g

INTERESTING EXTRAS

As a diet for a child is generally a long-term policy, include as many interesting extras as you can.

Above: Toad in the Hole; Norfolk Pudding. Right: Plain yogurt with fresh fruit

Most children enjoy plain *yogurt* which makes an excellent dessert with fresh fruit or fruit cooked with the minimum of sugar, honey or treacle (molasses). When buying plain yogurt look out for low-fat varieties and add fresh fruit to natural (plain) yogurt, rather than buying the rather sweet varieties available. There are many good plain yogurt makers on the market and it may well be worthwhile investing in one of these as home made yogurt is delicious.

Water ices are refreshing and can be varied throughout the year.

Iced lollies could not be more simple to make. You need to buy special 'Lolly Moulds'. Prepare a thin fruit purée or dilute fresh orange or lemon juice. Add sugar substitute to sweeten. Spoon the mixture into the lolly moulds and allow to set. Calories and carbohydrate content will vary but will be quite low.

Fresh fruit drinks and cordials save using high calorie types.

Special Needs

The Elderly

It is not easy to generalize on the needs of the elderly, for they vary so much in their way of life and their general health, particularly in the kinds of foods they find they can digest and also the foods that they can buy on what may be a restricted income.

One point, however, must be stressed: elderly people should not allow themselves to become overweight, any more than people in any other age group. If they are too heavy, they increase the possibility of heart trouble and may find it more difficult to take exercise and follow a normal routine.

What makes the recipes in this section different from other parts of the book? The first recipes are devised for two people, as in many cases the household will be a small one. The dishes on pages 158 to 159 are for 4 people and are the kind of simple, but unusual, food suitable for entertaining friends or family for a meal, or to provide two meals.

None of the recipes entails a great deal of preparation, for often as one becomes older the physical ability to beat, whisk or chop vigorously becomes impaired.

All the dishes are easy to digest; this does not mean they are too bland. Often there is the misconception that older people only require and enjoy food with little flavour. Many of the foods contain quite an amount of roughage, foods with natural fibre, for this is just as important for the older age group as for any other.

Older people should check that they have sufficient foods that give a good intake of protein and calcium and also include dishes high in vitamin C, i.e. fresh fruits, particularly oranges, grapefruit and blackcurrants, and lightly cooked or raw green vegetables; for this vitamin helps to build up resistance to infection.

None of the dishes, even those planned for a special occasion, are too expensive, and some are based on ready-cooked foods, which will save time and effort.

The suggestions made for low-cholesterol foods and dishes would also be of interest to the elderly, for wise precautions are always better than trying to effect a cure. These are to be found on pages 130 to 139.

If anyone enjoys milky foods and is trying to maintain a good weight, or even lose weight, they should choose skimmed rather than full-cream milk. It is a good idea to keep a can of the dried milk powder in the house, in case of bad weather and the inability to go shopping. This milk can be reconstituted with water and used in place of liquid milk. All recipes in this book using milk are based upon skimmed milk powder, unless stated to the contrary.

When using canned soups 1 × 15 ml spoon/1 tablespoon dried milk powder stirred into the hot, *but not boiling*, mixture adds extra protein in a very pleasant form.

A BOWL OF SOUP

You may well find that soup, followed by cheese or fruit, is enough for one of the meals in a day. You must, however, make quite sure that the soup contains a good balance of nutrients, while not adding too much to the calorie and carbohydrate content of the whole day's meals.

Golden Chicken Chowder; selection of green vegetables; Savoury Bread and Milk

154

Golden Chicken Chowder

■ 164/Kj687 □ 4.5 g

Metric/Imperial

1 chicken joint, giving about 100 g/4 oz edible flesh

600 ml/1 pint canned consommé or water with 1 chicken stock cube

2 medium carrots, grated

15 g/½ oz dried milk powder (optional)

salt

pepper

American

1 chicken joint, giving about ¼ lb edible flesh

2½ cups canned consommé or water with 2 chicken bouillon cubes

2 medium carrots, grated

⅙ cup dried milk solids

salt

pepper

❧If you have purchased a frozen chicken joint allow this to thaw before using. Put the chicken joint and consommé, or water and stock cube(s), into a saucepan. Cover the saucepan and simmer steadily for about 20 minutes or until the chicken joint is tender; lift this out of the pan onto a plate and cut the meat away from the bone, put it back into the liquid with the grated carrots and simmer for about 5 minutes. The carrots should still keep their firm texture. Take the saucepan from the heat and make sure the soup is no longer boiling; whisk in the milk powder, salt and pepper and stir until blended.

To serve: As a hot soup.

To freeze: This soup does not freeze well and is better freshly made.

Variation:

Use 100 g/4 oz/¼ lb minced (ground) raw beef in place of the chicken.

Savoury Bread and Milk

This turns a bowl of bread and milk into a light meal.

Put 450 ml/¾ pint/scant 2 cups milk into a saucepan. Heat carefully, for skimmed milk has more of a tendency to burn than full-cream milk. Remove from the heat and add a pinch of salt, shake of pepper and 25 g/1 oz/½ cup fresh breadcrumbs and 50 g/2 oz/½ cup grated Dutch cheese or other hard chesse.

To serve: As soon as prepared.

■ 236/Kj991 □ 17.5 g

Special Needs

FISH DISHES

The following recipes enable you to use fresh or frozen fish portions; the choice of white (lean) fish being a matter of availability and personal taste, but the best fish for each dish is suggested in the recipe.

Plaice (Flounder) in Mushroom Sauce

■ 122/Kj 510 □ 4.9 g

Metric/Imperial

2 portions plaice, each about 100 g/4 oz edible weight

1 small onion, chopped or 1 × 5 ml spoon/1 teaspoon dehydrated onion

150 ml/¼ pint milk

50 g/2 oz button mushrooms

1 × 5 ml spoon/1 teaspoon chopped or a pinch dried parsley or dill or fennel

salt

pepper

American

2 portions flounder, each about ¼ lb edible weight

1 small onion, chopped or 1 teaspoon dehydrated onion

⅔ cup milk

½ cup mushrooms

1 teaspoon chopped or a pinch dried parsley or dill or fennel

salt

pepper

Below: Plaice (Flounder) in Mushroom Sauce; Orange and Paprika Fish

❧If using frozen plaice (flounder) allow to thaw sufficiently to separate the portions. Put the chopped or dehydrated onion into a saucepan or deep frying pan (skillet) with the milk; if using dried onion, allow time to soak in the milk and soften. Add the washed whole mushrooms, there is no need to peel these, then the herbs, salt, pepper and the fish. Simmer gently for about 10 minutes, covering the saucepan with a lid; if you have no lid for the frying pan (skillet), then cover with a plate.

To serve: With vegetables.

To freeze: Better freshly cooked.

Variation:

Stir in 2–3 × 15 ml spoons/2–3 tablespoons plain yogurt, or top of the milk plus a little lemon juice, for a sharper flavour; do not boil after adding this.

Orange and Paprika Fish

■ 103/Kj 431 □ 6.0 g

Metric/Imperial

2 portions white fish, each about 100 g/4 oz edible weight

pinch paprika

salt

2 large oranges

American

2 portions lean fish, each about ¼ lb edible weight

pinch paprika

salt

2 large oranges

Chicken in a blanket

❧If using frozen fish allow to thaw completely, then drain and dry well. Sprinkle with paprika, a sweet, not hot flavour, and salt. Halve the oranges, cut one half into slices for garnish and squeeze out the juice from the three other halves. Sprinkle a little juice over the fish, cook under a hot grill (broiler) until tender. Put onto a hot flameproof serving dish (the type suitable to be put under the grill/broiler), add the rest of the orange juice and heat for 2 to 3 minutes under the grill (broiler).

To serve: Garnish with the sliced fruit.

To freeze: Better freshly cooked.

Variation:

Chicken joints can be cooked in the same way. Buy frying chicken. Naturally the cooking time will be a little longer than with fish.

MEAT DISHES

There are many meat dishes in this book, which are easy to prepare and economical. Having a freezer or a refrigerator means you can cook larger quantities of stews or casserole-type dishes and freeze the surplus or keep it until the next day in the refrigerator. *Do not* store cooked meat dishes without a refrigerator and even then use the food within 48 hours at the latest.

CHICKEN DISHES

Chicken is an ideal food today for a small family, for you can buy just the right amount of chicken portions and use these in a variety of ways.

If you steam chicken joints over a saucepan of boiling water they are ideal to use in salads or in the dish as below.

Chicken in a Blanket

Spread cooked chicken joints with a little made (Dijon) mustard or lemon juice, cover with mashed potato, you could use dehydrated potato, and heat for about 30 minutes in a moderate oven.

The chicken joints can be boned if preferred. The figures below are based on portions of 100 g/4 oz/¼ lb edible cooked chicken and 100 g/4 oz/½ cup mashed potato.

To serve: Garnish with watercress.

■ 357/Kj 1499 □ 20.8 g

VEGETABLES

These foods are important, they add both vitamins and roughage to the diet. Do not overcook vegetables, for you lose colour, texture and nutritional value. Try to eat raw vegetables in salads.

You may find some vegetables are not easy to digest, so sieve or purée in a blender after cooking.

Use the vegetable stock for gravies and sauces; important mineral salts are retained and this liquid does not increase either the calorific value or carbohydrate content of the dish.

Frozen and canned vegetables are also good foods, so use these when the fresh ones are not available.

DESSERTS

Avoid puddings based on high amounts of flour, fat or sugar. Choose fruit or light milky desserts. Rice has a moderate calorific value, but is easy to digest.

Rice Puddings

Cook 75 g/3 oz/½ cup pudding rice in 600 ml/1 pint/2½ cups skimmed milk with sugar substitute.

To serve: Have two portions hot, figures are based on this, with fruit. Cool rest and blend with plain yogurt. Top with fresh fruit as for a *Fruit Condé*.

To freeze: Do not freeze.

■ 127/Kj 531 □ 25.9 g

Mock Syllabub

The classic recipe is based on cream; if you are on a low-carbohydrate diet you can include cream. Low-fat plain yogurt has fewer calories, is cheaper and makes a good alternative. Yogurt has a higher carbohydrate value than cream.

Blend 300 ml/½ pint/1¼ cups plain yogurt with a very little grated lemon rind and the juice of 1 lemon, 2 × 15 ml spoons/2 tablespoons white wine, sugar substitute to taste.

To serve: Spoon into glasses and chill.

To freeze: Do not freeze.

■ 93/Kj 399 □ 8.5 g

Below: Mock Syllabub

Special Needs

Often as one becomes older one tends to lose contact with people, which is a pity, for it is when you are alone or with fewer interests that you are inclined to nibble and overeat; if you are interested in various activities and the company of friends, food becomes less important and it is easier to diet.

The recipes on these pages would be sufficiently interesting to serve when entertaining friends or family.

The pâté and mousse would be ideal for a light luncheon or supper and the Fish Bake is suitable for a main meal when served with vegetables.

Fish Bake

■ 401/Kj 1682 □ 3.5 g

Metric/Imperial

450 g/1 lb uncooked white fish

1 large egg

300 ml/½ pint milk

salt

pepper

1 × 2.5 ml spoon/½ teaspoon finely chopped parsley (optional)

TO GARNISH:
2 slices toast

American

1 lb uncooked lean fish

1 large egg

1¼ cups milk

salt

pepper

½ teaspoon finely chopped parsley (optional)

TO GARNISH:
2 slices toast

Above: Fish Bake

❧Cut the uncooked fish into neat pieces. Place at the bottom of a pie dish. Beat the egg, whisk in the hot, but not boiling, milk. Add a little salt and pepper and parsley if wished, then pour the custard over the fish. Stand the dish in another containing cold water and bake for approximately 35 to 45 minutes (until the custard is set) in the centre of a moderate oven (180°C/350°F, Gas Mark 4).

To serve: Cut the toast into triangles and arrange round the edge of the dish, serve at once.

To freeze: This dish is better eaten when freshly cooked.

Variations:

1: Add 25–50 g/1–2 oz/¼–½ cup cheese, grated, to the custard.

2: Add some finely chopped red and green pepper to the custard mixture.

Camembert Mousse

■ 241/Kj 1012 □ 9.5 g

Metric/Imperial

25 g/1 oz butter or margarine

25 g/1 oz flour

300 ml/½ pint milk

50 g/2 oz Camembert cheese, diced (without rind)

25 g/1 oz Parmesan cheese, grated

salt

cayenne pepper

1–2 × 5 ml spoons/1–2 teaspoons French mustard

1–2 × 5 ml spoons/1–2 teaspoons tomato purée

2 × 5 ml spoons/2 teaspoons powder gelatine

3 × 15 ml spoons/3 tablespoons water

2 eggs

TO GARNISH:
sprigs watercress

4 radish roses, prepared as on page 94

American

2 tablespoons butter or margarine

¼ cup flour

1¼ cups milk

½ cup diced Camembert cheese (without rind)

¼ cup grated Parmesan cheese

salt

cayenne pepper

1–2 teaspoons Dijon mustard

1–2 teaspoons tomato paste

2 teaspoons powder gelatin

3 tablespoons water

2 eggs

TO GARNISH:
sprigs watercress

4 radish roses, prepared as on page 94

Tie a wide band of double greaseproof (wax) paper round the outside of a 13-cm/5-inch soufflé dish, extending above the rim, brush the paper with a little of the butter or margarine. Melt the remaining butter or margarine, stir in the flour and cook for 2 minutes. Add the milk, bring to the boil and stir over a moderate heat until of a coating consistency. Add the Camembert and Parmesan cheeses, salt, cayenne pepper, mustard and tomato purée (paste), stir until smooth. Soften the gelatine in 1×15 ml spoon/1 tablespoon cold water, boil the remaining 2×15 ml spoons/2 tablespoons water, add the softened gelatine; stir until dissolved. Separate the eggs, beat the yolks into the cheese sauce, stir over a gentle heat for 1 to 2 minutes until the sauce thickens again. Whisk in the dissolved gelatine. Cool, stirring occasionally. Whisk the egg whites stiffly and fold in when the sauce has almost set. Spoon into the soufflé dish and allow to set.

To serve: Remove paper band, garnish with the watercress and radishes, serve with a mixed salad.

To freeze: Freeze for up to 3 weeks.

Variations:

1: Use 75 g/3 oz/¾ cup grated Cheddar cheese plus 1×15 ml spoon/1 tablespoon double (heavy) cream instead of Camembert.

2: For those on a low-carbohydrate diet, full cream milk can be chosen as this does not alter the carbohydrate content.

Below: Camembert Mousse

Above: Snowball Pâté

Snowball Pâté

■ 144/Kj606 □ 3.5 g

Metric/Imperial
225 g/8 oz liver sausage
100 g/4 oz cottage cheese
2×15 ml spoons/2 tablespoons lemon juice
2×15 ml spoons/2 tablespoons milk
salt, optional
pepper, optional
1 hard-boiled egg
lettuce
TO GARNISH:
2 tomatoes, sliced
1 lemon, sliced

American
½ lb liver sausage
½ cup cottage cheese
2 tablespoons lemon juice
2 tablespoons milk
salt, optional
pepper, optional
1 hard-cooked egg
lettuce
TO GARNISH:
2 tomatoes, sliced
1 lemon, sliced

Mash the liver sausage with the cheese. Gradually blend in the lemon juice and milk. Add salt and pepper if wished. Chop the yolk and the white of the egg separately, blend the yolk into the pâté.

To serve: Spoon the mixture onto a bed of lettuce and garnish with slices of tomato, the chopped egg white and lemon.

To freeze: Not suitable for freezing.

Variation:

Fish and Cheese Pâté: Use mashed cooked salmon or tuna instead of liver sausage.

Special Needs

Equipment

Special Equipment

In this section is advice on using various modern appliances. All of these can be of value to the person who is anxious to lose weight.
The first is the blender, or the type of mixer which achieves a similar result. This enables you to create *new* recipes that add interest to the diet.
Next is the pressure cooker, which can produce appetizing dishes in a matter of minutes. This is followed by the modern 'crock-pot' or slow casserole which will cook a variety of dishes.
Steamers and freezers complete this section.

Above: Tomato soup; Puréed strawberries make an excellent sauce for lemon water ice
Right: Milanese type soufflé, homemade meat pâté, and Cream of Vegetable Soup are all made in a blender

Blenders

No appliance can produce results so efficiently and rapidly as a blender.

You can make a purée of vegetables for soups, sauces or casserole dishes in a matter of seconds.

Fruits can be puréed for moulds, hot or cold soufflés, sauces and iced desserts in the same time.

Because of the speed of movement it is possible to purée acid fruits with milk for drinks and desserts without fear of curdling.

You can make low-calorie fish or meat purées (also low in, or with no, carbohydrate content), for satisfying moulds, pâtés and spreads.

Milk shakes can be included in some slimming diets, if fresh fruit and skimmed milk are used; these are quite delicious and are an excellent source of vitamins and protein.

Never overfill the blender. If the cutting blades do not turn well, stop the machine and remove some food.

MAKING SOUPS

The recipe that follows gives an idea of just how useful the blender will be in the preparation of soups. No longer will the vegetables need to be painstakingly chopped by hand.

Obviously, though, the ability of the blender to deal with *raw* vegetables does depend upon its size; the small models are, like the bigger ones, excellent for making a purée of cooked vegetables, but it may well prove difficult to use them for the initial chopping. If this is the case, remember you can chop or grate the vegetables more coarsely and unevenly than usual if the cooked mixture is to be puréed.

See also page 166.

Cream of Vegetable Soup

■ Varies □ Varies

Metric/Imperial
350 g/12 oz vegetables – carrots, potatoes, peas, mushrooms, onions, Jerusalem artichokes, etc. (use one vegetable or a mixture)
750 ml/1¼ pints water plus 1–2 chicken stock cubes (or use chicken stock) or water with yeast extract to flavour
salt
pepper
25 g/1 oz butter or margarine
25 g/1 oz flour or 15 g/½ oz cornflour
300 ml/½ pint milk

TO GARNISH:
3 × 15 ml spoons/
3 tablespoons single cream
chopped parsley

American

¾ lb vegetables – carrots, potatoes, peas, mushrooms, onions, Jerusalem artichokes, etc. (use one vegetable or a mixture)

3 cups water plus 2–3 chicken bouillon cubes (or use chicken stock) or water with yeast extract to flavor

salt

pepper

2 tablespoons butter or margarine

¼ cup flour or 2 tablespoons cornstarch

1¼ cups milk

TO GARNISH:
3 tablespoons light cream
chopped parsley

❧ Prepare the vegetables, feed into the blender and finely chop to save cooking time (and retain the maximum vitamins and mineral salts). Bring the water with the stock cubes or the stock or water and yeast extract to the boil. Drop in the vegetables and boil fairly quickly for about 10 to 15 minutes, adding salt and pepper to taste.

Meanwhile make a sauce with the butter or margarine, flour or cornflour (cornstarch) and milk. Add to the vegetable mixture and blend thoroughly. If you want a smooth creamy soup, put into a warmed blender and purée. Return to the saucepan and reheat.

To serve: Garnish with cream and parsley. Slimmers should be sparing with the cream topping and could have their portion of soup *without* the sauce mixture, but calories cover the basic soup.

To freeze: Cool then pack. This soup keeps well for 2 to 3 months. You could use less liquid to conserve space, then add the extra water etc. when necessary.

Equipment

163

MAKING SAUCES

The chapter that begins on page 80 gives a selection of sauces which are suitable for people on a diet, but the recipes that follow are prepared completely in a blender.

When making sauces, soups, drinks or anything containing a high percentage of liquid, remember that the blender must *not* be more than two-thirds full, for the mixture rises drastically as you switch on and this could easily force off the lid, often with unpleasant results.

Never put fruit containing stones (pits) or meat or poultry with tiny bones into the blender; check that these have been removed first.

If a sauce is not as smooth as desired, put it into the blender, switch on for a few seconds. The sauce will then be perfectly smooth, if a little thinner in consistency.

Mayonnaise

One of the most successful recipes to make in a blender is mayonnaise. You can use the whole egg, which is very satisfactory for slimmers, since the white accounts for only 11 calories. If you have a large blender you will need to double the quantities below, to cover the blades.

Put an egg, a pinch of salt, shake of pepper and dry mustard into the blender. Cover the blender, switch on for a few seconds. Remove the centre cap from the lid or use a foil lid with a hole in the centre. Keep the motor running on a low speed and add the oil **gradually**. In order to reduce calories the figures below are based upon 4 × 15 ml spoons/4 table-spoons – considerably less oil than usual. If you are on a low-carbohydrate diet you can increase the amount of oil.

After adding the oil gradually add up to 2 × 15 ml spoons/2 tablespoons lemon juice. This quantity gives 4 small portions.

To freeze: Mayonnaise is unsuitable for freezing.

■ 122/Kj 512 □ 0.0 g

BLENDER SAUCES

The joy of a blender is that you do not need a special recipe for many of the sauces you can produce, and this is of enormous value to people who normally love sauces over their foods. For example, you could take some of the vegetables cooked for the meal and put them into the blender with a little liquid. This could be meat stock (if clear, there are no appreciable calories to this) or milk, plain yogurt, tomato juice or skinned fresh tomato and blend gently until a smooth sauce. Then add salt and pepper to taste

Above: Mayonnaise

and you have a delicious sauce; here are some quick suggestions:

Carrot Sauce

Excellent with fish, poultry or meat dishes. Blend carrots with parsley and a little raw onion; moisten with stock, plain yogurt or milk and a squeeze of lemon juice.

Carrot Tomato Sauce

Blend equal amounts of cooked carrot and skinned fresh tomato, add chives plus a little vegetable stock to moisten. This sauce is good with white (lean) fish.

Onion Sauce

Blend cooked onions with a little stock and a small amount of plain yogurt. You could add a little sage and parsley too, plus a good pinch cayenne pepper as well as ordinary pepper. This savoury sauce blends with meat or poultry dishes.

Speedy Tomato Sauce

Skin 450 g/1 lb tomatoes, if you want to avoid any tiny particles of skin in the sauce; this stage is not essential. Halve or quarter the tomatoes. Skin a garlic clove, peel 2 to 3 spring onions (scallions) or peel and halve a small onion.

Put 3 × 15 ml spoons/ 3 tablespoons water into the blender, add the vegetables with a little salt and pepper. Blend gently until a smooth purée; there may be just a few seeds left in the mixture.
To serve: Either heat the mixture or serve cold. This sauce is a good accompaniment to many savoury dishes.
To freeze: Freezes well for 3 months.
Variations:
1: For a more definite taste add 1–2 × 15 ml spoons/ 1–2 tablespoons tomato purée (paste).
2: Add a little basil to the mixture; this herb is ideal with tomatoes.

■ 15/Kj62 □3.0 g

Orange Sauce

This recipe, based on the fresh fruit, can be adjusted to serve with savoury dishes, duck or pork in particular, or made into a sauce to have with plain yogurt.

Cut away the peel and pith from 4 medium oranges. If you like a tang to the sauce, which blends well with meat dishes, then use several small pieces of the orange skin, but check it is free from pith. Cut the fruit into segments, discard pips (seeds) and skin. Put 150 ml/¼ pint/⅔ cup stock (for savoury dishes) or water (for sweet dishes) into the blender, add the fruit, plus any rind being used and blend gently until a smooth purée. Taste and add a little sugar substitute and/or salt and pepper for savoury dishes.
To serve: Either hot or cold.
To freeze: Use within 3 months.

■ 36/Kj151 □9.6 g

Below from front: Speedy Tomato Sauce; Onion Sauce; Orange Sauce.

Making Savoury Spreads

These are ideal for sandwich spreads, and lower in calories than those you buy, as they contain no cereals.

Always put the melted fat and liquid into the blender first when using a blender; this is not essential when using the mixer with a cutting knife (the Magimix).

If you are using a small blender then you will need to deal with small quantities only at one time.

Potted Meat: Cut 225 g/ 8 oz/½ lb cooked meat or poultry into small pieces; melt 25 g/1 oz/2 tablespoons butter or margarine and put this into the blender with 2 × 15 ml spoons/ 2 tablespoons stock. Add the meat with salt, pepper and dry mustard to taste. Blend gently until a smooth purée. Spoon into a small dish, cover with foil and leave in

From right: Potted Meat; Fish spread; Cheese and tomato spread

the refrigerator until set.
To serve: As a filling or topping on crispbread.
To freeze: Cover well, use within 3 months.
Variations:
1: Add herbs or a little horseradish cream or spring onions (scallions).
2: Use cooked fish in place of meat or poultry. As this is softer than meat omit the stock and use just 1 × 15 ml spoon/1 tablespoon milk with 1 × 5 ml spoon/1 teaspoon lemon juice.
3: Skin and halve 2 tomatoes, put into the blender. Dice 225 g/8 oz/½ lb of any cheese, or use cottage cheese. Add salt and pepper to taste. Blend gently until a smooth purée.
Note: The calories etc. are based on lean beef.

■ 165/Kj693 □0.0 g

Equipment

165

Pressure Cookers

One of the great advantages of a pressure cooker is that it saves a great deal of fuel, since the cooking time for soups, stews, meat, poultry and vegetable dishes is drastically reduced.

It is always important to retain the essential vitamins and mineral salts in foods and this is even more essential when on a slimming diet, where the choice of foods may be somewhat restricted. If you use your pressure cooker *correctly* you will keep the essential nutrients quite as successfully as when you cook correctly by other methods.

As many of the recipes in this book can be adapted to pressure cooking, you will find general hints on adjusting the cooking times.

Another advantage for lone slimmers is that you put all the ingredients for the whole meal in the pressure cooker, so using only one cooking utensil.

USING THE PRESSURE COOKER

The capacity of even a small pressure cooker is sufficiently large to enable family-sized meals to be cooked, but if you have to plan two somewhat different menus, if one person is on a diet, you can easily put part of the meal in one container and another part in a separate dish. These dishes can be of metal or you can use ovenproof ware. If using the latter never cool the cooker rapidly with cold water, as you will crack the dish; always allow the pressure to reduce at room temperature.

The instruction book with your pressure cooker will give specific advice, but two general points to remember are:

Use an adequate amount of water in the pressure cooker to produce steam, then maintain the pressure without fear of the cooker boiling dry.

Unless recipes state to the contrary, bring up to pressure on a low heat, then reduce the heat to maintain the pressure.

ADAPTING COOKING TIMES

If you take one of your favourite dishes and cook it in a pressure cooker, you will be surprised at the vast difference in cooking time. Obviously this means that in recipes where a lot of water is normally used, i.e. in soups, stews, cooking dried fruits, you can reduce this (on an average by one-third) to compensate for the smaller evaporation of liquid during the shorter cooking period.

It is not easy to summarize on how much shorter the cooking time will be, but the following approximate times may prove helpful. These assume you are using a high heat, known as High/15 lb and are *pressure cooking, not total times*.

Soups: Will take about a quarter of the normal cooking time.

Stock: One of the problems of food on a slimming diet is that it can be dull, unless you take special pains to give flavour in ways that fit in with the particular diet. A good stock from bones can be made in the pressure cooker in about half-an-hour and, if this is skimmed of fat, it has virtually no calories, although a longer period produces a richer stock. You will find this good stock makes so much difference to the flavour of savoury dishes and it can be used as a clear soup, see page 28.

Fish: This cooks in a matter of 2 to 5 minutes depending upon the thickness of the fish. One of the interesting points about cooking different foods in the pressure cooker at one

time is that the smells and flavours do not intermingle, so you could cook fish, vegetables and a container of fruit and all would keep their individual taste and odour, see menu on page 170.

Meats: One can have the effect of pot roasting allowing just about 12 to 15 minutes per 450 g/1 lb in the case of pork and beef, 12 minutes for lamb and veal and only 5 minutes for chicken. Stews can be cooked in about 15 to 20 minutes.

Fruit and Vegetables: Take only a very few minutes and you can tenderize dried fruits and dried vegetables, such as haricot (navy) beans quite quickly, without pre-soaking if desired.

Various desserts can be prepared in the pressure cooker and egg custards can be set without fear of curdling, see the recipe on page 211.

Above: Smoked fish and spring greens can be cooked together in a pressure cooker, without the flavours transferring

Using a Microwave Oven

A microwave oven is another piece of equipment that will save both time, fuel and calories. If you own a microwave cooker you will find that it can be extremely helpful in following a slimming diet since many foods can be heated or cooked with little, if any, fat. The shorter cooking period will often provide more flavour to the dish. Follow the instructions in your manufacturer's book on the setting for defrosting and also for cooking various foods.

Equipment

Cod with Fennel
and Carrots
Compôte of Mixed Fruits

COD WITH FENNEL AND CARROTS

Put 300 ml/½ pint/1¼ cups water into the pressure cooker and place the trivet (rack) in position. Grease a soufflé or other ovenproof dish. Chop enough fennel leaves to give 1 × 15 ml spoon/1 tablespoon; dice the white part of the fennel very finely to give 50 g/2 oz. Skin and slice 4 large tomatoes, crush 1 garlic clove. Mix the fennel, tomato and garlic and put half into the dish. Top with 4 portions of cod, each weighing about 100 g/4 oz/ ¼ lb, add a little salt and pepper and the rest of the

Slimmer's Menu: 1

The following give some simple ideas of how you can use the pressure cooker for slimming meals and dishes.

Blanquette of Veal
with Brussels Sprouts
Apple Ginger

APPLE GINGER

The Apple Ginger is nicer cold, so prepare this first.

Peel and slice enough cooking (baking) apples to give 450 g/1 lb. Put 300 ml/ ½ pint/1¼ cups water into the pressure cooker with sugar substitute to taste, the finely grated rind and juice of a lemon and 1–2 × 5 ml spoons/ 1–2 teaspoons ground ginger. Put in the apples, fix the cover, bring to H/15 lb pressure and cook for one minute only. Reduce pressure under cold water.

To serve: Spoon the fruit into

a serving dish, then top with 25 g/1 oz/¼ cup flaked almonds.
To freeze: This freezes well; use within 3 months.
■ 95/Kj 397 □ 12.9 g

BLANQUETTE OF VEAL

Rinse out the cooker after preparing the fruit then proceed as follows:

Cut 450 g/1 lb stewing veal into pieces. Heat 25 g/1 oz/ 2 tablespoons fat (shortening) in the base of the pressure cooker. Fry the meat in this for 2 to 3 minutes, add 2 medium onions, cut into slices, fry for another 2 minutes, take care the meat and onions do not brown.

Add 300 ml/½ pint/1¼ cups stock (use white stock made from veal or chicken bones), 1 × 15 ml spoon/1 tablespoon lemon juice, salt and pepper and 1 × 15 ml spoon/ 1 tablespoon chopped parsley. Fix the cover, bring up to H/15 lb pressure, lower

Above: Blanquette of Veal with Brussels Sprouts and Apple Ginger

the heat, maintain for 9 minutes. Reduce the pressure by allowing cold water to run over the top, or stand it in the sink filled with cold water.

Remove the cover, put one of the separators into the pressure cooker, place 450 g/ 1 lb prepared Brussels sprouts in this with a very little salt. Bring up to H/15 lb pressure again, allow another 2 to 3 minutes cooking time. Reduce with cold water. Lift out the sprouts, then spoon the Blanquette into a serving dish.

To serve: Top with 150 ml/ ¼ pint/⅔ cup plain yogurt, chopped parsley and slices of lemon. The figures include garnish and sprouts.
To freeze: Not suitable for freezing, as veal does not freeze well.
■ 258/Kj 1083 □ 11.2 g

fennel mixture. Pour 2 × 15 ml spoons/2 tablespoons water into the dish. Cover with aluminium foil and stand on the trivet (rack). Cut 8 medium carrots into thin slices, put on the trivet (rack) round the dish containing the fish, add a little salt. Fix the cover of the pressure cooker. Bring up to H/15 lb pressure, reduce the heat and cook for 4 minutes. Allow pressure to reduce at room temperature.

To serve: With a green salad. Figures include the carrots but not the salad.

To freeze: Better freshly made.

■ 122/Kj511 □ 13.0 g

COMPÔTE OF MIXED FRUITS

These fruits can be cooked in the same way as the Apple Ginger on the left or you could put an assortment of fruits into another ovenproof dish, with a little water and sugar substitute to sweeten. When the fish comes out of the pressure cooker, you could place the dish containing the fruits in its place and allow about 3 to 4 minutes at H/15 lb pressure. You may, however, have a sufficiently large cooker for two dishes to be put in at one time, the first with the fish, the second with the fruit. The other alternative is to wrap the ingredients, including liquid, for the fish dish in foil and place this on the trivet (rack) with the carrots and then put the dish with the fruit on top.

■ □ Calories and carbohydrate content depend upon fruits selected.

Below: Cod with Fennel and Carrots; Compôte of Mixed Fruits

Cheese Custard

It makes a pleasant change to have a savoury instead of a sweet custard and this is very like the centre of a Quiche, but without the pastry, of course.

A sweet egg custard recipe is on page 211 and this can be cooked in the same way as the recipe below.

Blend 2 large eggs, a good pinch salt, pepper and dry mustard, 50 g/2 oz/½ cup Edam cheese, grated, and 450 ml/¾ pint/scant 2 cups warm skimmed milk together. Pour into a greased soufflé or other ovenproof dish. Cover the dish with greased greaseproof (wax) paper. Put 300 ml/½ pint/1¼ cups water into the base of the pressure cooker, place the trivet (rack) in position. Stand the dish containing the custard on this. Fix the lid and bring up pressure to H/15 lb. Lower the heat and maintain the pressure for 5 minutes only, reduce at room temperature.

To serve: Hot or cold with salad.

To freeze: Do not freeze.

■ 123/Kj517 □ 5.3 g

Above: Chicken Curry

Chicken Curry

Curries are very successful in the pressure cooker.

Dice enough chicken to give 450 g/1 lb. Heat 25 g/1 oz/2 tablespoons fat (shortening) in the base of the pressure cooker and fry 2 medium onions and 1 small apple, both peeled and finely chopped, together with 1–2 × 15 ml spoons/1–2 tablespoons curry powder, for 2 to 3 minutes. Add the chicken and 300 ml/½ pint/1¼ cups stock with salt, pepper and 1 × 15 ml spoon/1 tablespoon lemon juice. Continue as for the Blanquette of Veal, but allow only 5 to 6 minutes at H/15 lb pressure. Reduce the pressure under cold water.

To serve: With lemon slices and ½ cucumber, diced, blended with 300 ml/½ pint/1¼ cups plain yogurt. Figures include accompaniments.

To freeze: The basic curry, but not the cucumber, can be frozen for 2 months.

■ 267/Kj1119 □ 11.8 g

Equipment

Slow Casseroles (Crock-pots)

One of the interesting developments today is the desire to retain as much of the natural flavour of foods as possible, and to add to the fibre content of our diets by incorporating high roughage cereals such as bran, fresh vegetables and fruits. This trend is ideal when slimming and a slow casserole allows you to cook foods with the minimum of liquid so they retain their flavour and it is not lost in excess liquid.

Cooking with little liquid for a long period is often unsatisfactory in an ordinary saucepan, for the saucepan may well boil dry. This will not happen in the very low heat of an electric casserole,

often called a crock-pot.

Another advantage is that you can dispense with fat in cooking, if wished.

The short selection of recipes in this section can only give you an idea of *how* you cook in this special casserole (crock-pot). You can adapt many of the slimming recipes in this book for slow casserole (crock-pot) cooking.

When Using the Slow Casserole (Crock-pot)

Read the instructions given by the manufacturers on using and cleaning.

Always make sure the cover fits tightly.

In most slow casserole

models you have a LOW and HIGH setting. Use either setting for recipes in this section, or a combination of heats if this suits the time you have available.

As a small amount of liquid is used in cooking by this method you should be fairly sparing with salt and pepper.

If you want to brown foods first in fat this must be done on a higher heat in an ordinary saucepan. The food is then transferred to the electric casserole. This stage has been omitted in most recipes in this section, for it saves *at least* 220 calories (for an average family dish). This process could, of course, be incorporated into the preparation of suitable dishes if you are on a low-carbohydrate diet, for fats (shortenings) have no carbohydrates.

Pot Roast of Beef

Choose a lean joint, such as topside (top round), and no more than 1.5 kg/3 lb in weight.

Brown the meat on both sides in its own fat by cooking in an ordinary saucepan. Drain well. Put a layer of low-calorie vegetables, such as sliced onions, chopped celery and turnip in the slow casserole (crock-pot). Add 300 ml/ ½ pint/1¼ cups boiling stock, a little salt and pepper. Place the meat on top and allow 5 to 6 hours on HIGH. Use the liquid as a gravy.

Pot Roast of Beef. Inset: Pheasant and Grapes

170

Pheasant and Grapes

■ 421/Kj 1769 □ 9.2 g

Metric/Imperial
50 g/2 oz lean bacon
25 g/1 oz fat
1 young pheasant
100 g/4 oz celery, chopped
1 medium onion, sliced
150 ml/¼ pint stock
150 ml/¼ pint white wine
salt
pepper
175 g/6 oz green grapes
25 g/1 oz cottage cheese

American
2 oz lean bacon slices
2 tablespoons shortening
1 young pheasant
1 cup chopped celery
1 medium onion, sliced
⅔ cup stock
⅔ cup white wine
salt
pepper
1½ cups green grapes
2 tablespoons cottage cheese

♣ Cut the rind from the bacon, then cut this into matchstick-sized pieces. Heat the fat in an ordinary saucepan and brown the pheasant in this for a few minutes. Remove from the saucepan and toss the bacon in the saucepan for 2 to 3 minutes only. Transfer the bacon to the slow casserole (crock-pot), add the celery, onion, stock and wine with a little salt and pepper. De-seed and skin half the grapes, blend with the cottage cheese, stuff the pheasant with this mixture; place in the slow casserole (crock-pot). Cook on LOW for 9 to 10 hours or 4½ to 5 hours on HIGH.

To serve: Lift the pheasant onto a dish; garnish with the remaining grapes. Sieve or put in a blender the vegetables, bacon and liquid to make a sauce. The figures are based on about 100 g/ 4 oz/¼ lb cooked edible flesh.

To freeze: Better freshly cooked, but completely *thawed* pheasant could be used.

Variations:
1: Use a small chicken instead of pheasant.
2: Cook two plump pigeons instead of pheasant, substitute red for white wine.

Equipment

Slimmer's Jugged Hare

The traditional way of cooking Jugged Hare, with the inclusion of flour, redcurrant jelly and forcemeat balls gives a dish that is high in both calories and carbohydrate content. The version below is very good but quite different.

Use just the back (saddle) and cut into four portions; the legs could be used in the recipe for Country Rabbit.

Simmer the liver in a saucepan to give stock for that dish and the Jugged Hare; sieve or blend 25 g/1 oz of the liver, blend with 300 ml/½ pint/1¼ cups of stock, 2 × 15 ml spoons/ 2 tablespoons red wine, 1 × 5 ml spoon/1 teaspoon tomato purée (paste), a pinch

ground mace, salt and pepper to taste. Put the hare into the slow casserole (crock-pot), with an onion, sliced, and 2 carrots, sliced, add the liver mixture. Cook on LOW for 10 to 11 hours or for 5 to 5½ hours on HIGH.

Add 100 g/4 oz/¼ lb dessert plums, weight when halved and stoned (pitted), halfway through the cooking period.
To serve: Hot with a green vegetable or a salad. The figures are based on portions of 100 g/4 oz/¼ lb cooked edible flesh.
To freeze: This freezes well. Use within 3 months.

■ 295/Kj 1239 □ 6.8 g

Country Rabbit

■ 273/Kj 1146 □ 15.8 g

Metric/Imperial
1 small rabbit, jointed, with the liver
300 ml/½ pint stock, see method
salt
pepper
2 × 5 ml spoons/2 teaspoons made mustard
4 small dessert apples, peeled and cored
12 small onions or shallots
2 × 5 ml spoons/2 teaspoons white wine vinegar
1 × 15 ml spoon/1 tablespoon chopped parsley
1 × 5 ml spoon/1 teaspoon chopped tarragon

American
1 small rabbit, jointed, with the liver
1¼ cups stock, see method
salt
pepper
2 teaspoons Dijon mustard
4 small dessert apples, peeled and cored
12 small onions or shallots
2 teaspoons white wine vinegar

Above: Country Rabbit.
Right: Curried Vegetables

1 tablespoon chopped parsley
1 teaspoon chopped tarragon

♣ Wash the rabbit in cold water, drain and dry thoroughly. Put the liver into a saucepan with just enough water to cover, simmer until a good flavoured stock is obtained, strain and measure 300 ml/½ pint/1¼ cups. Add a little salt, pepper and the mustard. Add remaining incredients, then the hot liquid. Transfer to the slow casserole (crock-pot). Cook on LOW for 9 to 10 hours or 5½ to 6 hours on HIGH.
To serve: With a green vegetable. The figures are based on portions of about 100 g/4 oz/¼ lb cooked flesh.
To freeze: This freezes well; use within 3 months.

172

Curried Vegetables

■ 98/Kj 413 □ 21.5 g

Metric/Imperial

1 × 5 ml spoon/1 teaspoon cornflour

1 × 15 ml spoon/1 tablespoon curry powder

300 ml/½ pint water

salt

pepper

2 × 5 ml spoons/2 teaspoons lemon juice

1 × 15 ml spoon/1 tablespoon tomato purée

2 medium turnips, diced

4 medium onions, sliced

8 medium carrots, sliced

1 small cauliflower head, divided into even florets

150 ml/¼ pint plain yogurt

TO GARNISH:
1 × 15 ml spoon/1 tablespoon chopped parsley

American

1 teaspoon cornstarch

1 tablespoon curry powder

1¼ cups water

salt

pepper

2 teaspoons lemon juice

1 tablespoon tomato paste

2 medium turnips, diced

4 medium onions, sliced

8 medium carrots, sliced

1 small cauliflower head, divided into even florets

⅔ cup plain yogurt

TO GARNISH:
1 tablespoon chopped parsley

❧ Blend the cornflour (cornstarch) and curry powder with the water, salt, pepper and lemon juice. Stir over a medium heat in a saucepan until slightly thickened, add the tomato purée (paste). Place all the vegetables, except the cauliflower, in the slow casserole (crock-pot). Cover with the hot curry sauce. Cook on LOW for 7 to 8 hours or 3½ to 4 hours on HIGH. Stir once or twice during the cooking process. Add the cauliflower halfway through the cooking time and blend the yogurt into the sauce at the end of 6 to 7 hours if using LOW setting or 3 to 3½ hours if cooking on HIGH.

To serve: Sprinkle with parsley, serve with a little cooked rice. The figures do not include the rice.

To freeze: Better freshly made.

Orange Pears

■ 107/Kj 449 □ 28.0 g

Metric/Imperial

2 medium oranges

1 × 15 ml spoon/1 tablespoon lemon juice

little water, see method

sugar substitute (optional)

8 small cooking pears (about 75 g/3 oz each when peeled)

TO DECORATE:
1 orange, sliced

American

2 medium oranges

1 tablespoon lemon juice

little water, see method

sugar substitute (optional)

8 small baking pears (about 3 oz each when peeled)

TO DECORATE:
1 orange, sliced

❧ Grate the 'zest' of the orange finely. Squeeze the juice, blend with the lemon juice and water to give 300 ml/½ pint/1¼ cups. Heat this liquid with the orange

Above: Orange Pears

'zest', add sugar substitute if desired. Peel the pears, but do not slice or halve. Put into the slow casserole (crock-pot), add the hot liquid immediately. Cook for 5 to 6 hours on LOW or 2½ to 3 hours on HIGH. Spoon the liquid over the pears once or twice during cooking.

To serve: Hot or cold with the orange slices.

To freeze: This is a good way of preparing pears for freezing.

To thaw: Allow to thaw out steadily.

Variation:

Drain off the orange liquid, blend with a few drops orange colouring, 1 × 5 ml spoon/1 teaspoon arrowroot (arrowroot flour). Pour into a saucepan, stir over a low heat until thickened. Spoon over the pears.

Equipment

Steamers

This utensil is often under-estimated; a steamer enables you to conserve the flavour and texture of a great variety of foods. These are cooked *above* rather than *in* the liquid and therefore the natural taste is not diluted in any way.

Steaming is one excellent method of dealing with fish, although care must be taken when cooking white (lean) and some freshwater fish so they do not become dry and unpalatable.

Certain vegetables, particularly root vegetables, marrow (squash), leeks and onions are very good when they are cooked in a steamer, rather than in liquid. You can steam potatoes in their skins, which saves heating the oven to produce jacket potatoes. New potatoes are particularly delicious this way and

although they must be eaten sparingly on a slimming diet you do have the advantages of baked jacket potatoes outlined on page 150.

Young chickens or older fowls become deliciously tender when prepared in a steamer. If you put the ingredients for a meat stew into a bowl, with a very little liquid and any other foods used to flavour the meat, then cover this and steam the food, you achieve a quite exceptionally good flavour, rather like the taste of meat when cooked in a suet crust pastry for a meat pudding. Two examples are given on the page opposite.

Many fruits, particularly those with a high water content, have much more flavour if you put the prepared fruit, a little sugar, or sugar substitute into a bowl and cook in the steamer over boiling water.

Obviously a steamer is invaluable for cooking both savoury and sweet puddings, but these have little place in a book on slimming, although there is a recipe for a steamed Sponge Pudding on page 190.

When you are steaming a main dish, pack any suitable vegetables in the steamer too, so you can cook a complete

course or meal in the one utensil.

Always check there is sufficient water in the saucepan under the steamer and add more boiling water if the level has dropped. Add a little vinegar or lemon slices to this water, which you will find prevents the pan from discolouring.

Right: Liver and Tomato Ragoût
Below left: Chicken Dolmas

Steaming Chicken

The whole chicken can be steamed and served in salads or with a sauce as pages 78 to 81, but the following suggestions are for joints of young frying chicken and each serves 4 people. It is assumed that each portion gives about 100 g/4 oz/¼ lb of edible flesh when cooked. All these dishes are better freshly cooked. Allow the joints to thaw completely for these particular suggestions. Keep the water boiling fairly briskly to keep to the suggested cooking times.

Chicken in Lemon and Tarragon

Halve a lemon and rub the cut surfaces over four joints of chicken. Put into the steamer and sprinkle with a little salt, paprika and finely chopped tarragon. Steam for 30 minutes or until tender.
To serve: With chopped spinach. The figures do not include this.
■ 218/Kj916 □ 0.5 g

Spiced Chicken

Make several cuts in four chicken joints. Skin 2 garlic cloves, cut into slivers and insert these into the chicken. Rub a very little curry powder over the joints together with a *very little* salt. Steam for 30 minutes or until tender.
To serve: Hot with a little cooked rice and a tomato salad. The figures do not include these.
■ 220/Kj924 □ 0.4 g

Chicken Dolmas

Cook 4 large tender cabbage leaves in salted water for 3 minutes until pliable. Drain and lay flat. Chop 50 g/2 oz/ ½ cup mushrooms and 2 skinned tomatoes. Spread over the cabbage leaves. Bone four portions of chicken and place meat on the leaves, add a little salt and pepper to taste. Roll firmly and tie with fine cotton. Steam for 40 minutes or until tender.
To serve: Hot with a tomato sauce, see the recipes on pages 81 and 164. The figures do not include the sauce.
To freeze: Use within 2 months.
■ 225/Kj945 □ 1.6 g

STEAMING MEAT

The following are two suggestions for steaming meat dishes, but these could be adapted for other kinds of meat, such as heart, kidney, lamb or veal.

Liver and Tomato Ragoût

Prepare and slice 2 medium leeks very thinly. Skin and slice 4 medium tomatoes fairly thickly. Blend with the leeks and 1 × 2.5 ml spoon/ ½ teaspoon chopped lemon thyme, a little salt and pepper. Put half the mixture into an ovenproof bowl or dish. Cut 450 g/1 lb calf's liver into thin strips, place on the tomato mixture. Add 2 × 15 ml spoons/ 2 tablespoons of stock or water, with a very little salt and pepper. Top with the rest of the leek and tomato mixture. Cover the container with aluminium foil and place in the steamer.

Cook over rapidly boiling water for 30 minutes, or until the liver is just tender. Do not overcook.
To serve: Top with rings of raw leeks which are tender and delicious when young.
To freeze: Better freshly cooked, although frozen liver, which has thawed completely, could be used.
■ 185/Kj775 □ 6.0 g

Steak and Kidney Ragoût

Cube 450 g/1 lb good quality stewing steak and 225 g/8 oz/½ lb ox (beef) kidney neatly. Put into a bowl or ovenproof dish with a *little* salt and pepper and only just enough water to come just to the top of the meat. Cover very tightly with aluminium foil and steam over steadily boiling water for 2½ to 3 hours or until tender.
To serve: With green vegetables.
To freeze: Use within 3 months.
Variations:
1: Add chopped herbs and/or diced vegetables, such as mushrooms, celery, onions.
2: Those members of the family not slimming could have suet dumplings to serve with the meat. Cook these in boiling salted water.
■ 280/Kj1176 □ 0.0 g

Equipment

175

Freezers

There can be no doubt that a freezer is one of the most valuable appliances in the home, for, if used correctly, it can save time and money.

You will find information on freezing dishes given in this book. If you own a freezer it can be of great value when you are losing weight, for all too often one thinks it not worthwhile making a special dish and eats just what is being prepared, which can completely offset several days of hard dieting.

The freezer enables you to prepare larger quantities of special slimming dishes which freeze well. Divide the bulk quantity into smaller portions, wrap and freeze. If you are checking on calories and carbohydrates remember to label the containers with the name of the dish *plus* the calorie and/or carbohydrate content.

DISHES TO FREEZE

There is a great variety in the foods which can be frozen, but the suggestions below and on page 178 are for those that fit into a slimming routine.

Meal Starters

Freeze fresh grapefruit segments and citrus juices when at their cheapest, or when you have time to prepare them. This may well prevent you eating canned, sweetened grapefruit (although you can buy a variety which is unsweetened) or fruit cordials if you have no fresh fruit juice available. See the recipes in the section starting on page 24.

Soups

Homemade soups take time to prepare and must be chosen carefully if you are slimming. There are suitable soup recipes in the section starting on page 28. The time of storage will, of course, vary with the kind of soup. Mulligatawny soup, which follows, is worth freezing, for its good flavour depends upon using mutton stock which may not always be available. Because it has a certain amount of curry flavour it is better used within a comparatively short time, because the curry loses its potency with longer storage.

Fish

If you can obtain very fresh fish it is worthwhile preparing and freezing this. Cut into suitable-sized portions, weigh these so you know just how they will fit into your diet. Label each small package with all the relevant information. Separate fillets or cutlets of fish with squares of waxed paper so you can 'peel off' the desired number of portions. Information on freezing cooked fish dishes is given on the pages commencing with page 34 and elsewhere in this book.

Fish is an ideal food for most slimming diets, provided it is cooked in a suitable manner, but it is a food which can be difficult to obtain sometimes due to changes in weather and the particular season, so make good use of your freezer for fish.

Mulligatawny Soup

■ 138/Kj 581 □ 12.4 g

Metric/Imperial

1 apple, peeled and chopped

1 large carrot, chopped

2 onions, chopped

50 g/2 oz fat or mutton dripping

0.5–1 × 15 ml spoon/ ½–1 tablespoon curry powder

1.2 litres/2 pints stock made from mutton bones

1 × 15 ml spoon/1 tablespoon chutney

pinch sugar or sugar substitute

25 g/1 oz sultanas

salt

pepper

1 × 5 ml spoon/1 teaspoon lemon juice

25 g/1 oz flour

American

1 apple, peeled and chopped

1 large carrot, chopped

2 onions, chopped

¼ cup fat or mutton dripping

½–1 tablespoon curry powder

5 cups stock made from mutton bones

1 tablespoon chutney

pinch sugar or sugar substitute

scant ¼ cup seedless white raisins

salt

pepper

1 teaspoon lemon juice

¼ cup flour

❧ Toss the apple and vegetables in the hot fat or dripping, then work in the curry powder. Add most of the stock and the other ingredients, except the flour, cook together for about 45 minutes to 1 hour. Rub through a sieve or purée in a blender; return to the saucepan. Blend the flour with the remaining stock. Add to the soup and cook until thickened. Add more salt and pepper if necessary or a little extra sugar or lemon juice.

To serve: Hot, topped with desiccated coconut. Slimmers can have their soup without the thickening, but the calories etc. are for the basic recipe.

To freeze: Better frozen without thickening. Use within 6 weeks.

Variation:

Use 15 g/½ oz/2 tablespoons cornflour (cornstarch) instead of flour to reduce calories and carbohydrates.

TO FREEZE SOUPS

Prepare and cook the soup, then allow the soup to cool; either pour into polythene (styrofoam) boxes or use polythene (styrofoam) bags. To obtain a good shape stand the bag in a supporting carton or box, freeze, remove the bag from the container and you will have a good shaped package that stores well.

Always allow about 1 cm/ ½ inch of headroom in the container as soups contain a high percentage of liquid, which expands as it freezes.

To hasten thawing you can stand the box or bag in a bowl of cold water, then reheat the soup.

TO FREEZE FISH

Prepare the fish for cooking, then separate the portions, as described on the left, so making it easy to remove the amount needed for each meal.

Wrap the fish carefully, so that it keeps a good shape. Cooked dishes can be frozen in the cooking utensil, see page 178.

Below: Mulligatawny Soup

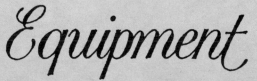

Equipment

MORE FOODS TO FREEZE

Meat

Many of you will bulk buy meat and save money by so doing. Take care to pack it in a practical manner so that you can take out just the amount needed for a meal.

If you pack in very large amounts, you need to thaw out the whole quantity in order to take out sufficient for one meal. This is particularly important for people on diets, for sometimes they will need just one chop or one piece of steak, when the rest of the family are having a meal that does not fit into the diet.

The following is the right way to pack small portions of raw or cooked meat.

Cut pieces of waxed paper just about the size of the chops, steaks, etc. Separate the individual portions with these pieces of paper, then pack in aluminium foil or polythene (styrofoam) bags or boxes.

The waxed paper makes it possible to 'peel off' exactly the quantity required.

Casserole Dishes

You can freeze these in the casserole used for cooking the food, but often this is troublesome, for you may need that particular casserole.

If you are cooking a casserole dish with the deliberate intention of freezing the food, line the ovenproof container with a double thickness of foil, *before* adding the various ingredients and keep the foil in the dish during the cooking period. Allow the food to cool, then freeze. When quite firm, lift the foil shape from the casserole and wrap well. When the time comes to reheat the food, simply place the foil package in the original cooking container.

If, on the other hand, you are only freezing a portion of the cooked dish you can put this into polythene (styrofoam) bags, boxes, etc., or use the same procedure as above, i.e. lining the dish after cooking in which you intend to reheat the food.

Below: Preparing vegetables to be frozen

Above: Preparing fruit to be frozen

FREEZING VEGETABLES

It is very wise to have a good supply of vegetables in your freezer when you are on a diet. As you will see from the tables and recipes in the vegetable section of this book, pages 58 to 69, many vegetables are low on calories and reasonably low in carbohydrate content too. These are the kind to buy or freeze yourself if you grow, or are able to purchase, prime vegetables. It is not worth freezing any foods that are not absolutely fresh and of first-rate quality; this applies to vegetables particularly. As most vegetables have a long storage life if prepared correctly for the freezer, you can be sure of having a good selection of green and other low-calorie vegetables at periods of the year when, through seasonal changes, or bad weather, they may not be available in their fresh form.

Your freezer instruction book will give you advice on blanching and packing the vegetables correctly.

Cooked vegetable dishes are ideal for appetizers and light snacks and you will find a selection in both the vegetable and vegetarian sections of this book together with the easy ideas on these pages.

FREEZING FRUITS

Fruits, like vegetables, fit into most diets and it is wise to freeze these when in season.

If some of the family are dieting and others are not, then freeze the fruits without sugar so that each person can sweeten the fruit as desired.

If you make fruit purées by sieving or blending raw ripe or cooked fruits you can pack a good quantity of fruit in a comparatively small space. The purée is ideal for various simple dishes, such as Fruit Fool or Fruit Snow.

Fruit purées also make good sauces to serve with plain yogurt or with various meats, e.g. apple sauce with pork and cranberry or orange sauce with poultry.

Courgettes (Zucchini) Lyonnaise

■ 18/Kj74 □3.4 g

Metric/Imperial
450 g/1 lb courgettes
225 g/8 oz onions, peeled
2 garlic cloves, peeled and crushed
150 ml/¼ pint chicken stock
salt
pepper
TO GARNISH:
2 × 15 ml spoons/ 2 tablespoons chopped parsley

American
1 lb zucchini
½ lb onions, peeled
2 garlic cloves, peeled and crushed
⅔ cup chicken stock
salt
pepper
TO GARNISH:
2 tablespoons chopped parsley

❧Wash the courgettes (zucchini) and cut away the tough ends, slice very thinly. Cut the onions into wafer-thin slices, and put the vegetables and garlic with the stock, salt and pepper into a saucepan and cover tightly, then simmer gently until tender.

To serve: Hot or cold topped with the parsley.

To freeze: If preparing for freezing keep the saucepan covered all the time, then when reheating cover until the vegetables are almost ready to serve. Lift the lid of the saucepan and allow the excess moisture to evaporate.

If freezing to serve cold then let this moisture evaporate at the end of the cooking time.

Variations:

1: If on a low-carbohydrate diet, toss the vegetables in a little butter before adding the stock.

2: Courgettes à la Grècque: Omit most of the stock and use a generous amount of lemon juice to flavour the dish.

3: Courgettes à la Provençale: Omit all the stock and add 450 g/1 lb skinned and sliced tomatoes. These will provide the necessary liquid for cooking the dish. This recipe would serve about 8.

Courgettes (Zucchini) Lyonnaise; Courgettes à la Provencale

Equipment

Family Menus

Family Menus

There is no doubt that continually having to prepare two entirely different types of meals can be time-consuming and difficult. At the same time, it is no use pretending that we can eat 'normal family meals' and still lose weight. There *must* be some adjustment and modification of everyday foods and menus.

In this section you will find a number of dishes which can form part of interesting meals for *every* member of the family. In some cases it is the person slimming who must make certain concessions; they will need to omit some of the ingredients that have a generous number of calories or a high carbohydrate content.

In other dishes the basic recipe is planned specifically for the slimmer and there are hints to make it more appealing or satisfying for the rest of the family. Slimming meals must be appetizing otherwise the diet stands a poor chance of being successful.

HAVE A GOOD BREAKFAST

This may sound strange advice when one is cutting down on food in order to slim, but it is sensible advice, particularly if you are dealing with overweight children. All too often the people who cannot face or have no time to eat breakfast feel hungry mid-morning, so have a cake, biscuits or sweetmeats (candies) to keep them going, plus a milky drink.

A *good* breakfast need not be a high-calorie meal; as you will see from the menus on pages 106 and 107, the kind of breakfast that the family enjoys can be adapted by anyone who is slimming.

Unsweetened fruit juice or fruit, which has the advantage that it takes longer to eat and is therefore more satisfying, would be a good choice. Beware though of too much fruit if you are following a low-carbohydrate diet; page 21 explains more fully about this.

There are cereals on the market with a lower, but not very low, calorie content. Have just a small helping, do not follow the example of the rest of the family if they heap their cereal bowls. Avoid sugar and use skimmed milk rather than full-cream milk.

Instead of a cereal choose a protein food, e.g. boiled, scrambled or poached eggs, cooked as pages 91 and 92, or an omelette (omelet) as the recipes which follow. Poached smoked haddock or cod makes a breakfast dish with plenty of flavour, which all the family will enjoy.

SEASONING AN OMELETTE (OMELET) PAN

Although the modern non-stick (silicone) finish makes seasoning an omelette (omelet) pan less necessary than in the old days, you may have invested in a new one, especially for omelettes (omelets), which does not have a special finish. It is therefore very important to prepare *this* pan before it is used and to take precautions when cooking in it, so that omelettes (omelets) do not stick.

To season a new pan, rub well with a little oil or fat (shortening), heat the pan and rub the oil or fat thoroughly into the surface. Next put a little salt into the warm pan and rub this in well, using soft tissue or absorbent paper that cannot scratch the surface of the pan. Tip out any surplus salt, but do not wash the pan. Put it away without using it for a day, then repeat the process. Rub away all salt and any fat on the surface of the inside of the pan, but again do not wash the inside of the pan.

Use the omelette (omelet) pan and wipe out the inside as soon as possible after use with a clean piece of soft paper.

In this way you never need to wash the inside of the pan and it will never cause omelettes (omelets) to stick. Store an omelette (omelet) pan carefully with a sheet of paper over it, so that other saucepans do not scratch the inside surface.

These precautions are helpful to slimmers for they do enable you to use less fat in cooking the egg mixture.

Plain Omelette

■ 113/Kj 473 □ Nil	
Metric/Imperial	
4 eggs	
salt	
pepper	
2 × 15 ml spoons/2 tablespoons water	
15 g/½ oz butter	
American	
4 eggs	
salt	
pepper	
2 tablespoons water	
1 tablespoon butter	

❧ Whisk the eggs with the salt, pepper and water. Do not overbeat this type of omelette (omelet); you are just blending the yolks and whites together. The water is not essential, but gives a lighter omelette (omelet) when cooked. Heat the butter in an omelette (omelet) pan about 13 cm/5 inches to 15 cm/6 inches; this is a small amount of butter, so it is important to use a well-seasoned pan or one with a non-stick (silicone) finish. Pour in the eggs, allow to cook for about half a minute, when the mixture should set at the bottom. Tilt the pan, at the same time loosening the egg mixture from the sides of the pan. Continue like this, this process is known as working an omelette (omelet), until set to personal taste. Fold or roll, away from the handle, and tip onto a hot dish.

Omelettes (Omelets) from left: Herb; Cheese; Mushroom

To serve: As soon as cooked.
To freeze: Must not be frozen.
Variations:
1: One-Egg Omelette (Omelet): If you are having just one egg, instead of two, heat the butter in the pan; pour in the beaten egg, then tilt the pan at once, so the egg covers only half the small pan, then continue working the omelette (omelet) over half the pan only.
2: Cheese Omelette (Omelet): Fill the omelette (omelet) with a very little grated or cottage cheese before folding.
3: Herb Omelette (Omelet): Blend chopped fresh herbs with the beaten egg.
4: Vegetable Omelette (Omelet): Mix finely chopped raw or cooked mushrooms with the beaten eggs or fill the omelette (omelet) with cooked low-calorie vegetables before folding.

Family Menus

LET US LOOK AT FAMILY MEALS

This paragraph is addressed to the non-slimming members of the family, if there are any. Modern statistics show that most people could benefit by losing weight even if it is just a few kilogrammes or pounds, so all the family may join in the campaign for a sensible and pleasant slimming routine with considerable benefit to their health and appearance.

Let us assume that there is no need for all the family to lose weight, but even so, please examine some typical family meals and see just *how* you can help people who need to slim.

Breakfast has been covered on the previous pages.

Mid-morning means no snacks at all, and tea or coffee without milk if possible or with the minimum amount of skimmed milk or a drink made with water and a beef or yeast extract.

Main Meals are so varied that it is difficult to be too dogmatic, but many dishes and menus can be adjusted. Here are some suggestions:

Appetizers should either be avoided or the suggestions on pages 24 to 27 should be followed.

Soups should be of the kind given on pages 28 to 33, but if the family are having a thickened soup this can be done at the end of the cooking period, and an unthickened portion of the soup, provided it is not high in both calories and carbohydrate content, given to the slimmer.

Stews can be treated in the same way. Often one fries the vegetables etc. in fat (shortening) first, blends in flour and then the liquid. This process can be changed around, as you will see in the recipe on page 191. The thickening is done at the very end by gradually adding a beurre mânié, a blending of fat and flour, so it is simple to take out an unthickened portion.

Roast joints are not a problem, provided a thickened gravy is not given; just offer any meat juices that flow from the meat in carving, or see the suggestions for making special sauces on pages 78 to 81 and 168. Some of these would make a pleasant change from the usual gravy.

Accompaniments, such as traditional stuffings, may have to be avoided while on a diet, but again one can have a new change of flavour with a less fattening mixture, see pages 50–1.

A Yorkshire pudding, to serve with beef, can be made with skimmed milk,

Right: Thickened and clear soups can be easily adapted for the slimmer

but even if you do this the pudding does add to the fattening quality of the meal, so it must be eaten sparingly. A recipe is given on page 152.

Vegetables are no great problem, for there is such a good variety from which to choose and the chapter on page 58 dealing with this subject will perhaps give new ideas that all the family will enjoy. Obviously one must avoid vegetables which are high in carbohydrate content.

Desserts and cakes are, on the whole, taboo, except for very special occasions. A recipe for making preserves follows.

Preserves for Slimmers

While it is better to avoid jams, jellies and marmalades, it may be difficult for adults or children to accept the fact that they must eat a slice of toast at breakfast-time *without* marmalade. There are two ways of dealing with the matter. Low-calorie jams are available; these have just about half the calories of home-made or commercial preserves made with the usual amount of sugar. It is possible, however, to prepare a preserve which could be combined with family jam-making.

Prepare and cook the fruit as usual.
For the slimmer: Take out a small quan-

tity of prepared hot fruit purée. Do not use too much at one time, since the slimmer's preserves will not keep for long.
For the family: The rest of the prepared fruit will then have sugar, any other ingredients (such as lemon juice) added and be boiled until set.
For the slimmer's preserve: Add sugar substitute to taste to the purée. For each 300 ml/$\frac{1}{2}$ pint/$1\frac{1}{4}$ cups allow 1×7.5 ml spoon/$\frac{1}{2}$ tablespoon/1 envelope gelatine. Soften this in 1×15 ml spoon/1 table-spoon cold water. Stir into the hot fruit purée until dissolved. Allow to cool, but not set, spoon into a jar. Use within a week to 10 days. Store in the refrigerator.
To freeze: Seasonal fruit purées can be frozen, stored for about 6 months and the preserves made regularly.

Family Menus

The recipes on these pages, together with pages 188–190, give a selection of dishes for main meals and a few starters.

Sweetbreads Princess

■ 361/Kj 1515 □ 7.3 g

Metric/Imperial

550 g/1¼ lb lambs' sweetbreads

water (see method)

300 ml/½ pint white stock

1 × 15 ml spoon/1 tablespoon lemon juice

100 g/4 oz button mushrooms

salt

pepper

15 g/½ oz cornflour

3 × 15 ml spoons/3 tablespoons milk

25 g/1 oz butter

3 × 15 ml spoons/3 tablespoons single cream

TO GARNISH:
paprika

little chopped parsley

American

1¼ lb lambs' sweetbreads

water (see method)

1¼ cups white stock

1 tablespoon lemon juice

¼ lb mushrooms

salt

pepper

2 tablespoons cornstarch

3 tablespoons milk

2 tablespoons butter

3 tablespoons light cream

TO GARNISH:
paprika

little chopped parsley

❧ First soak the sweetbreads in cold water for 1 hour. Put into a saucepan and and cover with fresh cold water. Bring the water to the boil and throw it away. This process is known as blanching the sweetbreads and whitens them. Return the sweetbreads to the saucepan with the stock, lemon juice, mushrooms, salt and pepper. Cover the saucepan tightly so the liquid does not evaporate too much, simmer for 30 minutes or until tender. Lift the sweetbreads from the stock retaining this in the saucepan, cool sufficiently to handle, then remove any skin and gristle. Blend the cornflour (cornstarch) with the 3 × 15 ml spoons/3 tablespoons cold milk, add to the stock together with the butter. Bring the sauce to the boil and cook steadily until thickened. Replace the sweetbreads and reheat thoroughly. Lastly stir in the cream and heat without boiling.

To serve for the slimmer: Lift the sweetbreads from the sauce and serve with the minimum of the thickened sauce and garnished with paprika and chopped parsley. Serve with broccoli or spinach.

To serve for the family: Garnish with piped creamed potatoes.

To freeze: The completed dish should not be frozen, but uncooked sweetbreads freeze well for 3 months and could be used in this dish. The blanching thaws them adequately.

Variation:

Sweetbread Brochettes: Blanch, then simmer the sweetbreads as above until tender. Remove from the stock, cut away any gristle and surplus fat. Divide the sweetbreads into neat pieces. De-rind several rashers (slices) of bacon, halve, form into rolls and put onto metal skewers with the sweetbreads. Cook steadily under a medium grill (broiler), turning once or twice until the bacon is crisp and the sweetbreads hot. Small mushrooms or tomatoes could be used with, or instead of, the bacon.

Sweetbreads Princess; Mimosa Liver

Mimosa Liver

■ 198/Kj831 □2.2 g

Metric/Imperial
2 hard-boiled eggs
225 g/8 oz lamb's or calf's liver
salt
freshly ground black pepper
pinch dry mustard
25 g/1 oz butter
2 or 3 sprigs parsley
lettuce
3 tomatoes, sliced

American
2 hard-boiled eggs
½ lb lamb's or calf's liver
salt
freshly ground black pepper
pinch dry mustard
2 tablespoons butter
2 or 3 sprigs parsley
lettuce
3 tomatoes, sliced

❧ Crack the shells of the eggs as soon as cooked, then plunge them into cold water (to avoid the formation of a dark line round the yolks), but do not allow the eggs to become quite cold. Cut the liver into thin slices to shorten the cooking time, and therefore keep the meat moist and tender; add salt and pepper to taste, and a pinch of dry mustard. Heat the butter in a saucepan, fry the liver for 1 to 2 minutes on either side.

Shell the *warm* eggs, remove the whites, Tip the liver onto a board with the egg whites and parsley, chop finely. Cool the mixture, but cover to prevent it becoming dry. Put the lettuce onto a flat dish with the tomatoes. Spoon the liver in a neat mound on the lettuce. Chop the egg yolks and sprinkle over the top.

To serve for the slimmer: Serve as a main dish.

To serve for the family: Serve as an appetizer.

To freeze: Frozen liver could be used; do not freeze the cooked dish, as hard-boiled eggs become tough.

Variation:

Cook the liver in a little well-seasoned stock instead of butter.

Family Menus

Jellied Turkey Salad

■ 187/Kj 784 □ 1.5 g

Metric/Imperial

3 × 15 ml spoons/3 tablespoons Oil and vinegar dressing, see page 81

0.75 kg/1½ lb cooked turkey, diced

3 × level 15 ml spoons/3 level tablespoons (40 g/1½ oz) powder gelatine

3 × 15 ml spoons/3 tablespoons cold water

600 ml/1 pint turkey stock or water and 2 chicken stock cubes

2 × 15 ml spoons/2 tablespoons lemon juice

1 × 15 ml spoon/1 tablespoon grated onion

1 × 5 ml spoon/1 teaspoon grated horseradish or horseradish cream

salt

pepper

2 × 15 ml spoons/2 tablespoons chopped red pepper (capsicum)

100 g/4 oz celery, diced

50 g/2 oz blanched almonds, flaked (optional)

2 hard-boiled eggs, chopped

TO GARNISH:
small lettuce

watercress

1 medium avocado

mayonnaise

American

3 tablespoons Oil and vinegar dressing, see page 81

1½ lb cooked turkey, diced

6 envelopes powder gelatin

3 tablespoons cold water

Gazpacho

■ 108/Kj 454 □ 10.8 g

Metric/Imperial

0.75 kg/1½ lb ripe tomatoes, skinned and chopped

2 medium onions, chopped

2 garlic cloves, chopped

1 green pepper (capsicum)

½ medium cucumber

salt

pepper

2 × 15 ml spoons/2 tablespoons lemon juice

1 × 15 ml spoon/1 tablespoon olive oil

iced water

American

1½ lb ripe tomatoes, skinned and chopped

2 medium onions, chopped

2 garlic cloves, chopped

1 green pepper

½ medium cucumber

salt

pepper

2 tablespoons lemon juice

1 tablespoon olive oil

iced water

🍃 Put the tomatoes, one of the onions and all the garlic into a saucepan. Simmer only until the tomatoes have softened slightly. Sieve or put into the blender, but remember you do not get rid of the seeds entirely in a blender. Dice the green pepper (capsicum), discard the core and seeds, skin the cucumber, if desired and dice, add half the pepper (capsicum) and half the cucumber to the tomato mixture with the salt, pepper, lemon juice, oil and enough iced water to give the consistency of a moderately thick soup. Chill. Keep the unused vegetables covered so they do not dry. Spoon the extra chopped onion, diced pepper (capsicum) and diced cucumber into separate dishes so that everyone can help themselves as a topping for the cold soup.

To serve for the slimmer: You can have all the soup ingredients as given, so spoon your portion into a chilled soup bowl.

To serve for the family: This recipe is good for slimmers, but it does reduce the oil, which is so much a part of the traditional Spanish soup, so anyone on a low-carbohydrate diet or the rest of the family could add another 1–2 × 15 ml spoons/1–2 tablespoons olive oil to the tomato mixture and add a dish of soft breadcrumbs to sprinkle on the soup with the diced vegetables.

To freeze: Freeze the tomato mixture and add the onions, garlic, pepper (capsicum) and cucumber when the mixture has thawed. Use within 6 months.

2½ cups turkey stock or water and 3 chicken bouillon cubes

2 tablespoons lemon juice

1 tablespoon grated onion

1 teaspoon grated horseradish or horseradish cream

salt

pepper

2 tablespoons chopped red pepper

1 cup diced celery

½ cup blanched flaked almonds (optional)

2 hard-boiled eggs, chopped

TO GARNISH:
small head lettuce

watercress

1 medium avocado

mayonnaise

🍂Combine oil and vinegar dressing and diced turkey; keep cool while preparing the other ingredients. Soften the gelatine in the cold water, then dissolve in the hot stock, or water and stock cubes; cool, then add the rest of the ingredients, except the garnish. Spoon into a large oiled mould and allow to set.

Invert the mould onto the serving dish; arrange a border of lettuce and watercress. Halve, skin and slice the avocado, blend with mayonnaise, spoon onto the lettuce.

To serve for the slimmer: Avoid the avocado and mayonnaise. The calories and carbohydrate content are based on a portion *without* these.

To freeze: This dish is not suitable for freezing.

Orange Cheese Cake

■ 411/Kj 1725 ☐ 36 g

Metric/Imperial

FOR THE BASE:
100 g/4 oz digestive biscuits

40 g/1½ oz butter

grated rind 2 oranges

25 g/1 oz sugar

FOR THE FILLING:
50 g/2 oz butter

grated rind 1 orange

50 g/2 oz sugar

2 eggs

15 g/½ oz cornflour

350 g/12 oz cottage cheese, sieved

2 × 15 ml spoons/2 tablespoons orange juice

TO DECORATE:
segments from 2 oranges

American

FOR THE BASE:
¼ lb Graham crackers

3 tablespoons butter

grated rind 2 oranges

2 tablespoons sugar

FOR THE FILLING:
¼ cup butter

grated rind 1 orange

¼ cup sugar

2 eggs

2 tablespoons cornstarch

1½ cups sieved cottage cheese

2 tablespoons orange juice

TO DECORATE:
segments from 2 oranges

🍂First prepare the base. Crush the biscuit crumbs with a rolling pin or put in a blender a little at a time. Cream the butter, orange rind and sugar. Add the biscuit crumbs and use to line the bottom of an 18–20 cm/7–8 inch cake tin – choose one with a loose base. Cream together the butter, orange rind and sugar for the filling. Separate the eggs and add the yolks, cornflour (cornstarch), cottage cheese and orange juice. Lastly fold in the stiffly whisked egg whites. Spoon onto the biscuit case and bake for approximately 1¼ hours in a moderate oven (160°C/325°F, Gas Mark 3) until firm but pale golden. Allow to cool in the oven with the heat turned off (this stops the cake sinking). Remove from the cake tin by lifting the base. Sprinkle icing sugar over the top of the cheese cake. Cut away the pith from the 2 oranges after grating the 'zest' for the base, and cut the fruit into neat segments, discarding the skin and pips (seeds). Arrange on top of the cheese cake.

To serve for the slimmer: Really only a special occasion dessert. You could reduce the calories by 182 and carbohydrates by 17.6 g if you did not eat the biscuit crumb base.

To freeze: Open-freeze, then wrap. Use within a month.

Variation:
Other fruits may be used in place of the orange. For a special occasion a fresh pineapple is a good choice.

Family Menus

Grilled Ham and Pineapple

■425/Kj 1783 □6.8 g

Metric/Imperial
4 gammon rashers (each 100 g/4 oz)
15 g/½ oz butter, melted
4 rings fresh pineapple (each 50 g/2 oz)
15 g/½ oz brown sugar
TO GARNISH:
watercress

American
4 ham slices (each ¼ lb)
1 tablespoon butter, melted
4 rings fresh pineapple (each 2 oz)
1 tablespoon raw sugar
TO GARNISH:
watercress

♣Cut away the rind from the gammon rashers (ham slices) and snip the fat at regular intervals. Brush the lean part of the gammon (ham) with the butter. Do not preheat the grill (broiler) since that causes the fat to curl and burn. Put the meat under the grill (broiler) and cook steadily on both sides until tender. Put the pineapple on the grill (broiler) pan, turn once so the fruit absorbs a little fat from the gammon (ham). Heat for 1 to 2 minutes then turn.

For the family: Sprinkle with sugar.
For the slimmer: Avoid the sugar, for one important point is to try and educate

Above: Grilled Ham and Pineapple.

your palate to enjoy tart tastes. Continue heating the pineapple for a minute.
To serve: Arrange the pineapple on the meat and garnish with watercress. The calories etc. given are for a portion *without* sugar.
To freeze: Do not freeze.

COOKING FRUIT

It is simple to poach fruit in a little water. Remove some of the fruit into a bowl and add sugar substitute to taste for the slimmer. Then stir sugar or honey into the fruit remaining in the saucepan; heat the sugar or honey for 1 to 2 minutes in the fruit and liquid to dissolve this for the family.

Steamed Sponge

■ 194/Kj 815 □28.2 g

Metric/Imperial
50 g/2 oz margarine
50 g/2 oz caster sugar
2 eggs
150 g/5 oz self-raising flour or plain flour with 1 × 1.25 ml spoon/1¼ teaspoons baking powder
little water to mix

American
¼ cup margarine
¼ cup caster sugar

Above: Steamed Sponge

2 eggs
1¼ cups self-rising flour or all-purpose flour with 1¼ teaspoons baking powder
little water to mix

♣Cream the margarine and sugar until soft and light. Gradually beat in the eggs. Sieve the flour, or flour and baking powder, then fold into the margarine mixture. Add enough water to make a soft dropping consistency. Put into a greased 1 litre/2 pint/5 cup bowl. Top with greased greaseproof (wax) paper and foil. Steam for 1¼ hours over boiling water; allow this to boil rapidly for the first 45 minutes to make sure the pudding is light.

To serve for the slimmer: Although this pudding really serves 4 only, the calculations are based on one-sixth of the pudding, so you have only a thin slice. Top the hot pudding with a fruit purée, sweetened with sugar substitute; the figures do not include this.

To serve for the family: This particular recipe is using a low proportion of margarine and sugar so you could be generous with a jam, golden (light corn) syrup or fruit topping.

Adding Sugar Substitute in Baking

Sugar plays an important part in lightening cakes and puddings, which sugar substitute cannot replace, see page 84.

Above right: Fruit Soufflé Omelette (Omelet); Ragoût of Beef

Ragoût of Beef

Dice 450 g/1 lb good quality stewing beef. Peel and slice 2 onions, 3 carrots, 2 tomatoes, chop 2 sticks (stalks) celery and enough parsley to give 2 × 15 ml spoons/2 tablespoons. Put the meat into a strong saucepan, heat for 2 to 3 minutes, turning once or twice. As no fat is used, be careful the meat does not burn. This initial searing seals in much of the meat juices. Add the rest of the ingredients, 600 ml/1 pint/2½ cups stock, or water with 2 beef stock (4 bouillon) cubes, and salt and pepper to taste. Bring just to boiling point, cover the saucepan, lower the heat. Simmer for approximately 2¼ hours, or until the beef is tender.

To serve for the slimmer: Lift out one portion of meat and vegetables, serve with a little unthickened liquid. The calories and carbohydrate count are based on this.

To serve for the family: Blend 25 g/1 oz/2 tablespoons fat (shortening) or butter with 25 g/1 oz/¼ cup flour. Drop tiny pieces into the boiling liquid; stir briskly until a smooth thickened sauce. Add a little wine or extra stock if too thick.

To freeze: Use within 4 months.

■ 398/Kj 1673 □9.2 g

Fruit Soufflé Omelette (Omelet)

■ 204/Kj 855 □4.2 g

Metric/Imperial
6 eggs
2 × 15 ml spoons/2 tablespoons milk
sugar substitute to taste
25 g/1 oz butter
225 g/8 oz strawberries
American
6 eggs
2 tablespoons milk
sugar substitute to taste
2 tablespoons butter
1¾ cups strawberries

Separate the eggs. Beat the yolks with the milk and a little sugar substitute. Whisk the whites until very stiff, fold into the yolks. Heat the butter in a large omelette (omelet) pan, pour in the egg mixture. Cook until the mixture sets at the bottom, then move the omelette (omelet) pan to the grill (broiler) and cook under a steady heat until set.

Mash and sweeten most of the strawberries. The purée can be heated if desired. Spread the fruit purée over the omelette (omelet) then fold *away* from the handle.

To serve: Tip onto a hot dish and decorate with whole strawberries. Serve at once.

To serve for the family: The basic recipe really does not need adjustment. Use sugar substitute and top your portion of the omelette (omelet) with sieved icing (confectioners') sugar.

To freeze: Unsuitable for freezing.

Variations:

1: Fill the omelette with fruit flavoured yogurt or plain yogurt, blended with diced fresh fruit.

2: Non slimmers can fill the omelette with hot mincemeat or a selection of dried fruit heated in a little rum or orange juice. This enables the fruit to swell as well as absorbing the flavour of the rum or orange juice.

3: Fill the omelette with spiced yogurt, add a little ground ginger, cinnamon and allspice to the yogurt.

4: Fill the omelette with cottage cheese blended with lemon or fruit juice or fruit of your choice.

Family Menus

191

Keeping Slim

Keeping Slim

If you have followed a fairly stringent diet, achieved your target and are now slim it is obviously important to assess just *how* you will keep this new figure.
All too often people think they can return to their 'old ways' of eating and trust to luck that all will be well.
Unfortunately one can gain weight just as rapidly as one can lose it, so plan your eating habits for the future years with care.
This maxim also applies to people who have been slim during their youth and as they tend to become less energetic gain those unwanted, and unwelcome, kilogrammes or pounds.
Often though a slimming diet has given one a new look towards food, you have probably lost the habit of going to the biscuit (cookie) tin at odd times, or taking the second helping you did not really need. This is splendid, for if you retain this habit you will have no problems in the future.

YOUR PLAN OF CAMPAIGN

It is much easier to lose an odd kilogramme or pound than to wait until it becomes a sizeable problem.

There are occasions when you have to eat the wrong food, or a little too much. It may be you had a splendid gastronomic vacation, or have been entertained rather a lot. Nothing is worse than the person who cannot eat delicious food at a party because they are dieting. Eat and enjoy the feast then plan to eat less for the next day or so. This chapter gives various ways of keeping slim.

On these two pages the dishes are based upon fruit and you could follow these ideas for a day or two, by which time that small weight increase should have vanished.

Fruit Cocktail

■ 45/Kj 189 □ 11.2 g
Metric/Imperial
2 oranges (each 100 g/4 oz)
1 grapefruit (175 g/6 oz)
2 tangerines or similar fruit (50 g/2 oz each)
squeeze lemon juice
150 ml/¼ pint water
sugar substitute to taste
1 firm ripe pear or apple (100 g/4 oz)
50 g/2 oz green grapes
American
2 oranges (each ¼ lb)
1 grapefruit (6 oz)
2 tangerines or similar fruit (each 2 oz)
squeeze lemon juice
⅔ cup water
sugar substitute to taste
1 firm ripe pear or apple (¼ lb)
2 oz white grapes

Cut the peel and pith from the citrus fruit. Cut the segments of fruit away from the skin, discard the pips (seeds). If you cut the fruit over a bowl the surplus juice drops into this. Put a little orange peel into a saucepan with the lemon juice, water and sugar substitute, simmer for 5 minutes, strain over the citrus fruit. Cool, then add the diced pear or apple and de-seeded grapes.

To serve: Chill well; spoon into glasses. These look attractive if the rims are dipped in cold water then into finely chopped parsley.

To freeze: Better eaten freshly made.

Orange Starter

■ 132/Kj554 □13.5 g

Metric/Imperial

150 ml/¼ pint unsweetened fresh or canned orange juice

1 egg

sugar substitute

TO GARNISH:

sprig fresh mint or little nutmeg, grated

American

⅔ cup unsweetened fresh or canned orange juice

1 egg

sugar substitute

TO GARNISH:

sprig fresh mint or little nutmeg, grated

Chill the orange juice thoroughly. Whisk the egg well. Whisk in the orange juice or emulsify in the liquidizer goblet. Add a little sugar substitute to taste, strain into one large or two smaller glasses.

To serve: Top with the mint or nutmeg.

To freeze: This is unsuitable for freezing.

Variation:

Other fruit juices can be used in place of the orange juice. Unsweetened apple juice is a good substitute. Pineapple juice or a mixture of equal quantities of pineapple and orange is also tasty. Lemon is refreshing, served well chilled on a hot summer's day. Apricot will make a special starter, with its smooth texture.

FRUIT SORBETS

A sorbet used to be a feature of banquets, when it was served between courses. Nowadays it can be served as a dessert, or a dish in a day on fruit.

Prepare either diluted fruit juice or make a thin fruit purée, sweeten with sugar substitute to taste. Freeze until the mixture is slightly mushy. To each 300 ml/½ pint/1¼ cups allow an egg white. Whisk this until stiff, fold into the half-frozen fruit mixture. Return to the freezer, leave until firm.

If storing for any length of time add gelatine (gelatin) (see comments page 196).

FRUIT SOUPS

These are a great favourite in many European countries and they are deliciously refreshing.

The most suitable fruits are apples (choose a fairly sharp cooking variety), plums, cherries (the cooking variety is better than the dessert type), rhubarb and any other fruits which have a strong taste when cooked or diluted with a fair amount of liquid.

Prepare the fruit for cooking, then simmer in water, or water and wine (remember the latter adds both calories and carbohydrates to your diet, so use sparingly), until a smooth thin mixture. Beat, sieve or purée in a blender until smooth, then add sugar substitute to taste. A fruit soup should always be sharp in taste. A little lemon juice can be added to most fruits to sharpen the taste. The lemon soup below is particularly good in hot weather.

Fruit Cocktail; Orange Starter; Lemon Soup

Lemon Soup

■ 28/Kj117 □Trace

Metric/Imperial

600 ml/1 pint water and 2 chicken stock cubes

2 × 15 ml spoons/2 tablespoons lemon juice

1 egg

salt

pepper

American

2½ cups water and 3 chicken bouillon cubes

2 tablespoons lemon juice

1 egg

salt

pepper

Heat the stock or water and stock cubes. Beat the lemon juice with the egg. Whisk into the stock together with salt and pepper to taste. Simmer *without boiling* for a few minutes.

To serve: Hot or very well chilled.

To freeze: Do not freeze.

Keeping Slim

PLAN ONE LIGHT MEAL

Another excellent way to control your weight is to have one really light meal each day. You may choose breakfast, or prefer a light mid-day luncheon or evening dinner.

You could serve a savoury ice, as the suggestions on this page, followed by a green or mixed salad or have a pâté *with* the salad. Other members of the family could add an extra course if they wished. Most people will enjoy these dishes, whether they are weight-watching or not.

SAVOURY ICES

We enjoy sweet ices and sorbets, why not savoury versions? These are delicious and make super first courses, light savouries, or an alternative to cheese and biscuits at the end of the meal.

Here are two quick and easy ideas, both of which are suitable for a slimming diet.

Adding gelatine (gelatin)

If you intend to freeze these ices or the sorbets on page 195 for more than a day it is a good idea to add gelatine (gelatin), for the dishes contain a high percentage of water. The gelatine (gelatin) prevents the mixture freezing with small splinters of ice in it.

If you have a clear unthickened liquid, as below, or diluted fruit juice in a sorbet allow:

2×5 ml spoons/2 teaspoons gelatine (gelatin) to 600 ml/1 pint/$2\frac{1}{2}$ cups liquid.

A thicker mixture, as the second recipe on the right or a fruit purée in a sorbet needs half this amount.

Soften gelatine (gelatin) in a little cold liquid then dissolve over hot water or in the hot liquid.

Consommé Ice

Make consommé as page 28, or buy canned consommé. Add a little lemon juice. Freeze lightly, then fold in 1 stiffly whisked egg white to each 300 ml/$\frac{1}{2}$ pint/ $1\frac{1}{4}$ cups consommé and re-freeze. Top with plain yogurt and herbs.

To freeze: Use within 2 months.

Frosted Mulligatawny

Blend canned or homemade mulligatawny soup, prepared as page 177, with enough yogurt or single (light) cream or milk to make a less stiff consistency. Freeze lightly, top with a little desiccated (shredded) coconut. The combination of the hot curry flavour and ice-cold temperature is very good.

Variation:

Blend the soup with a thin purée of cooked or canned apricots, garnish with apricot halves.

To freeze: Use within 2 months.

Crab and Avocado Pâté

■ 96/Kj 403 □2.2 g

Metric/Imperial

2×15 ml spoons/2 tablespoons lemon juice

1 ripe but firm avocado

175 g/6 oz fresh or canned crabmeat

1 tomato, skinned and chopped

salt

freshly ground pepper

pinch cayenne pepper (optional)

lettuce

TO GARNISH:

parsley

celery curls, see page 94

American

2 tablespoons lemon juice

1 ripe but firm avocado

6 oz fresh or canned crabmeat

1 tomato, skinned and chopped

salt

freshly ground pepper

pinch cayenne pepper (optional)

lettuce

TO GARNISH:

parsley

celery curls, see page 94

Put 1×15 ml spoon/1 tablespoon lemon juice into a basin, save the remainder. Halve the avocado, remove and discard the stone (pit), then spoon the pulp from the skin into the basin with the lemon juice; add the crabmeat and tomato, mash together. Add salt and pepper; gradually add enough of the remaining lemon juice to give a refreshing flavour. Wash and dry the lettuce leaves, arrange on a shallow dish.

To serve: Spoon onto the lettuce, garnish with parsley and curls of celery; serve as soon as possible after making or thawing.

To freeze: This pâté freezes well for 6–8 weeks.

To thaw: Allow to thaw in the refrigerator or other cold place.

Variations:

1: Avocado Cheese Pâté: Use cottage cheese in place of crabmeat, flavour mixture with a few drops Tabasco sauce.

2: Avocado Ham Pâté: Use finely chopped ham instead of crabmeat, flavour with a little horseradish cream.

Kipper and Horseradish Pâté

■ 207/Kj 869 □3.6 g

Metric/Imperial

4 kippers or 8 kipper fillets (450 g/1 lb)

150 ml/$\frac{1}{4}$ pint plain yogurt

1×5 ml spoon/1 teaspoon made mustard and 1×5 ml spoon/1 teaspoon horseradish cream *or* 2×5 ml spoons/ 2 teaspoons horseradish cream

3×15 ml spoons/3 tablespoons chopped chives or spring onions

shake of pepper

TO GARNISH:

lettuce heart

2 tomatoes, sliced

1 lemon, sliced

American

4 kippers or 8 kipper fillets (1 lb)

$\frac{2}{3}$ cup plain yogurt

1 teaspoon made mustard and 1 teaspoon horseradish cream or 2 teaspoons horseradish cream

3 tablespoons chopped chives or scallions

shake of pepper

TO GARNISH:

lettuce heart

2 tomatoes, sliced

1 lemon, sliced

From rear:
Consommé Ice;
Kipper and
Horseradish Pâté;
Crab and Avocado
Pâté; Frosted
Mulligatawny

Put the kippers into a dish. Cover with boiling water. Leave for 5 minutes, until softened but not overcooked, lift from the water. Mix the yogurt, mustard, horseradish, half the chives or spring onions (scallions) and pepper together. Flake the warm kippers and blend with the yogurt mixture. Put into a bowl or small mould, allow to cool. Turn out and garnish with the lettuce, tomatoes and lemon. Top with the remaining chives or spring onions (scallions).

To serve: As an appetizer.

To freeze: For a few days only. Add the garnish when thawed.

To thaw: For several hours in the refrigerator.

Variations:

1: Use bloaters or smoked haddock, both of which need cooking.

2: You can make a similar pâté with smoked trout, mackerel or eel, none of which need cooking. If using any of these three fish, blend with slightly more horseradish cream.

Keeping Slim

SERVE A SOUP

One can consider most soups under two categories. The light type, which make a good start to a meal, have few calories and are low in carbohydrate value too, and the sustaining soups which can be served as a complete light meal.

Both types are on this page and you will find other recipes on page 200 and in the soup section.

Melba Toast

Bread or toast seem essential accompaniments to soups. You can enjoy crisp, thin Melba Toast without adding too many calories to your meal.

Make the toast either by toasting ordinary sliced bread on both sides, then split this through the centre and crisp the untoasted sides, or cut wafer-thin slices of bread and crisp fairly slowly in the oven.

Clear Mushroom Soup

■ 5/Kj21 □Trace

Metric/Imperial

175 g/6 oz mushrooms, finely chopped

600 ml/1 pint chicken stock or water and 2 chicken stock cubes or 2 × 5 ml spoons/2 teaspoons yeast extract

salt

pepper

TO GARNISH:
chopped parsley

American

scant 2 cups mushrooms, finely chopped

2½ cups chicken stock or water and 2 chicken bouillon cubes or 2 teaspoons yeast extract

salt

pepper

TO GARNISH:
chopped parsley

❧Simmer the mushrooms for 5 to 10 minutes in the stock, or water and stock cubes or yeast extract, adding salt and pepper to taste.

To serve: Pour into hot soup cups and garnish with chopped parsley.

To freeze: Keeps well for 3 months.

From left: Cheese Soup; Clear Mushroom Soup; Beef and Tomato Consommé

Variations:

1: Use beef instead of chicken stock.

2: Sieve or purée the soup in a blender after cooking; this means the mushrooms do not need chopping before being added to the stock.

3: Creamy Mushroom Soup: Use half stock, or water and 1 stock (bouillon) cube, and half milk. Blend 1–2 egg yolks with a little extra milk or single (light) cream and whisk into the cooked soup. Reheat gently, without boiling.

Cheese Soup

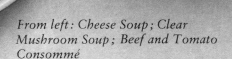

■ 131/Kj550 □8.2 g

Metric/Imperial

225 g/8 oz cottage cheese

600 ml/1 pint plain yogurt

salt

pepper

TO GARNISH:

1 × 15 ml spoon/1 tablespoon chopped parsley

2 × 5 ml spoons/2 teaspoons chopped chives

American

½ lb cottage cheese

2½ cups plain yogurt

salt

pepper

TO GARNISH:

1 tablespoon chopped parsley

2 teaspoons chopped chives

🍀Put the cheese, yogurt and a little salt and pepper into a blender and purée.

To serve: Very well chilled, topped with the herbs.

To freeze: Better freshly prepared.

Variations:

1: Use slightly less plain yogurt and add 2–3 skinned tomatoes to the mixture in the liquidizer. Blending does not remove *all* pips (pits), so the mixture would need sieving if you require an absolutely smooth mixture.

2: Add springs of parsley and/or other herbs to the cheese mixture.

Beef and Tomato Consommé

■ 55/Kj231 □3.9 g

Metric/Imperial

300 ml/½ pint beef consommé, as recipe page 28

300 ml/½ pint tomato juice

salt

pepper

celery salt

pinch dry mustard

2 ripe tomatoes, skinned and chopped

2–3 × 15 ml spoons/2–3 tablespoons grated cheese

1 × 15 ml spoon/1 tablespoon chopped chives

1 × 15 ml spoon/1 tablespoon chopped parsley

American

1¼ cups beef consommé, as recipe page 28

1¼ cups tomato juice

salt

pepper

celery salt

pinch dry mustard

2 ripe tomatoes, skinned and chopped

2–3 tablespoons grated cheese

1 tablespoon chopped chives

1 tablespoon chopped parsley

🍀Mix the consommé and tomato juice, season to taste. If serving hot, heat for 2 minutes only. If serving cold, whisk together then chill.

To serve: Top the hot or cold soup with the tomatoes, cheese and herbs.

To freeze: Freeze without the grated cheese or tomatoes, add these when serving. The herbs can be frozen in the consommé.

To thaw: Stand the container in cold water to speed thawing.

Keeping Slim

It is comparatively easy to produce interesting dishes that fit into a plan for healthy eating if you choose fish, for most fish have no carbohydrate value and are relatively low in calories.

Crab Vichyssoise

■ 159/Kj668 □14.7 g

Metric/Imperial

1 medium crab (225 g/8 oz flesh)

750 ml/1¼ pints water

salt

pepper

sprig parsley

2 medium leeks, sliced as method

1 medium onion, chopped

175 g/6 oz potatoes, diced

150 ml/¼ pint plain yogurt

2–3 × 15 ml spoons/2–3 tablespoons white wine (optional)

squeeze lemon juice

TO GARNISH:

chopped chives

chopped parsley

American

1 medium crab (½ lb flesh)

3 cups water

salt

pepper

sprig parsley

2 medium leeks, sliced as method

1 medium onion, chopped

6 oz potatoes, diced

⅔ cup plain yogurt

2–3 tablespoons white wine (optional)

squeeze lemon juice

TO GARNISH:

chopped chives

chopped parsley

Above: Crab Vichyssoise

Remove all the meat from the body and large claws of the crab. Discard the stomach bag and grey fingers. Put the crabmeat on one side, then place the small claws, shell of the body and large claws into a pan. Add the water, a little salt and pepper and the sprig of parsley. Simmer steadily for 15 to 20 minutes to give a good flavoured fish stock, then strain.

Remove most of the green part of the leeks, but save a little green. Slice the leeks thinly. Put the leeks, onion and potatoes into the fish stock and simmer for about 20 minutes until tender. Either sieve the mixture or purée in the warmed goblet of the blender.

To serve: Hot or cold; serve as soon as possible, as crab is highly perishable.

If serving hot, heat the vegetable purée, stir in the flaked crabmeat, yogurt, wine and lemon juice. Heat gently without boiling. Top with chopped chives and/or parsley.

If serving cold, stir the crabmeat into the smooth, warm vegetable mixture, allow to cool; whisk in the other ingredients. Serve topped with chives and/or parsley.

To freeze: This soup freezes well, but tends to separate slightly so emulsify or whisk before reheating or sieving.

To thaw: In the refrigerator.

Grilled Trout with Citrus Dressing

■ 321/Kj1348 □9.2 g

Metric/Imperial

FOR THE DRESSING:

2 medium oranges

1 medium lemon

1 × 2.5 ml spoon/½ teaspoon mustard powder

salt

pepper

1 × 5 ml spoon/1 teaspoon white wine vinegar

little sugar substitute (optional)

4 fresh trout (350 g/12 oz each)

TO GARNISH:

watercress

¼ cucumber, sliced

1 orange, sliced

American

FOR THE DRESSING:

2 medium oranges

1 medium lemon

½ teaspoon mustard powder

salt

pepper

1 teaspoon white wine vinegar

little sugar substitute (optional)

4 fresh trout (¾ lb each)

watercress

$\frac{1}{4}$ cucumber, sliced

1 orange, sliced

☙Grate the top 'zest' from the oranges and lemon. Be careful to use just the top coloured part of the rind and not the white pith, which makes any mixture slightly bitter. Squeeze out the juice and blend with the rind, mustard, salt, pepper and vinegar. Taste the dressing and add a little sugar substitute if the mixture seems very sharp. Pour into a shallow dish. Remove the heads and clean the fish, place into the dressing and leave for an hour. Remove the fish from the dressing, drain and grill (broil) for 10 to 12 minutes, until tender. Spoon any dressing left over the fish just before the end of the cooking time.

To serve: On a bed of watercress, garnished with cucumber and orange slices.

To freeze: Not suitable for freezing.

Variations:

1: Any oily fish can be used; herrings and mackerel are particularly suitable.

2: If using white (lean) fish add 1 × 15 ml spoon/1 tablespoon oil to the dressing.

Below: Grilled Trout with Citrus Dressing.

Above: Seafood Bisque

Seafood Bisque

■ 415/Kj 1747 □ 12.1 g

Metric/Imperial

225 g/8 oz white fish (weight without skin and bones)

50 g/2 oz butter or margarine

25 g/1 oz flour

450 ml/$\frac{3}{4}$ pint milk and 150 ml/$\frac{1}{4}$ pint single cream or 600 ml/1 pint milk

1 × 1.25 ml spoon/$\frac{1}{4}$ teaspoon paprika

peel from $\frac{1}{2}$ lemon

salt

pepper

1 large or 2 small raw scallops, sliced

75–100 g/3–4 oz shelled prawns

100 g/4 oz fresh crabmeat or 1 small can crabmeat

1 × 15 ml spoon/1 tablespoon lemon juice

1 × 15 ml spoon/1 tablespoon chopped parsley

American

$\frac{1}{2}$ lb lean fish (weight without skin and bones)

$\frac{1}{4}$ cup butter or margarine

$\frac{1}{4}$ cup flour

2 cups milk and $\frac{2}{3}$ cup light cream or 2$\frac{1}{2}$ cups milk

$\frac{1}{4}$ teaspoon paprika

peel from $\frac{1}{2}$ lemon

salt

pepper

1 large or 2 small raw scallops, sliced

3–4 oz shelled shrimp

$\frac{1}{4}$ lb fresh crabmeat or 1 small can crabmeat

1 tablespoon lemon juice

1 tablespoon chopped parsley

☙Cut the fish into 2.5 cm/1 inch cubes. Heat the butter or margarine in a saucepan, add the fish, cook until a delicate golden brown, then lift out of the pan, add the flour. Blend the milk and cream or milk with the paprika and stir into the 'roux'. Bring the sauce to the boil, stir until thickened, put in the thin strips of lemon rind and salt and pepper. Add the diced scallops, simmer for 5 minutes, then put in the rest of the ingredients, heat *gently* for a few minutes only, remove the lemon rind.

To serve: Hot with Melba toast, see page 198.

To freeze: This freezes well for up to a month. Add the lemon juice when reheating.

To thaw: Thaw by warming in the top of a double saucepan or basin over hot water. Do not overheat as this toughens the shellfish.

Variations:

1: Replace the lemon juice with 1 × 15 ml spoon/1 tablespoon dry sherry.

2: Top the soup with Parmesan cheese.

3: Substitute a pinch of chilli powder (this is very hot) for the paprika.

Keeping Slim

When you are maintaining your weight, rather than trying to lose excess kilogrammes or pounds, you will probably find it easier to choose foods rich in protein which have little, if any, carbohydrate and so avoid counting calories.

This means meals based upon fish, meat, poultry, eggs and cheese, avoiding foods high in carbohydrate value.

Plaice Provençal

■ 158/Kj 663 □ 4.2 g

Metric/Imperial

300 ml/½ pint tomato juice

1 onion, grated

2 × 5 ml spoons/2 teaspoons chopped parsley or basil

½ lemon

salt

pepper

4 large or 8 smaller fillets plaice (weight as recipe right)

American

1¼ cups tomato juice

1 onion, grated

2 teaspoons chopped parsley or basil

½ lemon

salt

pepper

4 large or 8 smaller fillets flounder (weight as recipe right)

❧Pour the tomato juice into a large frying pan, add the grated onion, parsley or basil, grated rind and juice of the lemon and a little salt and pepper. Fold the fillets, put into the liquid and bring this to boiling point. Lower the heat then simmer gently for 4 to 5 minutes, or until tender.

To serve: With the tomato mixture as a sauce.

To freeze: Better served freshly cooked.

Variation:

Use skinned sliced tomatoes plus a little water instead of the tomato juice.

Plaice with Creamed Mushroom Sauce

■ 364/Kj 1530 □ 1.3 g

Metric/Imperial

4 small whole plaice or large fillets of plaice (175 g/6 oz each)

25–50 g/1–2 oz butter or margarine

FOR THE SAUCE:

25 g/1 oz butter or margarine

50 g/2 oz fresh mushrooms

150 ml/¼ pint single cream

2 × 5 ml spoons/2 teaspoons lemon juice

salt

pepper

TO GARNISH:

parsley

American

4 small whole or large fillets of flounder (6 oz each)

2–4 tablespoons butter or margarine

FOR THE SAUCE:

2 tablespoons butter

½ cup fresh mushrooms

⅔ cup light cream

2 teaspoons lemon juice

salt

pepper

TO GARNISH:

parsley

❧Put the plaice (flounder) on the buttered rack of the grill (broiler) pan. Dot with butter or margarine and grill (broil) under a low heat for 5 minutes. Turn carefully, add the remaining butter or margarine and grill (broil) as before. Melt the 25 g/1 oz/2 tablespoons butter in a small saucepan and fry the mushrooms until tender. Add the cream, lemon juice and salt and pepper to taste and reheat.

To serve: Top the plaice with the sauce, garnish with parsley sprigs.

To freeze: Better freshly cooked.

COOKING SMOKED FISH

Smoked haddock or cod are excellent fish for breakfast or lunch. As the fish has so much flavour it just needs simmering in milk or water. Top with butter, or butter blended with chopped watercress or parsley and lemon juice, or a poached egg.

Spanish Liver

■ 335/Kj 1407 □ 9.5 g

Metric/Imperial

450 g/1 lb lamb's liver (in 4 slices)

4 large tomatoes, skinned and sliced

2 medium onions, finely chopped

100 g/4 oz mushrooms, sliced

50 g/2 oz fat

salt

pepper

little paprika

15 g/½ oz cornflour

450 ml/¾ pint brown stock

1 × 15 ml spoon/1 tablespoon sherry

2 × 15 ml spoons/2 tablespoons chopped parsley

American

1 lb lamb's liver (in 4 slices)

4 large tomatoes, skinned and sliced

2 medium onions, finely chopped

¼ lb mushrooms, sliced

¼ cup shortening

salt

pepper

little paprika

2 tablespoons cornstarch

2 cups brown stock

1 tablespoon sherry

2 tablespoons chopped parsley

Plaice Provençal; Plaice with Creamed Mushroom Sauce; Spanish Liver; Liver in Orange

❧Dry the liver on absorbent paper. Fry the vegetables in half the fat in a frying pan until soft. Add a little salt, pepper and paprika. Spread half over the liver slices. Roll and secure with wooden cocktail sticks or tie with fine string. Mix a little salt and pepper with the cornflour (cornstarch). Coat the liver rolls with the seasoned cornflour (cornstarch). Heat the remaining fat in a frying pan (skillet) and cook the rolls for 2 to 3 minutes, turning several times. Add the stock, remaining cooked vegetables, sherry and parsley. Cook in the open pan for 10 minutes, turning once or twice. Remove the cocktail sticks or string.

To serve: With a little cooked rice and a green vegetable.

To freeze: Freezes well for 2 months.

To thaw: Heat gently from the frozen state.

Variation:
Use thin slices of veal in place of liver. Boned chicken breasts could be flattened and rolled too.

Liver in Orange

■ 324/Kj 1361 □ 9.0 g

Metric/Imperial

450 g/1 lb lamb's or calf's liver

3 large oranges

salt

pepper

50 g/2 oz butter

American

1 lb lamb's or calf's liver

3 large oranges

salt

pepper

¼ cup butter

❧Cut the liver into strips. Grate the rind, squeeze out the juice from two oranges, slice the third. Sprinkle salt, pepper and grated orange rind over the liver. Heat the butter, fry the liver for 4 to 5 minutes, until tender. Add the juice and sliced orange for the last 2 minutes.

To serve: Top the liver with the orange-flavoured liquid and slices.

To freeze: Better freshly cooked.

ADD EXTRA FLAVOUR

Now you are maintaining, rather than losing, weight you may find you can have interesting 'extras', like a little honey, brandy, pâté, etc. Some flavours, such as Worcestershire or Tabasco sauce, can be used happily, as they do not affect either the calorie or carbohydrate content.

Keeping Slim

Tabasco Cream Chicken

■ 371/Kj 1559 □15.0 g

Metric/Imperial

4 joints frying chicken

50 g/2 oz butter or chicken fat

few drops Tabasco sauce

salt

pepper

150 ml/¼ pint soured cream or single cream and 1 × 15 ml spoon/ 1 tablespoon lemon juice

TO GARNISH:

4 tomatoes, halved

225 g/8 oz cooked sweetcorn

American

4 joints broiling chicken

¼ cup butter or chicken fat

few drops Tabasco sauce

salt

pepper

⅔ cup sour cream or light cream and 1 tablespoon lemon juice

TO GARNISH:

4 tomatoes, halved

½ lb cooked sweetcorn

🥄If using frozen chicken, thaw and dry thoroughly. Melt the butter or fat, add the Tabasco sauce, salt and pepper to taste. Brush the chicken with a little of the flavoured fat and grill (broil) for 5 to 6 minutes. Turn with tongs, brush with a little more fat and grill (broil) on the second side for 2 to 3 minutes. Blend the soured cream (sour cream) or cream and lemon juice with the remaining butter mixture, add a few more drops of Tabasco sauce, if you like a hot flavour, spread over each chicken joint; arrange the halved seasoned tomatoes round the chicken. Return to the grill (broiler), lower the heat and cook gently until tender (about 6 to 7 minutes).

To serve: Arrange the chicken in a border of sweetcorn and tomatoes.

To freeze: This is an excellent way to cook *thawed* frozen chicken (whole chickens must always be completely thawed before cooking, but in some recipes you can cook chicken joints from the frozen state). Do not freeze the completed dish.

Variation:

Small children may prefer their portion grilled (broiled) without flavouring, just with the butter or fat.

Kidneys Perigord

■ 351/Kj 1475 □15.3 g

Metric/Imperial

8 lamb's kidneys (about 50 g/2 oz each)

100 g/4 oz button mushrooms

50 g/2 oz butter

150 ml/¼ pint beef stock or water and ½ beef stock cube

4 × 15 ml spoons/4 tablespoons double cream

1 × 15 ml spoon/1 tablespoon brandy

salt

pepper

4 small slices bread (25 g/1 oz each)

25 g/1 oz Liver Pâté, as recipe page 25

American

8 lamb's kidneys (about 2 oz each)

¼ lb mushrooms

¼ cup butter

⅔ cup beef stock or water and 1 beef bouillon cube

¼ cup heavy cream

1 tablespoon brandy

salt

pepper

4 small slices bread (1 oz each)

1 oz Liver Pâté, as recipe page 25

🥄Skin and halve the kidneys. Wash, but do not skin the mushrooms, dry well. Heat the butter in a frying pan (skillet), toss the kidneys and mushrooms in this for 5 minutes. Add the stock or water and ½ (1) stock (bouillon) cube. Simmer gently for 5 minutes, then stir in the cream and brandy. Add salt and pepper, heat for 2 minutes *but do not boil*. Meanwhile toast the bread and spread with pâté.

To serve: Spoon the moist kidney mixture on to the toast and serve at once.

To freeze: Better served freshly made.

Steak Niçoise

■ 264/Kj 1110 □12.6 g

Metric/Imperial

450 g/1 lb tomatoes, skinned and chopped

1 onion, chopped

1–2 cloves garlic, chopped

150 ml/¼ pint water or stock

1 × 15 ml spoon/1 tablespoon tomato purée

salt

freshly ground black pepper

4 × 100 g/4 oz fillet or other grilling steak

American

1 lb tomatoes, skinned and chopped

1 onion, chopped

1–2 cloves garlic, chopped

⅔ cup water or stock

1 tablespoon tomato paste

salt

freshly ground black pepper

4 × ¼ lb fillet or other broiling steak

🥄Put the vegetables, water or stock and tomato purée into a large frying pan (skillet), simmer until the vegetables are soft. Add salt and pepper to both the sauce and the meat, then place the steaks in the tomato sauce and cook to personal taste. Turn the meat once or twice during the cooking period.

To serve: With a green salad, cooked spinach or broccoli. Non-slimmers would enjoy cooked noodles or rice with this dish.

To freeze: Do not freeze the completed dish but frozen tomato purée and frozen steaks can be used.

Variations:

1: Pork, lamb or veal can be cooked in the same way. If the meat has a fair amount of fat, then fry in its own fat slowly for a few minutes. Remove the meat from the pan, pour off any surplus fat (if counting calories), but this is not essential on a low-carbohydrate diet. Make the tomato sauce, replace the meat in the pan and complete cooking.

2: Steak Rossini: Top the cooked steak with liver pâté, as page 25, then serve at once.

Steak Niçoise; Kidneys Perigord; Tabasco Cream Chicken

Keeping Slim

The recipes on this page are chosen because they not only have an interesting flavour, but they are based upon foods that are particularly easy to digest. The Roulade gives a new way of serving tripe.

Roulade of Tripe

■ 465/Kj 1953 □ 19.8 g

Metric/Imperial

0.75 kg/1½ lb tripe (cut in one piece)

1 chicken stock cube

salt

pepper

FOR THE STUFFING:

2 large onions, chopped

50 g/2 oz fresh breadcrumbs

1 × 5 ml spoon/1 teaspoon chopped sage or 1 × 1.25 ml–1 × 2.5 ml spoon/¼–½ teaspoon dried sage

50 g/2 oz butter or margarine

FOR THE SAUCE:

40 g/1½ oz butter or margarine

2 medium onions, sliced

2 medium tomatoes, skinned and sliced

50 g/2 oz mushrooms, sliced

15 g/½ oz cornflour

American

1½ lb tripe (cut in one piece)

2 chicken bouillon cubes

salt

pepper

FOR THE STUFFING:

2 large onions, chopped

1 cup soft breadcrumbs

1 teaspoon chopped sage or ¼–½ teaspoon dried sage

¼ cup butter or margarine

FOR THE SAUCE:

3 tablespoons butter or margarine

2 medium onions, sliced

2 medium tomatoes, skinned and sliced

½ cup mushrooms, sliced

2 tablespoons cornstarch

❧ Wash and dry the tripe. Put into a pan. Cover with cold water. Bring the water to the boil then throw this away. This blanches and whitens the tripe. Replace the tripe in the pan with enough water to cover and the stock (bouillon) cube(s) and a very little salt and pepper. Cover the pan and simmer for about 45 minutes.

Meanwhile place the onions in a pan with just enough water to cover and a good pinch of salt and shake of pepper.

Cover the pan, simmer for 10 minutes. Strain off the surplus liquid (save this for the sauce). Blend the onions, crumbs, sage and butter or margarine. Lift the tripe from the saucepan, save the stock. Spread the tripe flat, spread with the stuffing. Roll firmly and tie with fine string, place into a casserole. Heat the 40 g/1½ oz/3 tablespoons butter or margarine, toss the onions, tomatoes and mushrooms in this for 2 to 3 minutes, then stir in the cornflour (cornstarch). Blend in the onion liquid and enough tripe stock to give 450 ml/¾ pint/2 cups. Stir over a moderate heat until thickened. Pour over the tripe. Cover the casserole and cook in the centre of a very moderate oven (160°C/325°F, Gas Mark 3) for 1 hour.

To serve: Remove the string and arrange on a dish with mixed root vegetables.

To freeze: Better eaten fresh although frozen tripe could be used.

Chaudfroid of Chicken; Arabian Honey Chicken

Chaudfroid of Chicken

■ 297/Kj 1251 □ 2.5 g

Metric/Imperial

0.5 × 15 ml spoon/½ tablespoon aspic
jelly powder

1 × 5 ml spoon/1 teaspoon powder
gelatine

300 ml/½ pint water

150 ml/¼ pint plain yogurt

salt

pepper

4 portions cooked chicken, each
approximately 175 g/6 oz

TO GARNISH:
3 tomatoes

2 hard-boiled eggs

4–6 gherkins or stuffed olives

lettuce

American

½ tablespoon aspic jelly

1 teaspoon powder gelatin

1¼ cups water

⅔ cup plain yogurt

salt

pepper

4 portions cooked chicken, each
approximately 6 oz

TO GARNISH:
3 tomatoes

2 hard-cooked eggs

4–6 sweet dill pickles or stuffed olives

lettuce

❧Mix the aspic jelly powder and the
powder gelatine (gelatin). Soften in
2 × 15 ml spoons/2 tablespoons of the
water. Heat the remaining water, stir in
the gelatine (gelatin) and continue stirring until dissolved, cool slightly. Whisk
the yogurt into the jelly, taste, and add a
little extra salt and pepper if necessary.
Allow the sauce to cool and become fairly
thick. Put the pieces of chicken on a wire
sieve, then coat carefully with the sauce,
leave to set. If using leg and thigh joints
of chicken, it is easier if you cut the bone
away with a sharp knife. Leave to set
more firmly then cut away any surplus
sauce from the bottom of each joint.
Garnish each piece with tiny pieces of
tomato, egg, gherkin or stuffed olives.

To serve: Arrange on a bed of lettuce.

To freeze: The portions of chicken
should be frozen *then* wrapped. Use
within 2 weeks.

To thaw: In the refrigerator.

Variations:

1: If wished a whole chicken can be
coated with the sauce and decorated.

2: For special occasions make up a
savoury butter by creaming a little
tomato ketchup (catsup) and paprika
pepper into butter; season well. Pipe a
border of this round each coated piece of
chicken. Avoid this if on a low-calorie
diet.

Arabian Honey Chicken

■ 355/Kj 1491 □ 14.2 g

Metric/Imperial

a 1 kg/2 lb chicken*

2 × 15 ml spoons/2 tablespoons honey

50 g/2 oz butter, melted

25 g/1 oz blanched almonds, chopped

TO GARNISH:
15–25 g/½–1 oz preserved ginger,
sliced (optional)

few fresh cherries, stoned

watercress

American

a 2 lb spring chicken*

2 tablespoons honey

¼ cup butter, melted

Roulade of Tripe

¼ cup chopped blanched almonds

TO GARNISH:
½–1 tablespoon sliced preserved ginger

few fresh cherries, pitted

watercress

*about 450 g/1 lb edible weight

❧Allow a frozen chicken to thaw out
completely, dry well. Prick the breast of
the chicken with a small sharp knife and
brush with some of the honey mixed
with the melted butter. Pour the remaining honey inside the bird, place in a
baking tin and roast just above the centre
of a moderately hot oven (190°C/375°F,
Gas Mark 5), allowing 20 minutes to
each 0.5 kg/1 lb and 20 minutes over.
Remove from the tin, cut the bird in half,
place on a hot serving dish. Sprinkle with
the almonds. Garnish with sliced ginger,
cherries and watercress.

To serve: Just before serving, pour any
honey and butter left over the chicken.

To freeze: This dish is better when
freshly cooked.

Keeping Slim

Most vegetables are low in calories (except potatoes and the pulses), so they enable you to add extra courses to your meals and maintain your ideal weight. Vegetables add essential roughage and vitamins to the diet too.

Cook vegetables lightly or serve raw to retain vitamins.

Savoury Pepper Slices

■ 87/Kj 365 □ 0.9 g

Metric/Imperial

2 medium green or red peppers (capsicums)

225 g/8 oz cottage cheese

2 × 5 ml spoons/2 teaspoons yeast extract

25 g/1 oz peanuts, chopped

1 × 15 ml spoon/1 tablespoon chopped parsley

8 starch-reduced crispbreads or biscuits (optional)

25 g/1 oz margarine

American

2 medium green or red peppers

½ lb cottage cheese

2 teaspoons yeast extract

¼ cup chopped peanuts

1 tablespoon chopped parsley

8 starch-reduced crispbreads or biscuits (optional)

2 tablespoons margarine

Wash and dry the peppers; leave them whole, but cut a slice from the top and remove the core and seeds (pits). Mix the cottage cheese, yeast extract, nuts and parsley together and stuff into the peppers. Cut each pepper into four slices.

To serve: Spread the crispbreads with the margarine, arrange a slice of pepper on each.

Note: The pepper slices can be topped with sliced tomatoes. To reduce calorie content omit the crispbread; the figures below have done so.

To freeze: The whole stuffed peppers can be frozen for about 2 months, but they lose their crispness.

To thaw: At room temperature.

Ratatouille; Savoury Pepper Slices; Health Salad

Ratatouille

■ 121/Kj 508 □ 9.6 g

Metric/Imperial
1 large aubergine (about 350 g/12 oz)

4 courgettes (about 225 g/8 oz)

450 g/1 lb tomatoes, skinned and sliced

225 g/8 oz onions, chopped

2 cloves garlic, chopped

1 × 15 ml spoon/1 tablespoon oil

2 × 15 ml spoons/2 tablespoons chopped parsley

salt

pepper

American
1 large eggplant (about ¾ lb)

4 zucchini (about ½ lb)

1 lb tomatoes, skinned and sliced

½ lb onions, chopped

2 cloves garlic, chopped

1 tablespoon oil

2 tablespoons chopped parsley

salt

pepper

❧ Wipe, then cube or slice the unpeeled aubergine (eggplant) and courgettes (zucchini). If you dislike the rather bitter taste of aubergine (eggplant) then score the vegetable skin with a sharp knife, sprinkle with a little salt and leave for at least 15 minutes, then drain and discard the liquid. The salt draws out the bitter juice. Discard the ends on the courgettes. Put the tomatoes, onion, garlic and oil into a pan, heat slowly until the tomato juice flows, add the aubergine (eggplant), courgettes (zucchini), half the parsley, salt and pepper to taste. Cover the pan, simmer steadily for 45 minutes until the mixture has thickened. Add the remaining parsley.

To serve: Hot or cold as an appetizer or vegetable.

To freeze: This is one of the most successful vegetable dishes for freezing. Use within 12 months.

To thaw: Allow to thaw at room temperature or reheat very slowly from frozen.

Variations:

1: Omit the oil.

2: Add 1–2 × 15 ml spoons/1–2 tablespoons tomato purée (paste).

Health Salad

■ 218/Kj 916 □ 20.0 g

Metric/Imperial
100 g/4 oz celery, chopped

salt

freshly ground black pepper

225 g/8 oz cottage cheese

2 large oranges

lettuce or chicory

watercress

12 drained cooked prunes

50–75 g/2–3 oz nuts, chopped

1 × 15 ml spoon/1 tablespoon chopped parsley

American
1 cup chopped celery

salt

freshly ground black pepper

1 cup cottage cheese

2 large oranges

lettuce or Belgian endive

watercress

12 drained cooked prunes

½–¾ cup nuts, chopped

1 tablespoon chopped parsley

❧ Add the chopped celery, salt and pepper to the cheese. Cut away the peel and pith from the oranges and cut the pulp into round slices, then half-circles. Arrange the cheese mixture on a bed of lettuce or chicory (Belgian endive) and watercress, surround with the prunes set on the half slices of orange. Top the cheese mixture with chopped nuts and scatter parsley over the top.

To serve: As a light main dish or meal starter.

To freeze: Do not freeze.

Variations:

1: Use grated Gouda, Cheddar or other hard cheese plus 2 × 15 ml spoons/ 2 tablespoons single (light) cream or yogurt.

2: Use cream cheese instead of cottage cheese.

Keeping Slim

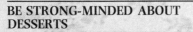

BE STRONG-MINDED ABOUT DESSERTS

If you know you have a tendency to gain weight easily you will be wise to avoid rich or over-sweetened desserts. The recipes in the slimming section, starting on page 82, are an ideal choice. Here are other basic recipes you can vary in many ways and adapt as necessary; you could omit the sugar and add sugar substitute instead, or return to skimmed milk in dishes, instead of ordinary full-cream milk.

ADAPTING JELLIES

You can turn a jelly, as the recipe right, into an interesting dessert.

Fruit Jelly: Add cubed fresh fruit to the jelly; be sparing with the liquid to compensate for fruit juice.

Jelly Cream: Use only half the amount of water in the jelly, cool, then add 300 ml/ ½ pint/1¼ cups plain yogurt or single (light) cream.

Lemon Snow: Add 2 stiffly whisked egg whites to the half-set jelly. You may need a little extra sugar or sugar substitute. Serve in glasses.

Fresh Lemon Jelly

■ 73/Kj 307 □ 16.5 g

Metric/Imperial
2 lemons
600 ml/1 pint water
1 × 15 ml spoon/1 tablespoon powder gelatine
50 g/2 oz sugar
few drops yellow colouring (optional)

American
2 lemons
2½ cups water
2 envelopes powder gelatin
¼ cup sugar
few drops yellow colouring (optional)

❧ Grate the yellow 'zest' only from the lemons. Be careful not to use any of the white pith, otherwise you will make the jelly bitter. Squeeze out the juice from the lemons. Put the lemon 'zest' with the water into a saucepan, simmer gently for 5 minutes, then strain and reheat. Soften the gelatine (gelatin) in the cold lemon juice, pour on enough boiling lemon liquid to make a total of 600 ml/1 pint/ 2½ cups. Stir until the gelatine (gelatin) has dissolved. Add the sugar to the hot liquid, together with the colouring, if wished. Pour the jelly into a rinsed mould or into glasses or spoon into orange halves, allow to set.

To serve: When set, turn out and decorate with slices of fresh fruit.

To freeze: Better freshly made but can be frozen for 1 or 2 weeks.

Variations:

1: Use sugar substitute instead of sugar.

2: Use 3 oranges instead of 2 lemons or a mixture of citrus fruits.

3: Purées of fruits make delicious jellies. Sieve ripe dessert fruits such as raspberries or strawberries and dilute with a little water, or cook harder fruits, like plums, damsons, rhubarb with enough water to give a purée which is just thick enough to coat a wooden spoon. As the purée is slightly thickened, allow 750 ml/ 1¼ pints/3 cups purée to the quantity of gelatine (gelatin) given in this recipe.

Baked Egg Custard

■ 203/Kj 853 □ 14.4 g

Metric/Imperial
4 eggs
600 ml/1 pint full-cream milk
25 g/1 oz sugar

American
4 eggs
2½ cups full-cream milk
2 tablespoons sugar

Fresh Lemon Jelly; Baked Egg Custard;
Apricot Soufflé

Beat the eggs lightly, then add the *hot*, but not boiling, milk and the sugar. Pour into a well-greased ovenproof basin, mould or dish. If when the milk is poured on there are tiny pieces of egg settling on the top, strain the mixture into the oven-proof dish. Stand the basin, mould or dish in another dish or tin containing cold water (a bain-marie). Bake for approximately 1 to 1½ hours (depending on the depth of the mixture) in the centre of a slow to very moderate oven (160°C/ 325°F, Gas Mark 3). If during cooking the water in the second container looks as if it is starting to boil, it should be replaced with more *warm* water. The custard may be baked at a lower tem-perature, when it will take longer to set.
To serve: Hot or cold with fruit.
To freeze: Only the uncooked liquid custard can be frozen. Use within a month, and thaw before baking as above.
Variations:
1: Use sugar substitute instead of sugar; remember 25 g/1 oz/2 tablespoons sugar gives about 112 calories and 29.7 gram-mes carbohydrate.
2: Flavour the custard with vanilla essence (extract) or coffee essence (ex-tract).
3: Steamed Custard: Cover the mould or dish with foil, stand in a steamer over

hot *but not boiling* water and steam for about 1 hour, until firm.
4: Use egg yolks only.
5: Bread and Butter Pudding: Pour the custard over thin slices of bread and butter; add a little dried fruit, flavour with spice, grated orange or lemon rind.
6: Flavour the basic mixture with cocoa powder to taste. Cook as above.
7: Make a spicy baked custard. Add ground spices such as cinnamon, nut-meg, cloves or allspice. If liked, dried fruit of your choice may be added as well.

Apricot Soufflé

■ 144/Kj685 □ 15.6 g
Metric/Imperial
225 g/8 oz thick apricot purée
15 g/½ oz cornflour
25 g/1 oz sugar
3 egg yolks
4 egg whites
2 × 5 ml spoons/2 teaspoons icing sugar, sieved

American
½ lb thick apricot purée
2 tablespoons cornstarch
2 tablespoons sugar
3 egg yolks
4 egg whites
2 teaspoons sieved icing sugar

Blend the apricot purée with the corn-flour (cornstarch), stir over a low heat until thickened. Add the sugar then remove from the heat and beat in the egg yolks; finally fold in the stiffly whisked egg whites. Spoon into a greased soufflé dish and bake in the centre of a moder-ately hot oven (190°C/375°F, Gas Mark 5), for 35 minutes until well risen and set.
To serve: Top with the icing sugar and serve at once.
Variations:
1: Top with browned almonds.
2: Use other well-flavoured fruits.
3: Be rather more generous with the sugar; or use sugar substitute to reduce calories and carbohydrates.

Keeping Slim

FOOD VALUE TABLES

Reading the Tables

On this and the following pages you will find a very comprehensive list of the calorific values of various everyday foods and drinks. This will enable you to plan your slimming routine.

There are certain points to observe:

(a) Both Calories, Kilojoules and Carbohydrate counts are given and in every case the accepted count refers to 28.35 g/1 oz, unless it is stated otherwise.

(b) **Biscuits (cookies and crackers):** Most biscuits are listed under weight *and* individual biscuits. As you will appreciate, manufacturers vary in the size they prepare these, so it is only an approximate guide.

(c) **Cakes:** I have shown the Calorie/Kilojoule count by weight and then by a small slice or individual cake. I felt this would help to show just what is indicated by a 'small slice' — in most cases not much over 28 g/1 oz.

(d) **Fruits:** Frequently you will find that the information is given under raw then stewed — this means cooked *without* sugar, i.e. using sugar substitute. Canned fruit, however, means the commercial type where sugar is used. In a few cases, where relevant, frozen fruits are mentioned.

(e) **Vegetables:** Where one is likely to eat the vegetable raw in salads, as well as cooked, there may be an appreciable difference in the Calorie/Kilojoule count, you will find the vegetable given under raw and boiled. In some instances a very popular method of cooking, e.g. fried onions (listed as onions, fried) is also given.

Unless otherwise stated, the food given means the edible portion, i.e. free from bone or skin or stones, etc.

Some foods have different names in Britain and America and the American names have been given, in brackets or listed separately if they are unobtainable in Britain.

If you read a book where the text refers to carbohydrate units, and you wish to compare them with the figures I give, simply remember that 5 grams of carbohydrate is equivalent to 1 carbohydrate unit.

As stated in point (a) above, calculations are given per 28.35 g/1 oz or 28.35 ml/1 fl oz, rather than in cups, spoons, etc., for this ensures a more accurate accessment. American readers should refer to handy cup measures on page 220 to help work out a familiar measure.

Item	Calories	Kilojoules	Carbohydrates
A			
Ale, brown – 568 ml/1 pint (2½ cups)	160	669	16.8
Ale, draught, mild – 568 ml/1 pint varies slightly	140	585	9.2
Ale, pale – 568 ml/1 pint varies slightly	160	669	11.2
All-Bran	69	289	16.5
Almond, shelled and flaked	172	719	1.0–2.0
Alpen	105	439	39.0
Anchovy fillets	40	168	0.0
Angel cake	118	493	25.9
Angel cake, small slice	133	556	30.0
Angel Delight, made up as packet	43	180	16.0
Angelica	90	376	16.2
Apples, raw	11–15	46–63	2.6–3.5
Apples, baked	9	38	2.8
Apples, dried	50	209	21.0
Apples, stewed	8	33	2.1
Apple purée or sauce	8	33	2.1
Apple dumpling	57	238	8.1
Apple juice	10	42	4.6
Apple pie, with top crust only	54	226	8.5
Apple pie, filling	22	92	5.0
Apple pudding	68	284	31.6
Apple tart, with top and bottom pastry	96	401	16.0
Apricot, raw	11	46	1.7
Apricot, stewed	17	71	1.5
Apricot, dried	50	209	12.3
Apricot, canned, halves	30	125	7.9
Apricot, canned, whole (with stone/pit)	14	59	4.0
Arrowroot	93	389	26.7
Artichoke, globe	4	17	0.8
Artichoke, Jerusalem	5	21	0.9

Item	Calories	Kilojoules	Carbohydrates
Asparagus	5	21	0.3
Asparagus soup, canned	9	38	2.1
Aubergine (Eggplant), raw	4	17	0.8
Aubergine (Eggplant), one slice, fried, no coating	50	209	0.8
Avocado pear	25	105	0.7
B			
Bacon, average lean	115	481	0.0
Bacon, gammon, very lean	92	385	0.0
Bacon, streaky, fair amount of fat	149	623	0.0
Bagel, one	125	522	32.5
Baked beans in tomato sauce	26	109	4.9
Baked beans and Frankfurters	37	155	4.9
Baked beans with pork and molasses	29	121	7.1
Bamboo shoots	9	38	2.26
Banana	22	92	5.5
Banana, one	80–100	334–418	34.5
Barley, raw	102	426	23.7
Barley, boiled	34	142	7.8
Bass, raw	29	121	0.0
Bass, boiled or steamed	36	150	0.0
Battenburg cake	105	439	17.2
Battenburg cake, one small slice	126	527	20.6
Beans, baked	26	109	4.9
Beans, broad (Fava)	15	63	2.0
Beans, French, runner (Green), raw	4	17	0.8
Beans, French, runner, boiled	2	8	0.3
Beans, haricot, (Butter), raw	100–120	418–502	12.9–14.2
Beans, haricot, (Butter), boiled	25–30	105–125	4.7–4.9
Beans, lima, raw	15	63	2.0
Beanshoot (Sprouts)	2–3	8–13	0.03
Beaujolais wine	19	79	0.07
Beef, good quality lean only (e.g. fillet)	50	209	0.0

Calories/kilojoules and **carbohydrate** counts are given per 28.35g/1oz or 28.35 ml/1 fl oz, unless otherwise stated.

Item	Calories	Kilojoules	Carbohydrates
Beef, good quality lean plus little fat (e.g. sirloin)	64	268	0.0
Beef, grilled (broiled) with minimum fat	86	359	0.0
Beef, lean stewing steak (e.g. chuck)	90	376	0.0
Beef (Steak) and kidney, pie	86–90	359–376	4.8
Beef (Steak) and kidney, pudding	69–74	288–309	5.2
Beefburger (Hamburger), varies	150–160	627–669	0.0 (all meat)
Some beefburgers are as low as home-made (see recipe page 45)	60–80	251–334	0.0 (all meat)
Beef paste (Spread), varies	43	180	1.2
Beef stock (Bouillon) cube	30	125	4.0
Beef stock (Bouillon) cube, one	10	42	1.3
Beer, Brown ale, etc., 568 ml/1 pint (2½ cups)	160	669	16.8
Beer, Draught ale, bitter 568 ml/1 pint (2½ cups)	180	752	12.8
Beer, Draught ale, mild 568 ml/1 pint (2½ cups)	140	585	9.2
Beer, Bottled light ale 568 ml/1 pint (2½ cups)	180	752	11.2
Beer, Stout 568 ml/1 pint (2½ cups)	210	878	23.8
Beer, Strong ale 568 ml/1 pint (2½ cups)	420	1756	34.8
Beetroot (Beet)	7	29	1.7
Beetroot, boiled	14	59	2.8
Beetroot, pickled	8	33	2.5
Bitter lemon drink, 170.4 ml/6 fl oz	56	234	3.0
Bitter lemon drink, Slimline (diet), 170.4 ml/6 fl oz	0.74 (1)	3	Trace
Biscuit, (cookie or cracker), plain	105	439	21.4
Biscuit, sweet	145	606	18.9
Biscuit, Bourbon	166	694	20.0
Biscuit, Bourbon, per biscuit	57	238	6–8
Biscuit, Breakfast	123	514	22.1
Biscuit, Breakfast, per biscuit	43	180	7.7
Biscuit, Chocolate, varies	130–172	546–722	18.0
Biscuit, Chocolate, per biscuit	62–86	260–361	6.0–9.0
Biscuit, Cornish wafer	155	648	17.1
Biscuit, Cornish wafer, per biscuit	46	192	5.0
Biscuit, Cream cracker	115	483	19.4
Biscuit, Cream cracker, per biscuit	36	150	5.00
Biscuit, Custard cream	140	585	17.0
Biscuit, Custard cream, per biscuit	58	242	7.0
Biscuit, Digestive (Graham cracker)	140	585	18.7
Biscuit, Digestive, per biscuit	49–56	205–234	5.4
Biscuit, Digestive, chocolate coated	138–142	577–594	17.6
Biscuits, Digestive, chocolate coated, per biscuit	79–80	330–334	10.1
Biscuit, Garibaldi	131	548	20.1
Biscuit, Garibaldi, per biscuit	32	134	4.9
Biscuit, Ginger nut (Gingersnap)	105	439	10.1
Biscuit, Ginger nut, per biscuit	33	138	3.2
Biscuit, Water biscuit (cracker)	114	477	20.7
Biscuit, Water biscuit, per biscuit	31	130	5.8
Blackberry, raw	8	33	1.8
Blackberry, stewed	6	25	1.4
Blackberry, canned	25	105	5.0
Blackberry and apple pie filling	34	142	8.0
Blackcurrant, raw	10–12	42–50	1.9
Blackcurrant, stewed	8	33	1.4
Blackcurrant, canned	30	125	6.0
Blackcurrant concentrate, varies a great deal	37–84	155–351	17.3
Black pudding (Blood Sausage)	68	284	5.0
Black treacle (Molasses)	84	351	19.1
Blancmange, made up as packet	31	130	5.3
Bloaters, raw	67	280	0.0
Bloaters, fried or grilled	73	305	0.0
Bloater paste	48	201	1.0–1.9
Blueberry [See Blackberry]			

Item	Calories	Kilojoules	Carbohydrates
Boiled sweets	130	543	24.8
Boysenberry [See Blackberry]			
Brains	29–31	121–130	0.0
Bran	89	373	16.5
Bran buds	76	319	17.5
Bran flakes	99	414	19.3
Brawn	56	234	0.0
Brandy	75	315	Trace
Bread, brown	67–70	280–293	14.2
Bread, white	70	293	14.9
Bread, wholemeal (Wholewheat)	65	272	13.4
Bread, toasted	85	355	18.4
Bread, fried	162	677	14.6
Bread, dried (Crumbs)	101	422	22.0
Bread, malt	71	297	14.0
Bread, currant	71	297	14.7
Bread, one average slice from small loaf, white, brown or wholemeal (Wholewheat)	60	251	11.3–11.9
Bread, rye, per slice	55	230	12.1
Bread, Pumpernickel, per slice	75	314	15.9
Bread, Vienna, per slice	54	226	10.4
Bread, slimmers', per slice	35–40	146–167	15.0
Breakfast sausage	82	343	4.8
Bream, raw	27	113	0.0
Bream, boiled or steamed	34	142	0.0
Brill, raw	26	109	0.0
Brill, boiled or steamed	33	138	0.0
Broccoli, raw	5	21	0.0
Broccoli, boiled	2–3	8–13	0.1
Broccoli, with Hollandaise sauce (see recipe page 80)	85	356	0.3
Brown bread	67–70	280–293	14.2
Brown flour	95–100	399–420	21.7
Brown sauce	28	117	7.2
Brussel sprouts, raw	9	38	1.3
Brussel sprouts, boiled	5	21	0.5
Buck rarebit	81	339	4.8
Buckwheat flour	35	147	17.7
Butter	260	1092	Trace
Buttermilk	10	42	1.4
Butterscotch	118	493	20.2

C

Item	Calories	Kilojoules	Carbohydrates
Cabbage and cabbage green, raw	5	21	0.9–1.1
Cake, bought, (home made tend to be higher in calories and sometimes lower in carbohydrates)			
Cake, plain, made with fat	75–90	314–376	15.2
Cake, iced (frosted), made with fat	110–120	460–502	17.9
Cake, sponge, made without fat	60–67	251–280	15.6
Cake, sponge, made with fat	134	560	16.3
Cake, Angel	118	493	27.6
Cake, Angel, small slice	133	556	30.0
Cake, Battenburg	105	439	17.2
Cake, Battenburg, small slice	126	527	20.6
Cake, cherry	129	539	16.1
Cake, cherry, small slice	169	706	22.1
Cake, chocolate cup cake	125	523	17.3
Cake, chocolate cup cake, one	150	627	20.7
Cake, chocolate eclair	133	556	12.0
Cake, chocolate eclair, one	143	598	14.0
Cake, chocolate-coated Swiss roll	119	497	13.4
Cake, chocolate-flavoured Swiss roll, cream-filled	99	414	11.8
Cake, custard tart	80	334	10.0
Cake, doughnut, jam-filled	100	418	13.8
Cake, doughnut, jam-filled, one	175	732	30.0
Cake, Dundee (varies)	110–120	460–502	17.7
Cake, Dundee, small slice	115–140	481–585	18.1

Calories/kilojoules and carbohydrate counts are given per 28.35g/1oz or 28.35 ml/1 fl oz, unless otherwise stated.

Item	Calories	Kilojoules	Carbohydrates
Cake, Eccles	126–147	527–614	14.5
Cake, Eccles, one	123–147	514–614	15.1
Cake, fairy	108	451	15.3
Cake, fairy, one	162	677	23.0
Cake, gingerbread	108	451	18.0
Cake, gingerbread, small slice	127	531	26.9
Cake, jam puff	154	644	16.8
Cake, jam puff, one	200	836	21.0
Cake, lemon curd tart	119	497	14.1
Cake, lemon curd tart, one	134	560	16.0
Cake, meringue	112	468	20.0
Cake, meringue, one	125	523	23.3
Cake, Swiss roll, jam	90	376	20.0
Cake, Viennese tart	147	614	16.6
Cake, Viennese tart, one	190	794	20.8
Campari	62.3	262	7.089
Candied peel	60	252	15.8
Caper	2	8	Trace
Capsicum [See Pepper entry]			
Carrot, raw, old	6	25	1.5
Carrot, raw, young	7	29	1.1
Carrot, boiled, old or young	6–7	25–29	1.2–1.3
Cashew nut	164	686	8.0
Cauliflower, raw	5	21	0.8
Cauliflower, boiled	2–3	8–13	0.3
Celeriac (Celery Root), raw	4	17	0.6
Celeriac, boiled	3–4	13–17	0.6
Celery, white celery, raw	3	13	0.4
Celery, canned or cooked	2–3	8–13	0.2
Champagne	21	88	0.4
Cheese, Cheddar and similar	105–120	439–502	Trace
Cheese, Brie	88	368	Trace
Cheese, Camembert	88	368	Trace
Cheese, Cheshire	110	460	Trace
Cheese, Cottage, low-fat	26	109	0.6
Cheese, Cottage, not labelled low-fat	29–31	121–130	Trace
Cheese, Cottage, with pineapple	60	251	0.6
Cheese, Cream	145–232	606–970	Trace
Cheese, Curd cheese	39	163	Trace
Cheese, Dairylea and similar cheese spreads	78	326	0.3
Cheese, Danish Blue	94	393	Trace
Cheese, Edam	88	368	Trace
Cheese, Gloucester	114	476	Trace
Cheese, Gorgonzola	95	397	Trace
Cheese, Gouda	96	401	Trace
Cheese, Gruyère	121–132	506–552	Trace
Cheese, Leicester	110	460	Trace
Cheese, Parmesan	118	493	Trace
Cheese, Philadelphia full-fat cheese spread	182	761	Trace
Cheese, Processed	103	431	Trace
Cheese, Roquefort	88	368	Trace
Cheese, Smoked cheese	78	326	Trace
Cheese, Stilton	135	564	Trace
Cheese, St Paulin	85	355	Trace
Cheese omelette (see recipe page 183)	102	426	Trace
Cheese pudding (see recipe page 135)	54	226	3.5
Cherry, fresh	11	46	3.0
Cherry, stewed	9–10	38–42	2.5
Cherry, glacé	62	259	15.8
Cherry cake	129	539	16.1
Cherry cake, small slice	169	706	21.5
Chicken, young, lean, raw	33	138	0.0
Chicken, young, fried or grilled (broiled), no coating	58	242	0.0
Chicken, young, boiled	54	226	0.0
Chicken, young, roast	54	226	0.0
Chicken, older fowl (Stewing chicken), raw	40	167	0.0
Chicken, older fowl (Stewing chicken), boiled	65	272	0.0

Item	Calories	Kilojoules	Carbohydrates
Chicken pie	80	334	6.0
Chicken or cream of chicken soup, canned	14–17	59–71	2.0
Chicken stock (Buillon) cube	30	125	6.0
Chicory (Endive)	3	12	0.4
Chilli, fresh [See Pepper entry]			
Chilli, dried	88	369	2.0
Chillo dessert, made up as packet	54–59	226–247	5.0
Chives	10	42	Trace
Chocolate, milk (varies)	120–167	502–698	15.5
Chocolate, plain	155–160	648–669	14.9
Chocolate, assorted	133–160	556–669	20.8
Chocolate peppermint creams, two pieces	117	489	5.0
Chocolate biscuit (varies)	130–172	546–722	18
Chocolate cake, plain	99	414	15.0
Chocolate cake, iced (See Cake entry)	125	523	17.3
Chocolate spread (varies)	88	368	20.0
Chopped ham loaf (varies)	70	293	1.2
Chopped candied peel	68	284	22.9
Christmas pudding, bought	92–100	385–418	15.0
Christmas pudding, home-made, (varies, but similar)			
Chutney	46–60	192–251	11.0–14.8
Cider, dry, 568 ml/1 pint (2½ cups)	200	836	0.75
Cider, sweet, 568 ml/1 pint (2½ cups)	240	1003	1.21
Cider, vintage, 568 ml/1 pint (2½ cups)	560	2340	2.07
Citrus fruits (orange, etc.)	6–9	25–38	0.9–2.4
Clam, flesh only	23	96	0.0
Clam chowder, canned	7–8	29–33	6.2
Coca-Cola, etc., 184.28 ml/6½ fl oz	80	334	21.9
Cocoa powder (unsweetened)	100	418	9.9
Coconut, fresh	100	418	1.1
Coconut, dried (desiccated/shredded)	180	752	1.8
Coconut, milk	none	none	1.4
Cod, raw	16	67	0.0
Cod, boiled or steamed	23	96	0.0
Cod, fried or grilled (broiled)	40–45	167–188	0.0–0.8
Cod, smoked	22	92	0.0
Cod roe, fried	59	277	0.9
Cod roe, steamed or canned	28–30	117–125	0.0
Crispy cod fry, one	25	105	2.5
Condensed milk, full cream	100	418	15.9
Coffee, black	negligible	negligible	negligible
Coffee, made with average amount of milk and 1 teaspoon sugar; 1 cup	85	355	4.8
Coleslaw (see recipe page 73)			
Consommé, home made (see recipe page 28), skimmed of fat	negligible	negligible	0.0
Consommé, canned	3–6	13–25	0.0
Corn, [See Sweetcorn entry]			
Cooking fat (varies)	240	1003	0.0
Corn cob	15	63	5.0
Corn, canned creamed	28	117	5.0
Corn syrup, [See Golden syrup entry]			
Cornflakes	104–108	435–451	25.2
Cornflour (Cornstarch)	100	418	26.2
Cornish pasty	108	451	6.0–10.0
Corn oil	255	1066	0.0
Courgette (Zucchini) [See Marrow (Squash) entry]			
Crab, cooked	37	155	0.0
Crab, canned	32–36	134–150	0.31

Calories/kilojoules and **carbohydrate** counts are given per 28.35g/1oz or 28.35 ml/1 fl oz, unless otherwise stated.

Item	Calories	Kilojoules	Carbohydrates
Crab, paste	42	176	0.5
Cranberry, fresh	4	17	1.0
Cranberry sauce	35	146	9.0
Cream, double (Heavy)	100–128	418–535	0.6
Cream, single (Light)	51	213	0.9
Cream, dairy soured (Sour)	53	222	0.6
Cream, canned	66–67	276–280	0.6
Cream, imitation, (varies)	76	318	2.0
Creamed rice, canned	30	125	5.2
Crème de Menthe	90	376	6.0
Crème de caçao	90	376	6.0
Crispbread, (varies)	90–115	376–481	9.0–23.0
Crumpet	54	226	12.0
Crumpet, one	79	330	17.5
Cucumber	3	13	0.5
Currant, dried	76	318	18.0
Currant, fresh, black, red, white	8–12	38–50	1.2–1.9
Currant bread	71	297	14.7
Currant bun	87	364	15.4
Custard apple	20	84	5.1
Custard, canned	30	125	5.0
Custard, with powder, made-up	30	125	5.0
Custard powder, dry	100	418	26.2
Custard, egg (see recipe, page 211)	18	69	1.2
Curry powder	67	280	7.4

D

Item	Calories	Kilojoules	Carbohydrates
Dab (Small sole) [See Plaice entry]			
Damson, fresh (with stone/pits)	9	38	2.4
Damson, stewed (with stone/pits)	8	33	2.1
Date, dried (without stone/pits)	75	314	18.1
Date, dried (with stone/pits)	50–60	209–251	15.6
Dill pickle	2	8	
Doughnut, jam-filled	100	418	13.8
Doughnut, jam-filled, one	175	732	30.0
Drambuie	65	272	1.2
Dream topping, made up as packet	34	142	3.7
Dried breadcrumbs	101	422	22.0
Dried skimmed milk, 568 ml/1 pint (2½ cups)	200	836	30.0
Dry ginger	2	8	1.4
Dry ginger ale	4	17	2.62
Dubonnet	50	209	4.0
Duck, raw, medium lean	47–62	196–259	0.0
Duck, roast	89	372	0.0
Dundee cake	115	481	17.7

E

Item	Calories	Kilojoules	Carbohydrates
Eccles cake	126–147	527–614	14.5
Eccles cake, one	123	514	14.1
Eel, young (elver), raw	20	84	0.0
Eel, silver, raw	90	376	0.0
Eel, silver, stewed	106	443	0.0
Egg, one, small fried or scrambled	140	585	Trace
Egg, white, one small, raw or boiled	11	46	Trace
Egg, yolk, one small, raw or boiled	69	288	Trace
Eggplant [See Aubergine entry]			
Endive (Chicory)	3	13	0.3
Energen crispbread, bran	90	376	9.0
Energen crispbread, rye	105	439	10.0
Energen crispbread, wheat	116	485	13.0
Energen rolls	105	439	12.0
Evaporated milk	45	188	3.5

F

Item	Calories	Kilojoules	Carbohydrates
Faggot	79	330	6.0
Fairy cake	108	451	15.3
Fairy cake, one	162	677	23.0
Farex	97	405	20.7
Fat (Shortening) (varies)	240	1003	0.0
Fava	15	63	2.0
Ferveil	5	21	0.8
Fig, green, raw	12	50	2.7
Fig, dried	108	451	15.0
Fig, dried, stewed	30	125	7.5
Filbert	108	451	1.9
Fish cake, made with white fish (see recipe page 148)	34–61	142–255	2.8
Fish cake, one	65–110	272–460	9.4
Fish cake, made with salmon, one	82	343	9.4
Fish in batter, frozen	52	217	2.8
Fish in batter, one portion approx.	210	878	11.2
Fish in breadcrumbs	27–48	113–201	1.65
Fish in breadcrumbs, one portion (varies with fish)	135	564	6.50
Fish finger (Stick), depends on coating	50	209	1.65–5.0
Fish finger, one, depends on coating	54	226	1.87–5.1
Fish paste, anchovy	40	167	1.0–1.9
Fish paste, bloater	48	201	1.0–1.9
Fish paste, crab	42	176	1.0–1.9
Fish paste, salmon and anchovy	51	213	1.0–1.9
Fish pie, average	65	272	9.0
Flatbread, per slice, varies	12	50	2.7
Flatbread, per 28.35 g/1 oz	98	410	21.9
Flounder, raw	20	84	0.0
Flounder, boiled or steamed	27	113	0.0
Flounder, fried	42	176	1.8
Flour, white	95–100	399–420	22.0
Frankfurter	70	293	0.5
French fries	68	284	10.6
Fried bread	162	677	14.6
Frogs' legs	18	75	0.0
Fruit-flavoured jelly, made with water	18	75	17.7
Fruit juice, bottled grapefruit, orange pineapple, tomato [See under various flavours]			
Fruit pastille	80	334	17.6
Fruit pie filling, apple	22	92	5.0
Fruit pie filling, apple and blackberry	34	142	8.0
Fruit pie filling, other, approx.	34–38	142–159	8.0
Fruit, soft (blackberry, raspberry, strawberry, etc.) See also under individual fruits	6–8	25–33	1.6–1.8
Fruit salad, canned	25	105	7.1
Fruit salad, fresh (see recipe page 84) [Depends on contents]			
Fruit squash and cordial (average needed 56.7–85 ml/2–3 fl oz)	32–39	134–163	9.6–10.2
Fudge (varies)	80–110	334–460	25.6

G

Item	Calories	Kilojoules	Carbohydrates
Garlic, 1 medium clove	5	21	0.4
Gelatine, (gelatin)	70	294	0.0
Gherkin	2	8	Trace
Gin	60	251	0.0
Ginger, stem (preserved)	80	334	24.7
Ginger beer, 170.4 ml/6 fl oz	70	293	12.0
Gingerbread	108	751	18.0

Calories/kilojoules and carbohydrate counts are given per 28.35g/1oz or 28.35 ml/1 fl oz, unless otherwise stated.

Item	Calories	Kilojoules	Carbohydrates
Glacé cherries	62	259	15.8
Glucose	110	460	24.0
Golden syrup	84	351	22.4
Goose, raw	62–64	259–268	0.0
Goose, roast	92	385	0.0
Gooseberry, raw, dessert	10	42	2.6
Gooseberry, raw, green	4	17	1.0
Gooseberry, stewed	3	13	0.7
Gooseberry, canned	22	92	5.0
Grape	15	63	3.7–4.6
Grape juice	14	59	5.2
Grapefruit	6	25	1.5
Grapefruit segments, canned (varies)	11–22	46–92	5.0
Grapefruit juice, fresh	9	38	2.9
Grapefruit juice, canned	10–14	42–59	3.8
Grapefruit juice, canned, low-calorie	9	38	Trace
Graves (see also under Wines)	21	88	0.95
Green pea soup	8–17	33–71	1.5–3.0
Greengages, raw	14	58	3.4
Greengages, stewed	11	46	2.6
Grits, raw	99	416	22.0
Grits, cooked, ½ cup	51	92	13.3
Ground almond	184	769	1–2
Grouse, raw	29	121	0.0
Grouse, roast	49	205	0.0
Guava, raw	15	51	3.25
Guinea fowl [See Chicken entry]			

H

Item	Calories	Kilojoules	Carbohydrates
Haddock, fresh, raw	20	84	0.0
Haddock, boiled or steamed	28	117	0.0
Haddock, fried	50	209	1.0
Haddock, smoked, raw	20	84	0.0
Haddock, smoked, boiled or steamed	28	117	0.0
Hake, raw	23	96	0.0
Hake, boiled or steamed	30	125	0.0
Hake, fried	53	222	1.5
Halibut, raw	30	125	0.0
Halibut, boiled or steamed	37	155	0.0
Ham, raw (cured or smoked)	142	594	0.0
Ham, boiled, lean only	62	259	0.0
Ham, boiled, lean and fat	123	514	0.0
Hare, stewed	55	230	0.0
Hare, roast	55	230	0.0
Heart, lambs'	45	188	0.0
Heart, ox	20	84	0.0
Heart, pig's	27	113	0.0
Heart, roasted with minimum fat	66	276	0.0
Hermasetas tablets	0	0	25.0
Herring, raw	67	280	0.0
Herring, soused	54	226	0.0
Herring, fried in oatmeal	67	280	0.4
Herring, fried or grilled (broiled) without coating	73	305	0.0
Herring, canned	67	280	0.0
Herring, in tomato, canned	45	188	2.0
Herring, pickled	65	272	0.0
Herring roe, fried	74	309	1.3
Herring roe, steamed	35–40	146–167	0.0
Honey	82	344	21.7
Horseradish, fresh	36	151	2.1
Horseradish cream (average helping 1–2 × 5 ml spoons/1–2 teaspoons)	28	117	0.0

I

Item	Calories	Kilojoules	Carbohydrates
Ice cream, (varies), average	31–60	130–251	5.6

Item	Calories	Kilojoules	Carbohydrates
Ice cream, family raspberry ripple, whole block	537	2245	48.2
Ice cream, family vanilla block, whole block	309	1292	47.1
Iced cake, with fat, average	110–120	460–502	17.9
Iced lolly, per lolly (varies)	60–140	251–585	12.9
Iced lolly, chocolate covered	140	585	14.5
Instant Whip, made up as packet	31	130	46.0

J

Item	Calories	Kilojoules	Carbohydrates
Jam, average	74–80	309–334	19.6
Jam, very high sugar content (conserves)	120	502	21.6
Jam, very high sugar content (conserves), teaspoon	37–40	155–167	8.8
Jam, low-calorie (diabetic-type)	50	209	12.0
Jam puff	154	644	16.8
Jam puff, one	200	836	21.0
Jelly, fruit-flavoured, made with water	18	75	5.4
Jello, fruit-flavoured, made with water	18	75	5.4
Jumbo shrimp [See Scampi entry]			

K

Item	Calories	Kilojoules	Carbohydrates
Kedgeree	43	180	2.8
Kidney, lambs', ox, pork	30	125	0.0
Kidney, lambs', fried or grilled (broiled) with minimum fat	57	238	0.0
Kidney soup, canned	12	50	1.0–2.0
Kippers, raw	67	280	0.0
Kippers, jugged (cooked in water)	54	226	0.0
Kippers, baked	57	238	0.0
Kohlrabi, raw	14	59	2.1
Kohlrabi, boiled	11	46	1.25

L

Item	Calories	Kilojoules	Carbohydrates
Lamb, good quality, lean only (e.g. leg, cutlet)	40–60	167–251	0.0
Lamb, mixture of lean with little fat (e.g. loin chop)	90	376	0.0
Lard	240	1003	0.0
Lean (White) fish, average	20	84	0.0
Leek, raw	6	25	1.7
Leek, boiled	5	21	1.3
Lemon, juice	2	8	0.5
Lemon, whole	4	17	0.9
Lemon, PLJ juice	4	17	0.6
Lemonade, commercial, aerated	7	29	1.6
Lemonade shandy	7	29	5.0
Lemonade shandy, canned	2	8	3.0
Lemon curd	86	359	12.0
Lemon curd, tart	119	497	14.1
Lemon squash	11–24	46–100	9.6
Lentil, dry	80	334	15.1
Lentil, boiled	27	113	5.2
Lentil soup, canned	12–29	50–121	2.0–2.9
Lettuce	4–5	17–21	0.5
Lime [See Lemon entry]			
Liqueur, most liqueurs, including brandy	75	314	0.0
Liqueur, Crème de menthe	90	376	6.0
Liqueur, Crème de cacao	90	376	6.0
Liqueur, Drambuie	65	272	6.0
Liquorice allsorts	90–91	376–380	21.0
Liver, calves', lambs', ox, pigs'	40	167	0.0
Liver, fried or grilled (broiled) with minimum fat	74	309	0.7–1.1

Calories/kilojoules and **carbohydrate** counts are given per 28.35g/1oz or 28.35 ml/1 fl oz, unless otherwise stated.

Item	Calories	Kilojoules	Carbohydrates
Liver sausage, Continental	83	347	0.0
Loganberry, fresh	6	25	1.0
Loganberry, stewed	5	21	0.7
Loganberry, canned	27	113	7.4
Lucozade (Glucose drink)	19	79	5.1
Luncheon meat, canned	95	397	1.4

M

Item	Calories	Kilojoules	Carbohydrates
Macaroni, raw	102	426	22.6
Macaroni, boiled	32	134	7.2
Macaroni, canned	21	88	7.2
Macaroni, creamed, canned	30	125	4.0
Macaroni, in cheese sauce	35	146	9.0
Mackerel, raw	76	318	0.0
Mackerel, cooked [See Herring entry]			
Malt bread	71	297	14.0
Mango	16	67	4.6
Maple syrup	84	351	12.8
Margarine	220	920	0.0
Marmalade, varies according to fruit	74–80	309–334	19.8
Marmalade, low-calorie	50	209	12.0
Marrow, (Squash), raw	2–3	8–13	0.4
Marrow, (Squash), boiled	1–2	4–8	0.4
Marshmallow	94	393	23.0
Marzipan	116	485	16.0
Mayonnaise, average	110	460	0.4
Mayonnaise, low-calorie	50	209	0.4
Medlar	11	46	3.0
Melon	4	17	0.9
Meringue	112	468	20.0
Meringue, each	125	523	23.3
Milk, fresh, whole	19	79	1.4
Milk, fresh, skimmed	10	42	1.4
Milk, dried, skimmed, powder	93	389	14.0
Milk, dried, skimmed, reconstituted	10	42	1.4
Milk, dried, whole powder (used as baby food)	145–150	606–627	11.0
Milk, dried, whole powder, reconstituted (depends on strength)	from 15	from 63	from 1.4
Milk, buttermilk	10	42	1.4
Milk, evaporated, full cream	45–47	188–196	3.5
Milk, condensed, full cream	100	418	15.9
Milk, condensed, skimmed	75	314	17.0
Mincemeat	37	155	7.2
Mince pie	111	464	12.5
Minestrone soup, canned, (varies)	10–20	42–84	2.0–3.0
Minestrone soup, dehydrated	6	25	1.0
Mixed candied peel and fruit	68	284	16.9
Molasses [See Treacle entry]			
Mousse, frozen	42–53	176–222	7.0
Mousse, frozen, 1 person portion	123–125	514–523	15.0
Muesli, breakfast cereal, (varies according to ingredients)	100–107	418–447	39.0
Mulberry	9	38	2.3
Mulligatawny soup, canned	18	75	2.2
Mushroom, raw	1–2	4–8	0.0
Mushroom, fried	77	322	0.0
Mussels, cooked in water	25	105	Trace
Mustard powder	132	552	5.9
Mutton, lean	75	314	0.0
Mutton, mixture lean and fat	up to 154	644	0.0

N

Item	Calories	Kilojoules	Carbohydrates
Navy beans, dry	100–120	418–502	12.9–14.2
Navy beans, boiled	25–30	105–125	4.7–4.9

Item	Calories	Kilojoules	Carbohydrates
Nectarine	13	54	3.2
Noodle, boiled	32	134	7.2
Nuts, (without shells), almond	168	702	1.2
Nuts, (without shells), Brazil	180	752	1.2
Nuts, (without shells), cashew	164	686	8.3
Nuts, (without shells), chestnut	49	205	10.4
Nuts, (without shells), cobnut or filbert	113	472	1.9
Nuts, (without shells), hazelnut	108	451	2.0
Nuts, (without shells), nuts mixed with raisin	108	451	12.2
Nuts, (without shells), peanut	160–178	669–744	2.4
Nuts, (without shells), salted cashew	161	673	8.3
Nuts, (without shells), salted peanut	173–180	723–752	2.4
Nuts, (without shells), walnut	156	652	1.4

O

Item	Calories	Kilojoules	Carbohydrates
Oatmeal, raw	115	481	20.6
Oatmeal, as porridge	13	54	2.3
Okra	8	33	1.5
Olive	30	125	Trace
Olive oil	264	1104	0.0
Olive oil, tablespoon	100	418	0.0
Omelette, (varies) (see recipe page 183)			
Onion, raw	6	25	1.5
Onion, spring (Scallion), raw	6	25	2.4
Onion, boiled	5	21	0.8
Onion, fried	93	389	2.9
Onion, pickled	4–6	17–25	1.0
Onion soup, clear, canned	6	25	0.5
Onion soup, home-made (see recipe page 125)	2	8	0.5
Onion soup, dehydrated, reconstituted	10	42	1.1
Orange	9	38	2.4
Orange juice, fresh	10	42	2.7
Orange juice, canned	11–17	46–71	2.7–4.0
Orange juice, low-calorie, canned	9	38	2.7
Orange squash	24	100	10.2
Outline (low calorie spread)	110	460	0.0
Ovaltine powder and similar products	100–113	418–472	20.6
Oxtail	25	104	0.0
Oxtail soup, canned (varies)	9–20	38–84	1.0–4.0
Oxtail soup, dehydrated powder	5–10	21–42	1.0–1.5
Ox tongue	84–88	351–368	0.0
Oyster, raw	14	59	Trace

P

Item	Calories	Kilojoules	Carbohydrates
Paella, (including rice)	25	104	4.0
Paella, (including rice), 2 portions	865	3616	137.4
Pancake, without filling	85	355	10.6
Parsnip, raw	14	59	3.2
Parsnip, boiled	16	67	3.8
Passion fruit, raw	9	38	1.8
Pasta, raw, (varies)	95–102	399–426	19.8–22.6
Pasta, cooked	29	123	6.0
Peaches, raw	10	42	2.6
Peaches, dried	58	242	15.0
Peaches, dried, stewed	20	84	5.0
Peaches, canned	25	105	6.5
Peanut [See Nut entry]			
Peanut butter	170	711	6.0
Peanut brittle	133	556	15.6
Pear, raw, dessert	11	46	3.0
Pear, raw, cooking	10	42	2.6

Calories/kilojoules and **carbohydrate** counts are given per 28.35g/1oz or 28.35 ml/1 fl oz, unless otherwise stated.

Item	Calories	Kilojoules	Carbohydrates
Pear, dried	50	209	15.0
Pear, dried, stewed	18	75	5.0
Pear, canned	20	84	5.7
Pea, fresh	19	79	3.0
Pea, dried	85	355	14.2
Pea, dried, boiled	28	117	5.4
Pea, canned	24	100	4.7
Pea, frozen	20	84	3.0
Pepper (Capsicum), raw	10	42	0.0
Pepper, green, stuffed, one, medium, (see recipe page 67)	175	732	12.2
Pepper, powder	88	368	0.0
Persimmon	12	50	4.9
Pheasant, roast	61	255	0.0
Piccalilli (Mustard pickles)	12	50	3.6
Piccalilli, sweet	37	155	10.0
Pigeon, roast	66	276	0.0
Pigeon, stewed	62	259	0.0
Pilchard, canned	54	226	0.0
Pilchard, in tomato	43	180	1.0
Pineapple, raw	10	42	3.3
Pineapple, canned	16–22	67–92	5.7
Pineapple juice, canned	16–17	67–71	3.8
Pineapple juice, canned unsweetened	11	46	3.0
Plaice, (Flounder), raw	22	92	0.0
Plaice, boiled or steamed	29	121	0.0
Plaice, fried	66	276	2.0
Plain cake, with fat	75–90	314–376	16.3
Plum, raw, dessert	10	42	2.7
Plum, raw, cooking	7	29	1.8
Plum, stewed, (with stone/pit)	5	21	1.4
Plum, canned (with stone/pit)	22	92	3.0
Pomegranate pulp (seeds are not edible)	12	50	3.3
Pork (difficult to avoid fat)			
Pork, lean only	67	280	0.0
Pork, fat only	112	468	0.0
Pork luncheon meat	78	326	1.4
Port wine, ruby	43	180	3.24
Port wine, tawny	45	188	3.55
Potato, raw	25	105	5.9
Potato, old, boiled	24	100	5.6
Potato, new, boiled	21	88	5.2
Potato, old, fried, chips	68	284	10.6
Potato, old, baked in skins, pulp only	30	125	7.0
Potato, old, baked in skins, with skin	24	100	5.8
Potato, old, mashed	34	142	5.1
Potato, sweet [See Yam entry]			
Potato crisps	159	665	14.0
Potato croquettes	22	92	7.0
Potato, dehydrated	100–105	418–439	21.0
Prawn, (Shrimp), cooked, peeled	30	125	0.0
Prawn, (Shrimp), cooked, with shell	11	46	0.0
Prawn Curry, (including rice), two portions	792	3311	125.8
Preserved ginger	80	334	24.7
Primula crispbread, per slice	17	71	3.9
Prune, with stone/pit	37	155	9.5
Prune, without stone/pit	46	193	11.4
Prune, stewed	19	79	4.8
Prune, canned	34	142	7.0
Puffed Wheat	104	435	21.4
Pumpernickel, per slice	75	314	20.5
Pumpkin, raw	4–6	17–25	1.0
Pumpkin, boiled	2–3	8–13	0.4

Q

Item	Calories	Kilojoules	Carbohydrates
Quaker Oats	114	477	21.0

Item	Calories	Kilojoules	Carbohydrates
Quick Whip dessert, made with 568 ml/1 pint/2½ cups milk (4 portions)	664	2776	103.0
Quince, raw	7	29	1.8
Quince, stewed	5	21	1.2

R

Item	Calories	Kilojoules	Carbohydrates
Rabbit, stewed	51	213	0.0
Radish	2	8	0.8
Raisin, seedless	70	293	18.3
Raspberry, raw	6	25	1.6
Raspberry, canned	22	92	6.0
Raspberry, frozen	18	75	7.9
Ratatouille, (see recipe page 209)	6	25	1.2
Ravioli, canned	30	125	4.0
Red cabbage	2	8	1.0
Redcurrant, raw	8	33	1.2
Redcurrant, stewed	7	29	1.0
Red wine, [See Wine entry]			
Rhubarb, stewed	1	4	0.2
Rhubarb, canned	22	92	5.0 .
Ribena, see also blackcurrant concentrate	84	351	17.3
Rice, raw	102	426	24.6
Rice, boiled	35	146	8.4
Rice, creamed, canned	33	138	5.0
Rice Krispies	100	418	24.2
Rissole, average	92	385	6.0
Roe, cod, fried	59	247	0.9
Roe, herring, fried	74	309	1.3
Rolled oats, raw	100–115	418–481	21.0
Roll, as Bread			
Roll, slimmers', one	18–27	75–113	12.0
Root vegetables, see under individual names			
Rose hip syrup, sweetened	95	397	19.0
Rum	78	326	0.0
Rutabaga [See Swede entry]			
Rye bread, one slice	55	230	12.1
Rye-King, light rye, per slice	28	117	4.1
Rye-King, rye, per slice	32	134	4.2
Rye-King, wheat, per slice	42	176	6.0
Ryvita, per slice	29	121	4.1

S

Item	Calories	Kilojoules	Carbohydrates
Sago, creamed, canned	27	113	3.0
Salad dressing, (varies)	108–124	451–518	5.0
Salad dressing, low-calorie, see recipes pages 80, 81			
Salami, lean, average	83	347	0.37
Salmon, raw	50	209	0.0
Salmon, poached or steamed	57	238	0.0
Salmon and anchovy paste	51	213	1.0–1.9
Salmon and shrimp paste	40	167	1.0–1.8
Salmon, smoked	47–60	196–251	0.0
Salsify	5	21	0.7
Sardine, in oil	84	351	0.0
Sauerkraut	2–3	8–13	0.2–0.4
Sausage, beef, raw	60	251	3.7
Sausage, beef, one, fried	81	339	4.5
Sausage, pork, raw	72	301	2.8
Sausage, pork, one, fried	93	389	3.6
Sausage, carbohydrates depends on crumb content			
Sausage roll, one	134–142	560–594	10.1–11.4
Scallion [See Spring onion entry]			

Calories/kilojoules and carbohydrate counts are given per 28.35g/1oz or 28.35 ml/1 fl oz, unless otherwise stated.

Item	Calories	Kilojoules	Carbohydrates
Scallop, steamed	30	125	Trace
Scallop, boiled	30	125	Trace
Scampi, coated in batter, fried, one	83	347	0.5
Scanda Crisp, per slice	19	79	3.9
Scone, (Biscuit), one	90	376	16.3
Scotch egg, carbohydrate count depends on coating	49–75	205–313	2.9
Scotch pancakes	73	305	9.9
Seedless white raisins [See Sultana entry]			
Semolina, raw	100	418	22.0
Semolina, creamed, canned	27	113	3.0
Shepherd's pie, small amount potato	30	125	2.7
Sherry, dry	33	138	0.39
Sherry, sweet	36	150	1.95
Shrimp, shelled	32	134	0.0
Shrimp, potted	29	121	0.0
Shrimp, dry pack	36	150	0.0
Shrimp, in liquid	25	105	0.0
Skate [See Plaice entry]			
Slimline (Diet) bitter lemon and tonic	1	4	0.0
Sole [See Plaice entry]			
Soup, canned:			
Soup, Asparagus	9	38	2.1
Soup, Chicken, cream of	14–17	58–71	2.0
Soup, Clam chowder	7–8	29–33	1.4
Soup, Cream of asparagus	18	75	2.2
Soup, Cream of celery	13	54	2.3
Soup, Cream of mushroom	16	67	2.2
Soup, Cream of tomato	19	79	2.6
Soup, Cream of vegetable	13	54	2.3
Soup, Green pea	8–17	33–71	1.5–3.0
Soup, Kidney	12	50	1.0–2.0
Soup, Lentil	12–29	50–121	2.0–2.9
Soup, Minestrone	10	42	2.0–3.0
Soup, Mulligatawny	18	75	2.2
Soup, Onion	6	25	0.5
Soup, Oxtail	9–10	37–42	1.0–4.0
Soup, Scotch broth	6–16	25–67	1.5
Soup, Thick vegetable and beef	19	79	8.9
Soup, Tomato	10	42	2.9
Soup, Vegetable	9–10	37–42	2.3
Soup mix, dehydrated, (varies)	95–100	397–418	16.7
Soup mix, reconstituted:			
Soup mix, Chicken and leek	13	54	2.1
Soup mix, Chicken noodle	4	17	5.0
Soup mix, Minestrone	6	25	3.0
Soup mix, Thick onion	10	42	4.0
Soya bean flour	123	514	3.8
Soya Choice, chunks	33	141	2.9
Soya Choice, mince	32	137	2.6
Soya Extenders	92	386	9.1
Sparkling orange drink			
28.35 ml/1 fl oz	12–17	50–71	23.9
170.4 ml/6 fl oz	88	368	143.4
Spaghetti, raw	104	435	23.9
Spaghetti, boiled	33	138	7.0
Spaghetti, in tomato and cheese sauce	20	84	3.5–5.0
Spaghetti, Bolognese	20	84	2.0
Spice, (varies)	60–100	252–420	7.0–12.0
Spinach	5–7	21–29	0.4
Sponge cake, without fat	60–67	251–280	15.6
Sponge cake, with fat	134	560	16.3
Sprat, raw	125	522	0.0
Sprat, fried	126	527	0.0
Sprat, smoked	91	380	0.0
Squash [See Marrow entry]			
Squash, fruit-flavoured, (vary enormously)			
Squash, lower calories	11–24	76–100	3.2

Item	Calories	Kilojoules	Carbohydrates
Squash, higher calories	32–39	134–163	10.2
Squid (Octopus)	14	58	0.0
Steak [See Beef entry]			
Steak and kidney pie	86–90	359–376	4.8–6.0
Steak and kidney pudding	69–74	288–309	4.8–6.0
Stem ginger	80	334	2.0
Stew pack (Vegetable)	6	25	1.2
Stout, 568 ml/1 pint (2½ cups)	210	878	Trace
Stock (Bouillon) cube	30	125	4.0–6.0
Strawberry, raw	7	29	1.8
Strawberry, canned	22	92	3.0
Strawberry, frozen in sugar	12	50	2.5–7.5
Stuffing, (varies)	100	418	22.0
Suet	260	1087	0.0
Suet pudding	105	439	12.0
Sugar, Barbados	108	751	29.6
Sugar, coffee crystals	112	468	29.7
Sugar, dark brown	108	451	29.6
Sugar, icing (Confectioners')	112	468	29.7
Sugar, light brown and demerara	112	468	29.6
Sugar, white	112	468	29.7
Sultana (Seedless White Raisins)	76	318	18.4
Swede (Rutabaga), raw	6	25	1.2
Swede (Rutabaga), boiled	5	21	1.1
Sweetbread, stewed	51	213	0.0
Sweetcorn, canned or cooked	15	63	5.0
Sweetheart dessert made up with 284 ml/½ pint/1¼ cups milk, (2 portions)	560	2341	79.0
Swiss breakfast food	112	468	39.0
Syrup, golden (Corn) or maple	84	351	22.4

T

Item	Calories	Kilojoules	Carbohydrates
Tangerine and similar fruit, raw	9	38	2.3
Tangerine, canned (Mandarin orange)	18	75	4.7
Tapioca, raw	100	418	27.0
Tapioca, creamed, canned	21	88	4.0
Tea, black, no sugar	negligible	negligible	0.4
Tea, made with average amount of milk and 1 teaspoon sugar; 1 teacup	75	314	4.4
Tea cake	87	364	17.0
Textured vegetable protein (T.V.P.) [See Soya Choice and Extender entry]			
Thousand Island dressing	114	476	0.4
Toad-in-the-hole	82	343	5.3
Toast	85	355	18.4
Toffee, average	113	472	25.6
Tomato, raw	4–5	17–21	0.8
Tomato, fried	20	84	1.0
Tomato juice	6	25	1.0
Tomato ketchup	25–32	105–134	6.8
Tomato purée (Paste)	15	63	3.0
Tomato soup, canned	10	42	2.6
Tongue, fresh	84	355	0.0
Tongue, salted, boiled or canned	84–88	351–368	0.0
Tonic water, 28.35 ml/1 fl oz	10.1	42	1.0
170.4 ml/6 fl oz	66	276	6.0
Tonic water, Slimline (diet):			
28.35 ml/1 fl oz	0	0	0.0
170.4 ml/6 fl oz	0.74 (1)	3	0.0
Treacle (molasses) [See Black treacle entry]			
Trifle	50	209	6.0
Tripe	17–29	71–121	0.0

Calories/kilojoules and carbohydrate counts are given per 28.35g/1oz or 28.35 ml/1 fl oz, unless otherwise stated.

Item	Calories	Kilojoules	Carbohydrates
Trout, raw	31	130	0.0
Trout, boiled or steamed	38	159	0.0
Trout, smoked	36	150	0.0
Trout, smoked, one	220	920	0.0
Tuna, canned	76	318	0.0
Tuna, fresh	45	188	0.0
Turbot, raw	21	88	0.0
Turbot, boiled or steamed	28	117	0.0
Turnip, raw	5	21	1.1
Turnip, boiled	3	13	0.7
Turkey, boiled	29	121	0.0
Turkey, roast	56	234	0.0
Twiglets	114	477	20.7

V

Item	Calories	Kilojoules	Carbohydrates
Veal, very lean	31	130	0.0
Veal, fried with minimum fat	61	255	1.3
Veal and ham paste	58	242	1.2
Veal and ham pie	111	464	7.0
Vegetable soup, canned	9–10	38–42	2.3
Vegetable and beef soup, canned	19	79	8.9
Venison, roast	56	234	0.0
Vermouth, dry	40	167	Trace
Vienna bread, one slice	54	226	10.4
Viennese tart	147	614	22.0
Vinegar	1	4	0.2
Vitawheat, one slice	32	134	3.1
Vodka	66	276	0.0

W

Item	Calories	Kilojoules	Carbohydrates
Waffles	60	251	8.0
Waffles, one	216	903	28.4
Walnut, shelled	156	652	1.4
Walnut, pickled	10	42	2.0
Watercress	4	17	0.2
Watermelon [See Melon entry]			
Welsh rarebit	102	426	7.5
Wheat, Shredded, 1 portion	102	426	22.7
Wheat, Puffed, 1 portion	104	435	21.4

Item	Calories	Kilojoules	Carbohydrates
Whisky	63	263	0.0
Whiskey (Irish)	66	276	0.0
Whitebait, fried	152	635	1.5
White bread	70	293	14.9
White currants	6	25	1.6
White sauce, (see recipe page 78)			
White wines [See Wine entry]			
Whiting, raw	19	79	0.0
Whiting, boiled or steamed	26	109	0.0
Whiting, fried	55	230	2.0
Wholemeal bread (Wholewheat)	65	272	13.4
Wine, average wineglass holds about 113.4 ml/4 fl oz			
Wine, Champagne	21	88	0.4
Wine, dry white, e.g. Graves	21	88	0.95
Wine, sweet white, e.g. Sauternes	26	109	1.67
Wine, red, e.g. Beaujolais	19	79	0.07
Wine, red, e.g. Burgundy	20	84	0.11
Wine, red, e.g. Chianti	18	75	0.05
Wine, red, e.g. Medoc	18	75	0.08
Wine, Madeira	32–44	134–184	1.0
Wine, Port	43–45	180–188	3.24–3.55
Wine, Sherry	33–36	138–150	0.39–1.95
(See entries under Beer, Stout, Liqueurs, etc. for alcoholic drinks)			
Winkles, raw	5	21	Trace
Winkles, boiled	20	84	Trace
Worcestershire sauce	3	13	2.7

Y

Item	Calories	Kilojoules	Carbohydrates
Yam, boiled	23	96	5.7
Yeast, extract	negligible	negligible	0.0
Yeast, compressed	13	55	0.0
Yogurt, low-fat	15	63	1.4
Yogurt, fat-free	10	42	1.4
Yogurt, flavoured	20–29	84–121	4.0
Yorkshire pudding	60	251	8.0

Z

Item	Calories	Kilojoules	Carbohydrates
Zweiback, one piece	25	104	5.1
Zucchini [See Courgette entry]			

These cup measures are for American readers and include common food store items, fruits and vegetables.

Cup measure chart

Food		Cup	Ounces	Food		Cup	Ounces
Almonds,	shelled	1	6	**Cheese,**	dry	1	4
Almonds,	flaked	1	4	Cheese,	freshly shredded	1	4
Apples,	cubed	1	4	Cheese,	blue, crumbled	1	4
Apples,	dried	1	5½	Cheese,	cottage	1	8
Apples,	stewed	1	8	**Cooking fat**		1	8
Apple purée,	sauce	1	8	**Cranberries,**	fresh	1	4
Apricots,	stewed	1	5½	Cranberries,	sauce	1	9
Apricots,	dried	1	5 to 6	**Dried breadcrumbs**		1	4
Apricots,	canned	1	5	**Dried skimmed milk**		1	3
Bamboo shoots		1	2	**Ground almonds**		1	4
Beans, dried,	kidney	1	7	**Lentils,**	dry	1	8
Beans, dried,	lima	1	7	Lentils,	boiled	1	3
Beans, dried,	navy	1	8	**Mushrooms,**	fresh	1	2 to 3
Beetroot,	pickled	1	6	Mushrooms,	fried	1	8
Blueberries,	fresh	1	4	**Prunes,**	without pits	1	7
Brazil nuts,	shelled, whole	1	4	Prunes,	stewed	1	8
Butter		1	8	**Rice,**	raw	1	7
Cabbage,	raw, shredded	1	4	Rice,	boiled	1	5½
Cabbage,	red, raw, shredded	1	4	**Rice Krispies**		1	1
				Shrimp,	cooked, shelled	1	8

Index

Acknowledgments

The publishers would like to thank the following companies for their help in providing equipment for photography. The Prestige Group for a pressure cooker; Thorn Domestic Appliances for a Kenwood Electronic Blender and Tower Housewares for a Slo-Cooker.

The publishers would also like to thank the following companies for the loan of accessories for the photography in this book: Casa Catalan; Elizabeth David; David Mellor; Paperchase; Craftsmen Potter and Tupperware.

Photography by: Bryce Attwell 188–9; courtesy of the British Turkey Federation 52–3; Buxted Advisory Bureau 54–5 above; Dutch Dairy Bureau 150 above; Melvin Grey 1–5, 6 above, 7, 8 above, 10–37, 44–54 left, 55 right, 81, 100–19, 125 right, 128–49, 154–69, 174–5, 180–1, 192–211; Paul Kemp 6 below, 8 below, 9, 38–43, 82–99, 120–5 left, 126–7, 150 below, 151–3, 170–3, 176–9, 182–7.